EFFECTIVE ACCOUNTING MANAGEMENT

Effective Management
Series Editor: Alan H. Anderson

Effective Personnel Management
Alan H. Anderson

Effective Business Policy
Alan H. Anderson and Dennis Barker

Effective General Management
Alan H. Anderson

Effective Organizational Behaviour
Alan H. Anderson and Anna Kyprianou

Effective Labour Relations
Alan H. Anderson

Effective Marketing
Alan H. Anderson and Thelma Dobson

Effective International Marketing
Alan H. Anderson, Thelma Dobson and James Patterson

Effective Marketing Communications
Alan H. Anderson and David Kleiner

Effective Entrepreneurship
Alan H. Anderson and Peter Woodcock

Effective Enterprise Management
Alan H. Anderson and Dennis Barker

Effective Accounting Management
Alan H. Anderson and Eileen Nix

Effective Financial Management
Alan H. Anderson and Richard Ciechan

EFFECTIVE ACCOUNTING MANAGEMENT

a skills and activity-based approach

ALAN H. ANDERSON
and
EILEEN NIX

Copyright © Alan H. Anderson and Eileen Nix 1994

The right of Alan H. Anderson and Eileen Nix to be identified as authors of this work has been asserted in accordance with the Copyright, Designs and Patents Act 1988.

First published 1994

Blackwell Publishers, the publishing imprint of

Basil Blackwell Ltd
108 Cowley Road
Oxford OX4 1JF
UK

Basil Blackwell Inc.
238 Main Street
Cambridge, Massachusetts 02142
USA

All rights reserved. Except for the quotation of short passages for the purposes of criticism and review, no part of this publication may be reproduced, stored in a retrieval system, or transmitted, in any form or by any means, electronic, mechanical, photocopying, recording or otherwise, without the prior permission of the publisher.

Except in the United States of America, this book is sold subject to the condition that it shall not, by way of trade or otherwise, be lent, resold, hired out, or otherwise circulated without the publisher's prior consent in any form of binding or cover other than that in which it is published and without a similar condition including this condition being imposed on the subsequent purchaser.

British Library Cataloguing in Publication Data

A CIP catalogue record for this book is available from the British Library.

Library of Congress Cataloging-in-Publication Data

Anderson, Alan H., 1950-
    Effective accounting management: a skills and activity-based approach / Alan H. Anderson and Eileen Nix.
      p. cm. – (Effective management)
    Includes bibliographical references and index.
    ISBN 0-631-19121-6
    1. Managerial accounting. 2. Activity-based costing. I. Nix, Eileen. II. Title. III. Series: Effective management (Oxford, England)
HF5657.4 A527 1994   94-1739
658. 15'11 – dc20   CIP

Designed and typeset by VAP Group Ltd., Kidlington, Oxfordshire

Printed in Great Britain by TJ Press Ltd., Padstow, Cornwall

This book is printed on acid-free paper

This book is dedicated to our families.

Contents

List of Figures	viii
List of Tables	ix
List of Boxes	x
List of Activities	xi
Introduction to the Series	xiii
The Series: Learning, Activities, Skills and Compatibility	xvii
Preface	xxvii
Concept	xxvii
Learning Aims	xxviii
Format and Content	xxviii
An Outline of the Units	xxviii
Acknowledgements	xxxi
Unit One **Introduction: the Context of Accounting**	1
Unit Two **Recording Financial Information**	37
Unit Three **Costs and Their Classifications**	79
Unit Four **Budgeting for Planning and Control**	115
Unit Five **Accounting Information for Decision Making**	163
Unit Six **Measuring Performance with Accounting Information**	213
Conclusion	248
A Lay Guide to Accountancy Terms	249
Select Bibliography and Further Reading	263
Index	267

Figures

Figure SK.1	Series skills matrix: functional and generic skills	xviii
Figure SK.2	Series learning strategy	xxi
Figure SK.3	Series knowledge and skills related to an educational classification	xxii
Figure SK.4	Series knowledge and skills related to a training classification	xxiii
Figure SK.5	Series knowledge and skills related to Management Charter Initiative (MCI) competencies	xxiv
Figure SK.6	Series knowledge and skills related to Training Commission/Council for Management Education (CMED) competencies	xxv
Figure 0.1	Contents flowchart	xxix
Figure 1.1	A typical large accounting department	8
Figure 1.2	The regulatory framework	17
Figure 2.1	Straight line depreciation	60
Figure 2.2	Reducing balance depreciation	62
Figure 3.1	Variable costs	87
Figure 3.2	Fixed costs	88
Figure 3.3	Semi-variable costs	88
Figure 3.4	Step costs	89
Figure 3.5	Job costing	92
Figure 3.6	Process costing	97
Figure 3.7	The overhead allocation process	106
Figure 3.8	Organization structure and personnel	112
Figure 4.1	The planning and control cycle	123
Figure 4.2	The planning cycle	123
Figure 4.3	Typical budgets and relationships in a manufacturing company	131
Figure 4.4	Feed-forward control	140
Figure 4.5	A feed-back control system	140
Figure 4.6	Monthly operating expenses report	144
Figure 5.1	Fixed costs as a percentage of total costs	181
Figure 5.2	Break even chart	182
Figure 5.3	The economist's chart (a) and the accountant's chart (b): a comparison	187
Figure 5.4	Costs and revenue for two manufacturing methods	189
Figure 5.5	Bluebell NPVs at increasing rates of interest	202
Figure 5.6	NPVs for projects A and B	208
Figure 6.1	Stock turnover	236

Tables

Table 2.1	Straight line depreciation	60
Table 2.2	Reducing balance depreciation	61
Table 4.1	Planning levels	126

Boxes

Box AM1.1	Nature of accounting 1	7
Box AM1.2	Standards	22
Box AM1.3	Creative accounting – at an end?	23
Box AM1.4	Balance sheet	29
Box AM1.5	The profit and loss statement	33
Box AM2.1	Debits and credits – *aide-mémoire*	43
Box AM3.1	Job sheet – example	93
Box AM3.2	Goods received note – example	98
Box AM3.3	Material requisition – example	99
Box AM3.4	Stock record card – example	100
Box AM3.5	Stores ledger account – example	100
Box AM3.6	Calculating overhead recovery rates	107
Box AM4.1	Definitions of planning and control	122
Box AM4.2	The planning cycle	123
Box AM4.3	Budgetary control	142
Box AM4.4	'Featherbedding' or 'the best laid plans of mice and men'	157
Box AM5.1	Factors affecting the time value of money	199

Activities

Activity AM1.1	The limits of accounting	14
Activity AM1.2	A management accountant: job and person profiles	18
Activity AM1.3	Terminology	35
Activity AM2.1	Ken College	50
Activity AM2.2	The Green Stores partnership	71
Activity AM2.3	Green Stores Limited	75
Activity AM2.4	Principles of the profit and loss account – retail example	77
Activity AM3.1	Debate on advertising costs	85
Activity AM3.2	Breaking down costs	86
Activity AM3.3	Small Engineering Limited	90
Activity AM3.4	Domsec	94
Activity AM3.5	Definitions and examples	110
Activity AM3.6	The Paper Mill	111
Activity AM4.1	Budgets	136
Activity AM4.2	Budgets and variance 1	146
Activity AM4.3	Budgets and variance 2	147
Activity AM4.4	Budget variance at the newspaper	155
Activity AM4.5	The value of accounting management in business planning at Malmö	160
Activity AM5.1	The Albion	171
Activity AM5.2	TEFL	184
Activity AM5.3	The London Brewing Company	194
Activity AM5.4	Gift Ideas Ltd and profitability	209
Activity AM6.1	Ratio analysis in the retail organization	227
Activity AM6.2	Ratios and their implications	229
Activity AM6.3	Ratios and organizational health	239
Activity AM6.4	A company assessment	242
Activity AM6.5	Ratio analysis: definitions and comment	248

Introduction to the Series

> "He that has done nothing has known nothing."
>
> *Carlyle*

The Concept

In this series 'effective' means getting results. By taking an action approach to management, or the stewardship of an organization, the whole series allows people to create and develop their skills of effectiveness. This interrelated series gives the underpinning knowledge base and the application of functional and generic skills of the effective manager who gets results.

Key qualities of the effective manager include:
- **functional expertise** in the various disciplines of management;
- an understanding of the **organizational context**;
- an appreciation of the **external environment**;
- **self-awareness** and the power of **self-development**.

These qualities must fuse in a climate of **enterprise**.

Management is results-oriented so action is at a premium. The basis of this activity is **skills** underpinned by our qualities. In turn these skills can be based on a discipline or a function, and be universal or generic.

The Approach of the Series

These key qualities of effective management are the core of the current twelve books of the series. The areas covered by the series at present are:

People	*Effective Personnel Management*
	Effective Labour Relations
	Effective Organizational Behaviour
Finance	*Effective Financial Management*
	Effective Accounting Management
Marketing and sales	*Effective Marketing*
	Effective International Marketing
	Effective Marketing Communications
Operations/Enterprise	*Effective Enterprise Management*
	Effective Entrepreneurship
Policy/General	*Effective Business Policy*
	Effective General Management

xiv INTRODUCTION TO THE SERIES

The key attributes of the effective manager are all dealt with in the series, and we will pinpoint where they are emphasized:

- *Functional expertise.* The four main disciplines of management – finance, marketing, operations and personnel management – make up nine books. These meet the needs of specialist disciplines and allow a wider appreciation of other functions.
- *Organizational context.* All the 'people' books – the specialist one on *Effective Organizational Behaviour*, and also *Effective Personnel Management* and *Effective Labour Relations* – cover this area. The resourcing/control issues are met in the 'finance' texts, *Effective Financial Management* and *Effective Accounting Management*. Every case activity is given some organizational context.
- *External environment.* One book, *Effective Business Policy*, is dedicated to this subject. Environmental contexts apply in every book of the series: especially in *Effective Entrepreneurship*, *Effective General Management*, and in all of the 'marketing' texts – *Effective Marketing*, *Effective International Marketing* and *Effective Marketing Communications*.
- *Self-awareness/self-development.* To a great extent management development is manager development, so we have one generic skill (see later) devoted to this topic running through each book. The subject is examined in detail in *Effective General Management*.
- *Enterprise.* The *Effective Entrepreneurship* text is allied to *Effective Enterprise Management* to give insights into this whole area through all the developing phases of the firm. The marketing and policy books also revolve around this theme.

Skills

The functional skills are inherent within the discipline-based texts. In addition, running through the series are the following generic skills:
- self-development
- teamwork
- communications
- numeracy/IT
- decisions

These generic skills are universal managerial skills which occur to some degree in every manager's job.

Format/Structure of Each Book

Each book is subdivided into six units. These are self-contained, in order to facilitate learning, but interrelated, in order to give an effective holistic view. Each book also has an introduction with an outline of the book's particular theme.

Each unit has *learning objectives* with an overview/summary of the unit.

Boxes appear in every unit of every book. They allow a different perspective from the main narrative and analysis. Research points, examples, controversy and theory are all expanded upon in these boxes. They are numbered by unit in each book, e.g. 'Box PM1.1' for the first box in Unit One of *Effective Personnel Management*.

Activities, numbered in the same way, permeate the series. These action-oriented forms of learning cover cases, questionnaires, survey results, financial data, market research information, etc. The skills which can be assessed in each one are noted in the code at the top right of the activity by having the square next to them ticked. That is, if we are assuming numeracy then the square beside Numeracy would be ticked (✓), and so on. The weighting given to these skills will depend on the activity, the tutors'/learners' needs, and the overall weighting of the skills as noted in the appendix on 'Generic Skills', with problem solving dominating in most cases.

Common cases run through the series. Functional approaches are added to these core cases to show the same organization from different perspectives. This simulates the complexity of reality.

Handbook

For each book in the series, there is a *handbook*. This is not quite the 'answers' to the activities, but it does contain some indicative ideas for them (coded accordingly), which will help to stimulate discussion and thought.

Test bank

We are developing a bank of tests in question-and-answer format to accompany the series. This will be geared to the knowledge inputs of the books.

The Audience

The series is for all those who wish to be effective managers. As such, it is a series for management development on an international scale, and embraces both management education and management training. In management education, the emphasis still tends to be on cognitive or knowledge inputs; in management training, it still tends to be on skills and techniques. We need both theory and practice, with the facility to try out these functions and skills through a range of scenarios in a 'safe' learning environment. This series is unique in encompassing these perspectives and bridging the gulf between the academic and vocational sides of business management.

Academically the series is pitched at the DMS/DBA types of qualification, which often lead on to an MA/MBA after the second year. Undergraduates following business degrees or management studies will benefit from the series in their final years. Distance learners will also find the series useful, as will those studying managerial subjects for professional examinations. The competency approach and the movement towards Accredited Prior Learning and National Vocational Qualifications are underpinned by the knowledge inputs, while the activities will provide useful simulations for these approaches to management learning.

This developmental series gives an opportunity for self-improvement. Individuals may wish to enhance their managerial potential by developing themselves without institutional backing by working through the whole series. It can also be used to underpin corporate training programmes, and acts as a useful design vehicle for specialist inputs from organizations. We are happy to pursue these various options with institutions or corporations.

The approach throughout the series combines skills, knowledge and application to create and develop the effective manager. Any comments or thoughts from participants in this interactive process will be welcomed.

Alan H. Anderson
Melbourn, Cambridge

The Series: Learning, Activities, Skills and Compatibility

The emphasis on skills and activities as vehicles of learning makes this series unique. Behavioural change, or learning, is developed through a two-pronged approach.

First, there is the **knowledge-based (cognitive)** approach to learning. This is found in the main text and in the boxes. These cognitive inputs form the traditional method of learning based on the principle of receiving and understanding information. In this series, there are four main knowledge inputs covering the four main managerial functions: marketing/sales, operations/enterprise, people, and accounting/finance. In addition, these disciplines are augmented by a strategic overview covering policy making and general management. An example of this first approach may be illustrative. In the case of marketing, the learner is confronted with a model of the internal and external environments. Thereafter the learner must digest, reflect, and understand the importance of this model to the whole of the subject.

Second, there is the **activity-based** approach to learning, which emphasizes the application of knowledge and skill through techniques. This approach is vital in developing effectiveness. It is seen from two levels of learning:

1 The use and application of *specific skills*. This is the utilization of your cognitive knowledge in a practical manner. These skills emanate from the cognitive aspect of learning, so they are functional skills, specific to the discipline.

   For example, the learner needs to understand the concept of job analysis before he or she tackles an activity that requires the drawing up of a specific job evaluation programme. So knowledge is not seen for its own sake, but is applied and becomes a specific functional skill.

2 The use and application of *generic skills*. These are universal skills which every manager uses irrespective of the wider external environment, the organization, the function and the job. This is seen, for example, in the ability to make clear decisions on the merits of a case. This skill of decision making is found in most of the activities.

There is a relationship between the specific functional skills and the generic skills. The specific functional skills stand alone, but the generic skills cut across them. See figure SK.1.

In this series we use activities to cover both the specific functional and the generic skills. There are five generic skills. We shall examine each of them in turn.

xviii ACTIVITIES, SKILLS AND COMPATIBILITY

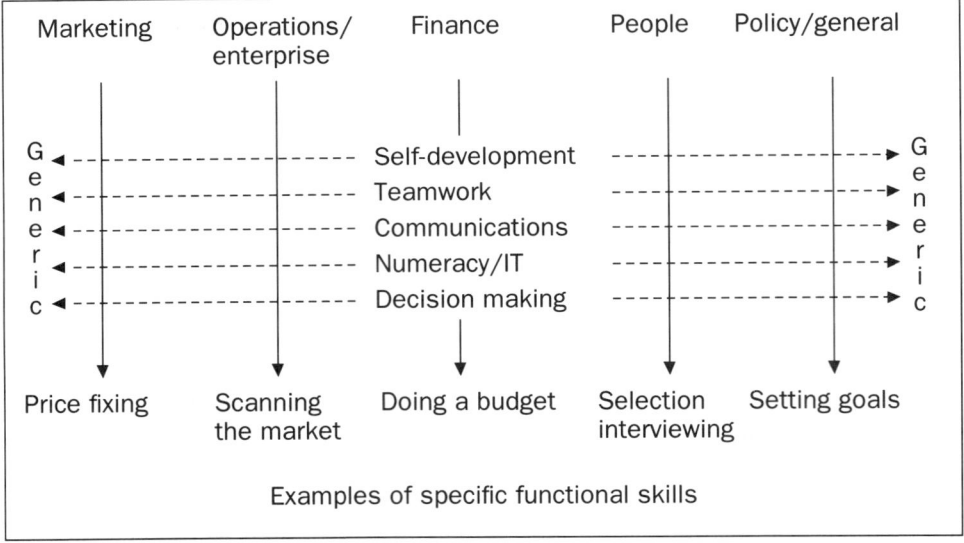

Figure SK.1 Series skills matrix: functional and generic skills.

Self-development

The learner must take responsibility for his or her learning as well as 'learning how to learn'. Time management, work scheduling and organizing the work are involved in the procedural sense. From a learning perspective, sound aspects of learning, from motivation to reward, need to be clarified and understood. The physical process of learning, including changing knowledge, skills and attitudes, may be involved. Individual goals and aspirations need to be recognized alongside the task goals. The ultimate aim of this skill is to facilitate learning transfer to new situations and environments.

Examples of this skill include:
- establishing and clarifying work goals;
- developing procedures and methods of work;
- building key learning characteristics into the process;
- using procedural learning;
- applying insightful learning;
- creating personal developmental plans;
- integrating these personal developmental plans with work goals.

Teamwork

Much of our working lives is concerned with groups. Effective teamwork is thus at a premium. This involves meeting both the task objectives and the socio-emotional processes within the group. This skill can be used for groups in a training or educational context. It can be a bridge between decision making and an awareness of self-development.

Examples of this skill include:
- clarifying the task need of the group;
- receiving, collating, ordering and rendering information;
- discussing, chairing and teamwork within the group;
- identifying the socio-emotional needs and group processes;
- linking these needs and processes to the task goals of the group.

Communications

This covers information and attitude processing within and between individuals. Oral and written communications are important because of the gamut of 'information and attitudinal' processing within the individual. At one level communication may mean writing a report, at another it could involve complex interpersonal relationships.

Examples of this skill include:
- understanding the media, aids, the message and methods;
- overcoming blockages;
- listening;
- presenting a case or commenting on the views of others;
- writing;
- designing material and systems for others to understand your communications.

Numeracy/IT

Managers need a core mastery of numbers and their application. This mastery is critical for planning, control, co-ordination, organization and, above all else, for decision making. Numeracy/IT are not seen as skills for their own sake. Here, they are regarded as the means to an end. These skills enable information and data to be utilized by the effective manager. In particular these skills are seen as an adjunct to decision making.

Examples of this skill include:
- gathering information;
- processing and testing information;

- using measures of accuracy, reliability, probability etc.;
- applying appropriate software packages;
- extrapolating information and trends for problem solving.

Decision making

Management is very much concerned with solving problems and making decisions. As group decisions are covered under teamwork, the emphasis in this decision-making skill is placed on the individual.

Decision making can involve a structured approach to problem solving with appropriate aims and methods. Apart from the 'scientific' approach, we can employ also an imaginative vision towards decision making. One is rational, the other is more like brainstorming.

Examples of this skill include:
- setting objectives and establishing criteria;
- seeking, gathering and processing information;
- deriving alternatives;
- using creative decision making;
- action planning and implementation.

This is *the* skill of management and is given primary importance in the generic skills within the activities as a reflection of everyday reality.

Before we go about learning how to develop into effective managers, it is important to understand the general principles of learning. Both the knowledge-based and the activity-based approaches are set within the environment of these principles. The series has been written to relate to Anderson's sound principles of learning which were developed in *Successful Training Practice*.

- *Motivation* – intrinsic motivation is stimulated by the range and depth of the subject matter and assisted by an action orientation.
- *Knowledge of results* – ongoing feedback is given through the handbook for each book in the series.
- *Scale learning* – each text is divided into six units, which facilitates part learning.
- *Self-pacing* – a map of the unit with objectives, content and an overview helps learners to pace their own progress.
- *Transfer* – realism is enhanced through lifelike simulations which assist learning transfer.
- *Discovery learning* – the series is geared to the learner using self-insight to stimulate learning.
- *Self-development* – self-improvement and an awareness of how we go about learning underpin the series.

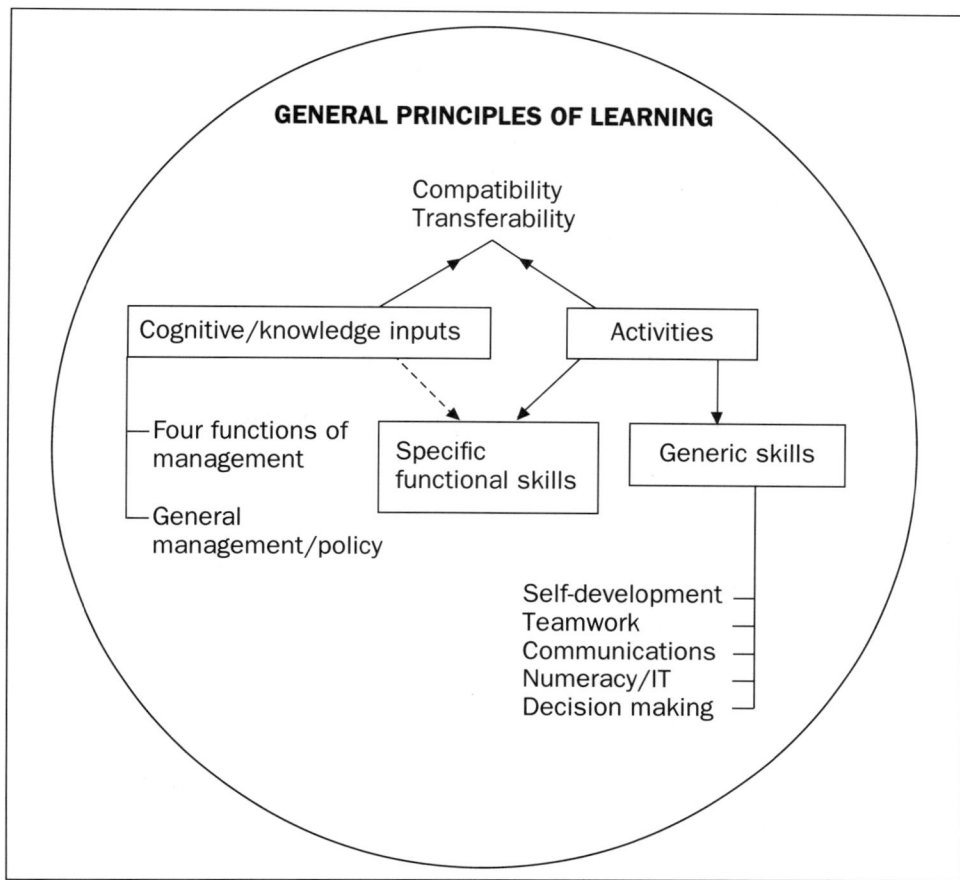

Figure SK.2 Series learning strategy.

- *Active learning* – every activity is based upon this critical component of successful learning.

From what has been said so far, the learning strategy of the series can be outlined in diagrammatic form. (See figure SK.2.)

In figure SK.2, 'compatibility and transferability' are prominent because the learning approach of the series is extremely compatible with the learning approaches of current initiatives in management development. This series is related to a range of learning classification being used in education and training. Consequently it meets the needs of other leading training systems and learning taxonomies. See figures SK.3–SK.6.

xxii ACTIVITIES, SKILLS AND COMPATIBILITY

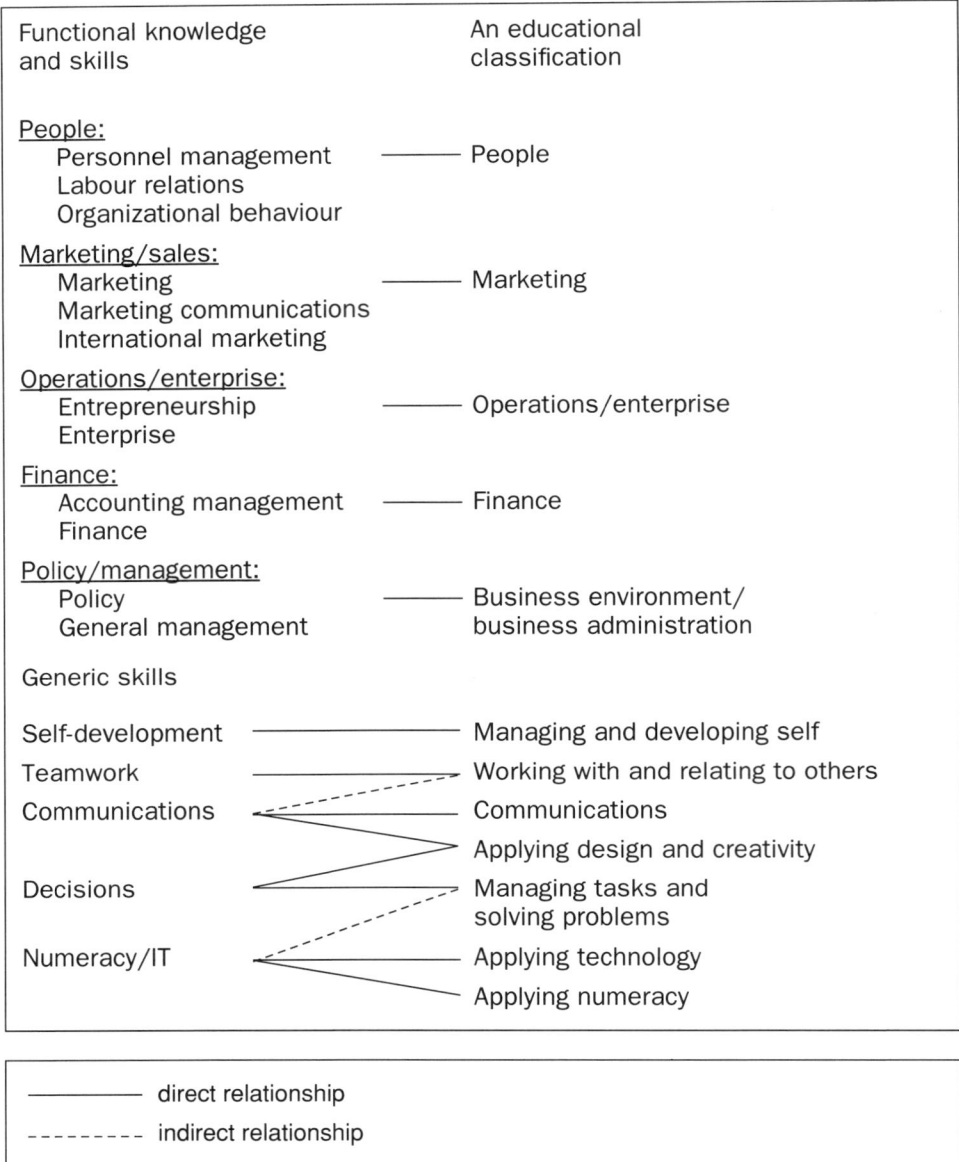

Figure SK.3 Series knowledge and skills related to an educational classification.

Source: Adapted from Business Technician and Education Council, 'Common skills and experience of BTEC programmes'.

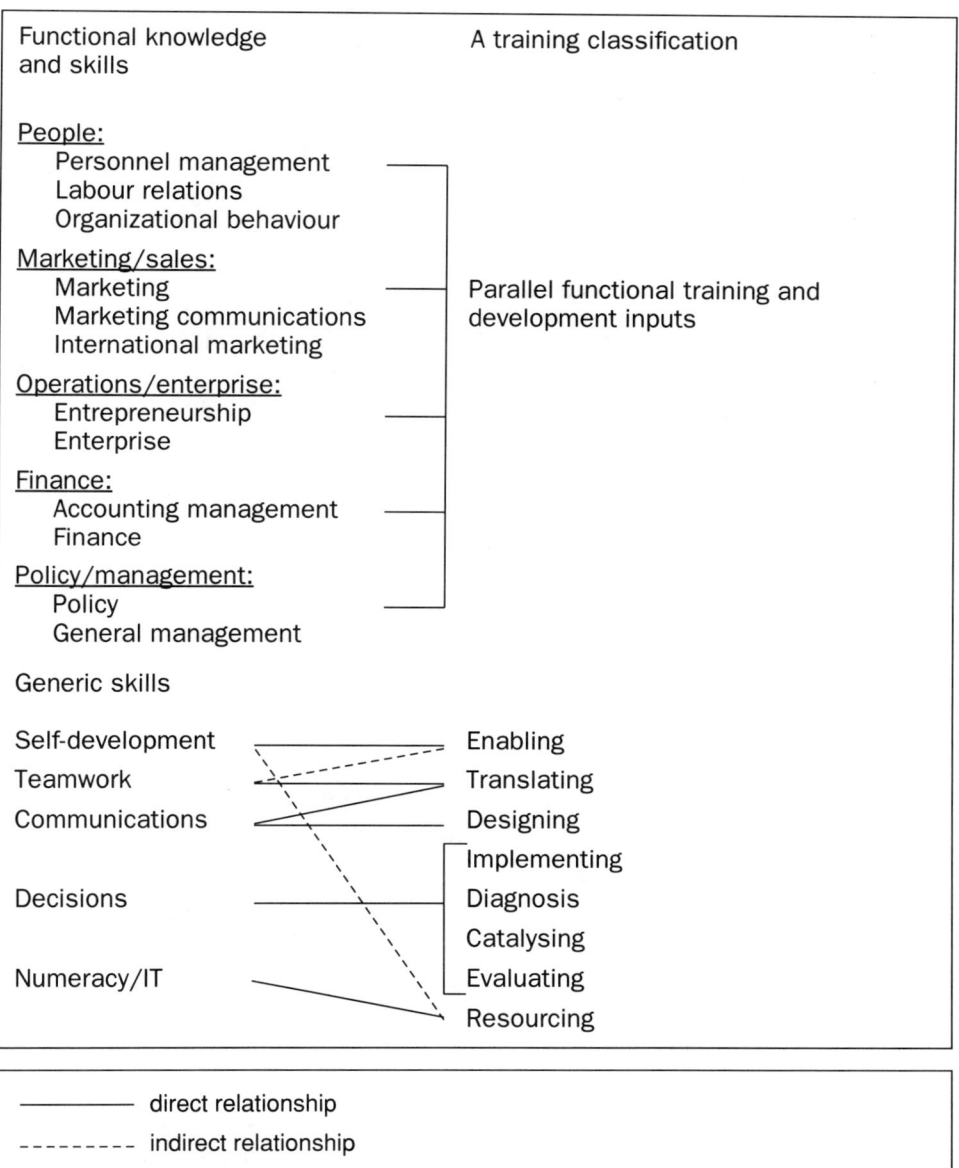

Figure SK.4 Series knowledge and skills related to a training classification.

Source: Adapted from J.A.G. Jones, 'Training intervention strategies' and experience of development programmes.

Functional knowledge and skills	MCI competency
People:	Managing people
Personnel management	
Labour relations	
Organizational behaviour	
Marketing/sales:	
Marketing	
Marketing communications	Managing operations and
International marketing	managing information
Operations/enterprise:	(plus new texts pending)
Entrepreneurship	
Enterprise	
Finance:	Managing finance
Accounting management	
Finance	
Policy/management:	Managing context
Policy	
General management	
Generic skills	
Self-development	Managing oneself
Teamwork	Managing others
Communications	Using intellect
Decisions	Planning
Numeracy/IT	

——— direct relationship
- - - - - indirect relationship

Figure SK.5 Series knowledge and skills related to Management Charter Initiative (MCI) competencies.

Source: Adapted from MCI diploma guidelines.

ACTIVITIES, SKILLS AND COMPATIBILITY xxv

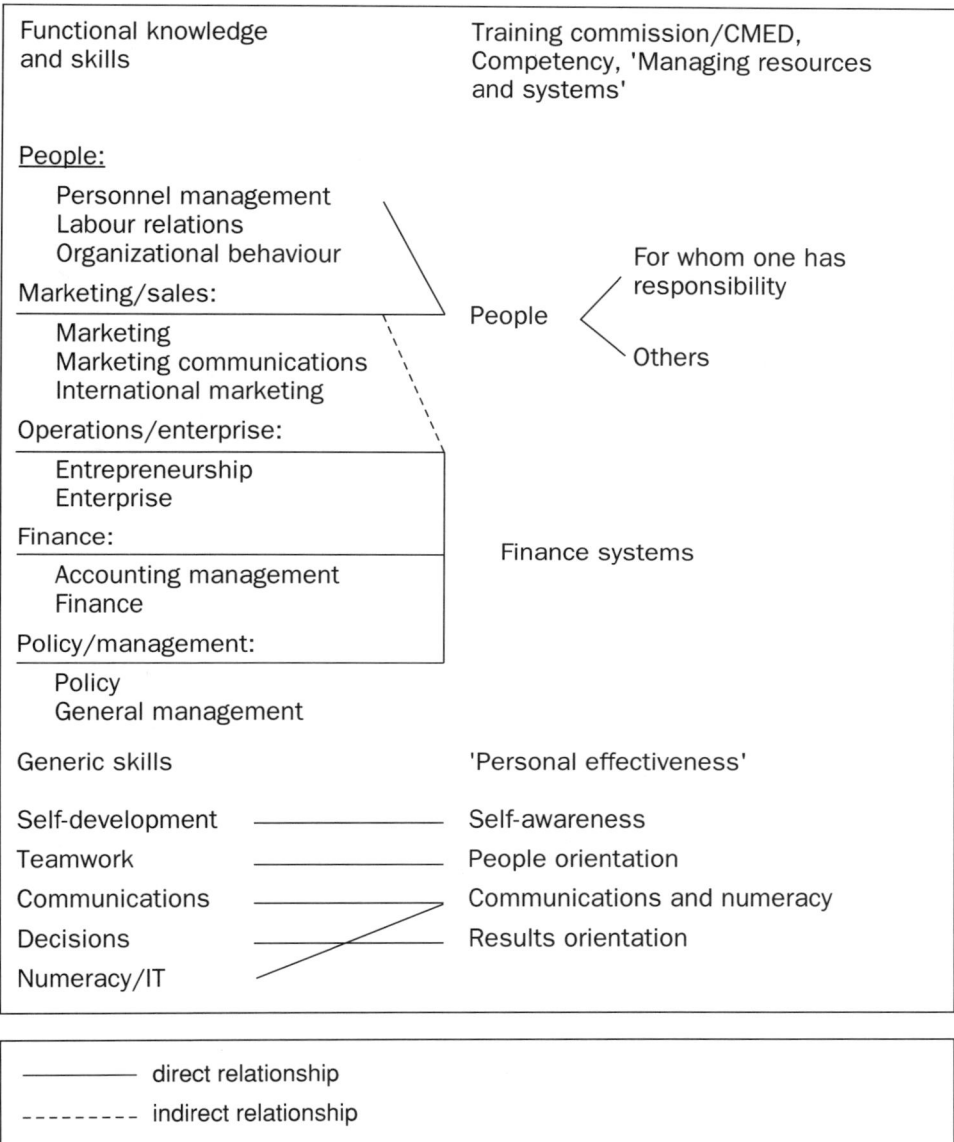

Figure SK.6 Series knowledge and skills related to Training Commission/Council for Management Education (CMED) competencies.

Source: Adapted from Training Commission/CMED, 'Classifying the components of management competencies'.

Preface

Concept

Accounting is the language of business. This book, like its sister volume *Effective Financial Management*,[1] does not aim for the fluency of a native speaker. It seeks a wider *appreciation* of the main concepts and techniques of accounting. This will help the non-accountant to become a better team manager in his or her dealings with specialists and give the non-accountant an overview of perhaps one of the most critical components of the organization, its financial resources.

Accountancy still remains a mystery to many managers and students of business. Others see it as a difficult subject, and the numbers put people off. More cynical people see it as common sense deliberately wrapped up in impenetrable conventions and formats, so that specialists can keep their monopoly.

The real purpose of this book is to unravel these mysteries in a clear format that reduces complexity without oversimplification. As to the numbers block, an understanding of the concepts, the issues and the various formats open to the specialist gives the numbers a context. We develop the *framework* to give the numbers more of a meaning. Basic numeracy is developed in another intended text of the series, *Effective Information Management*.[2]

More specifically, this book introduces the learner to issues of accounting. What are we trying to achieve in accounting? Whose responsibility is it? What documentation is needed? How can it help management control, management planning and decision making? How can we measure the relative financial effectiveness of an organization from an internal organizational perspective?

We are concerned with its *application to management* rather than with accounting from a purist's perspective. Consequently, we do not become enmeshed with intricate debates about accounting. You do not have to understand all these debates to be able to use the concepts, understand financial documentation and apply a range of accountancy techniques. To draw an analogy, we do not have to understand how all parts of a motor car work in order to drive a vehicle. This book is about driving, not mechanics. It sets out to allow the learner to monitor how the vehicle is doing on the road by helping the learner to read the appropriate dials and signals. Hence this book will give us signals about how the business organization is progressing. Remedial action or improved performance can result through this monitoring process.

Learning Aims

The learning aims of the book are as follows:
- to place accounting into its business context;
- to record accounting information and data;
- to give an understanding of basic accounting concepts and practices;
- to prepare appropriate documentation;
- to apply data to managerial tasks of control, planning and decision making;
- to analyse the internal organizational 'health' of an organization using appropriate accounting methods.

Format and Content

The format, or how we do things in the book, follows on from the aims. We deliberately set out to simplify complexity. Footnotes, academic treatises and accounting debates have been asided. Even the bibliography runs to only a few pages of 'additional reading'.

The activity-based approach, as in the whole series, underpins the knowledge base. The five generic skills are evident throughout the six units. The core cases of the series apply in this volume as well.

Boxes are minimized in the text and are replaced to some extent by *worked examples*. These detailed exercises show the concept or principle and are aligned with figures, tables etc. to demonstrate a step by step approach to learning. Again this is in keeping with the overall aims of the book.

In addition to these activities and worked examples, scope is given to mini-activities, still based on the generic skills, with room to respond to a specific accounting skill or technique.

An Outline of the Units

The content dovetails into the aims and format.

Unit Topic	*Theme*
Unit One Introduction and Context to Accounting	A brief historical background is given. The nature of accounting is examined. The context of the regulatory framework provides an important backcloth. 'Boundary rules' linked to financial statements conclude this unit.

PREFACE xxix

Unit Topic	*Theme*
Unit Two Recording Financial Information	A summary of accounting records is given as a background to information in accounting. We then bring our books to 'trial balance'. A discussion occurs on period end adjustments and we conclude by preparing the final accounts for different types of organizations.
Unit Three Costs and Their Classifications	We must be able to identify costs and put them into distinct compartments. This classification allows us to examine the make-up of costs. Various types of production systems are considered with their cost implications. We then record these costs and conclude by looking at overheads.
Unit Four Budgeting for Planning and Control	We are now applying these accounting principles to managerial tasks. Budgets, planning cycles and horizons are linked to systems of control. The physical preparation of budgets is important. Performance and variance analysis conclude this unit.
Unit Five Accounting Information for Decision Making	This whole unit concerns both the identification of financial data for decision making and the evaluation of these data.
Unit Six Measuring Performance with Accounting Information	This concluding unit is involved with performance management. Ratio analysis and a commentary on effective financial performance conclude the book.

Figure 0.1 shows the 'flows' of the book.

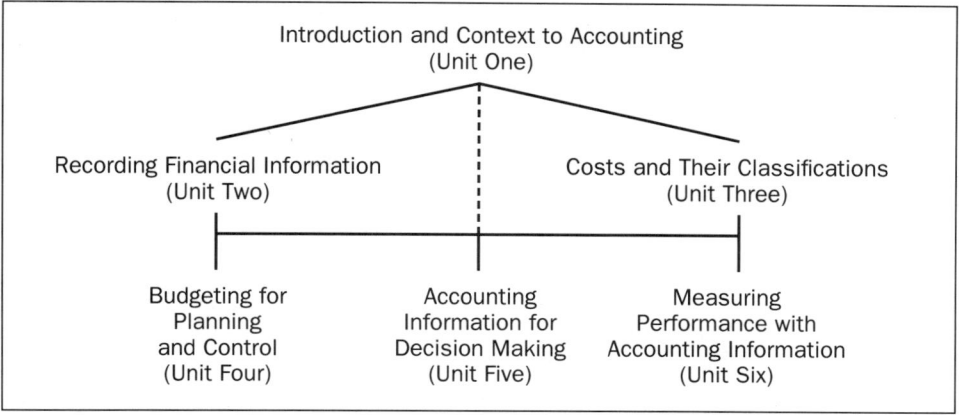

Figure 0.1 Contents flowchart.

Notes
1 See Anderson and Ciechan, *Effective Financial Management*.
2 There is a new book scheduled: Anderson and Thompson, *Effective Information Management – Decision Analysis*.

Acknowledgements

The authors and publisher would like to thank Richard Denison, Priscilla Kendal and Andrew Younger for their advice and assistance in the development of this book. In addition, both authors express their gratitude to Maureen Anderson for helping to pull the strands together and to Richard Ciechan for reading the proofs.

Unit One

Introduction: the Context of Accounting

Learning Objectives

After completing this unit you should be able to

- understand the factors that have influenced the development of accounting in the UK;
- identify the major users of company accounting information, and discover what this information is used for and the extent to which accounting information can be useful;
- identify the sources of regulation on financial reporting;
- appreciate the difference between financial accounting and management accounting;
- understand the concepts of wealth and profit, and how accounting information attempts to measure these concepts;
- read the main financial statements and understand the information they convey;
- apply the generic skills.

Contents

Overview

Introduction to Accounting

The Context of Accounting

Historical Background

Who Are the Users of Accounts?

- ▶ Investors and owners
- ▶ Lenders
- ▶ Creditors
- ▶ Business contact groups
- ▶ Employees
- ▶ Analysts and advisors
- ▶ Rivals
- ▶ The government
- ▶ The general public
- ▶ Management

Accounting Today

The Job of an Accountant

The Regulatory Framework

- ▶ The Companies Acts
- ▶ The accounting profession
- ▶ The stock exchange

Measuring Wealth and Profit

- ▶ Historic cost
- ▶ Historic cost less depreciation
- ▶ Net realizable value
- ▶ Replacement cost
- ▶ Economic value

Boundary Rules

The Financial Statements

Conclusion

Unit One

> " The accountancy profession appears more and more like a scavenger feeding on the carcasses of ailing companies. "
>
> D. Schulke[1]

Overview

This unit is a scene setter. It sets out to give a brief historical appreciation of accounting and tells the story up to the present day. The users of accounting information are discussed alongside the nature of accountancy.

A wider context is then given, with a discussion on the regulatory framework, the measures of wealth and profit and the 'rules' of the game. A brief introduction to financial statements concludes this unit as a 'taster' of things to come.

Introduction to Accounting

Why are effective managers so concerned about the financial performance of their companies? To understand their concern it is first necessary to understand the relationship that exists between the directors and those who own the business. Directors (and subordinate managers) are appointed to manage the business, ultimately for the benefit of the owners, the investors. The rewards, that is the money earned, go to the investors. To understand the concerns of managers to please the shareholders it is necessary to understand a little about the objectives of investors and the rewards they seek.

Think of yourself as someone with a small amount of money that you would like to save for the future (invest). There are a range of options, all competing for your money. One option is to buy a share in a company, another is to put your money into a building society. Why would you choose to buy a share in preference to the building society? It's a risky thing to do, and you might end up losing all your money. The building society is nice and safe, and you are virtually guaranteed to get your money back with interest. The reason why people invest in shares is that company shares on the whole give a better return than the building society. Those who buy shares are prepared to accept the higher risk in return for the higher return.

Shares are risky investments, but you should be able to avoid the worst of the risk by looking at the performance of the company. If you don't like the performance you can sell the share. If lots of people don't like the performance they will sell their shares too. If this happens the price will fall. The shareholders who still own shares will become unhappy because the value of their investments has decreased. They may not want to sell their shares but there is another course of action open to them. At the company's annual general meeting they vote on the composition of the board of directors. They can replace directors with ones they think will manage the business better. Existing directors are concerned that shareholders be kept happy so that they can keep their positions.

Which aspects of performance are the investors interested in? They may be concerned that the company is being a good 'citizen', but what is more likely to be of paramount importance is the amount of money returned to the investor. This is one of the major reasons for directors and managers being so concerned with financial performance. Directors make reports to investors, which enable them to make judgements. They will be concerned that these statements show their management in the best possible light.

How do you assess performance? For a start you can look at the past. Evidence from the past is often useful for predicting the future. A company that has had a good record in the past tends to do well in the future. The purpose of financial accounting is to give financial information from which investors can make assessments.

Much publicity has been given in recent years to financial scandals and frauds. How can accounting still be held in high regard? First, these frauds are rare: there are one million companies in the UK and in most cases there is no problem. Second, it is the complexity of business that makes financial frauds possible, not accounting in itself. Third, it is the directors who have the ultimate authority to choose how to report information, not accountants.

There are many different sorts of accountants. Some provide specialist services such as taxation and insolvency advice. The majority are information providers. Financial accountants serve people 'outside' the organization. We will focus on the 'internal' perspective of management accountant, although we take a wider view in Unit Six and to some extent in Unit Five.

Why are managers in not-for-profit organizations also interested in financial performance? The desire to report good performance has become prevalent in all organizations. A charity wants to show donors that funds are being used effectively. A local authority wants to show the local tax payers that it is providing services which are both efficient and effective. Many organizations are being made more 'accountable' by government. For example, in the UK the National Health Service is being made to report, so that greater visibility is given to activities and the cost of those activities. Even if profitability is not the objective, as a minimum position costs must be met for all organizations – profit or non-profit making.

The Context of Accounting

To understand where any subject stands at a particular point in time it is useful to look into the background of how and why it has developed. The way accounting has developed differs in various countries and this has resulted in widely differing practices around the world. UK accounting developed in a different way from that in other European Community nations. Differences and their causes were not fully appreciated until the European Community attempted to harmonize accounting practice in member nations. It was only then that the full extent of the fundamental differences was appreciated. The reasons for these differences lie in the social, economic, cultural and historical backgrounds of the nations. This section looks at these influences primarily from a UK perspective, with specific regard to conventions and the regulatory framework. Some of the wider principles may be transferable elsewhere, and the core concepts should be of value to Commonwealth countries or states based on the English framework. Before we go any further we should define the nature of our subject and look at an example of what it means to a firm. Please refer to Box AM1.1.

Historical Background

Accounting has been around for a very long time, before money was known to exist. Records have been found in Assyria from about 4500 BC, recording payment of taxes, which were made in gems, produce and

---

BOX AM1.1

Nature of accounting 1

Accounting is one of the key aspects of a business. The American Accounting Association has summed up the nature of the profession as 'the process of identifying, measuring and communicating economic information to permit informed judgements and decisions by users of the information'.

In summary, accounting is a tool for decision makers or managers, it helps with resource allocation and deployment, it allows control of resources and it is an aid to monitoring performance. Every manager must feel at least comfortable with the concepts and techniques. Of course, accounting spreads across all types of firms, from the sole proprietor and the partnership (which is quite common) to larger organizations. With size, specialism is more evident so a typical 'large' accounting department in a large company may look like that in figure 1.1.

8 EFFECTIVE ACCOUNTING MANAGEMENT

```
                          DIRECTOR
                                    SERVICES -------------
    ┌──────────┬──────────┼──────────┬──────────┐
MANAGEMENT    COST      FINANCIAL   INTERNAL   FINANCIAL
ACCOUNTING  ACCOUNTING  ACCOUNTING   AUDIT    MANAGEMENT
                                             (See other text
                                                in series)
```

MANAGEMENT ACCOUNTING	COST ACCOUNTING	FINANCIAL ACCOUNTING	INTERNAL AUDIT
Really a management information system being applied in a broad fashion. May include cost elements.	Collection/ presentation of detailed information for management to apply to control/resourcing/ decision making.	Maintenance/ preparation function of the main transactions.	Reporting internally to senior managers regarding accounting/ management procedures.

EXTERNAL ADVISORS

— *Trusts*
More individual than corporate on estate management/disposal.

— *Taxation*
Specialists in tax affairs (avoidance, not evasion).

— *Audit (external)*
External checkers on procedures/methods/standards (anti-fraud).

— *Financial*
Periodic financial data are published, e.g. for shareholders, government.

— *Liquidation etc.*
Bankruptcy, liquidation and receivership. Role and asset realization or 'company doctor' if in receivership, to allow the possibility of continuation of business.

Figure 1.1 A typical large accounting department.

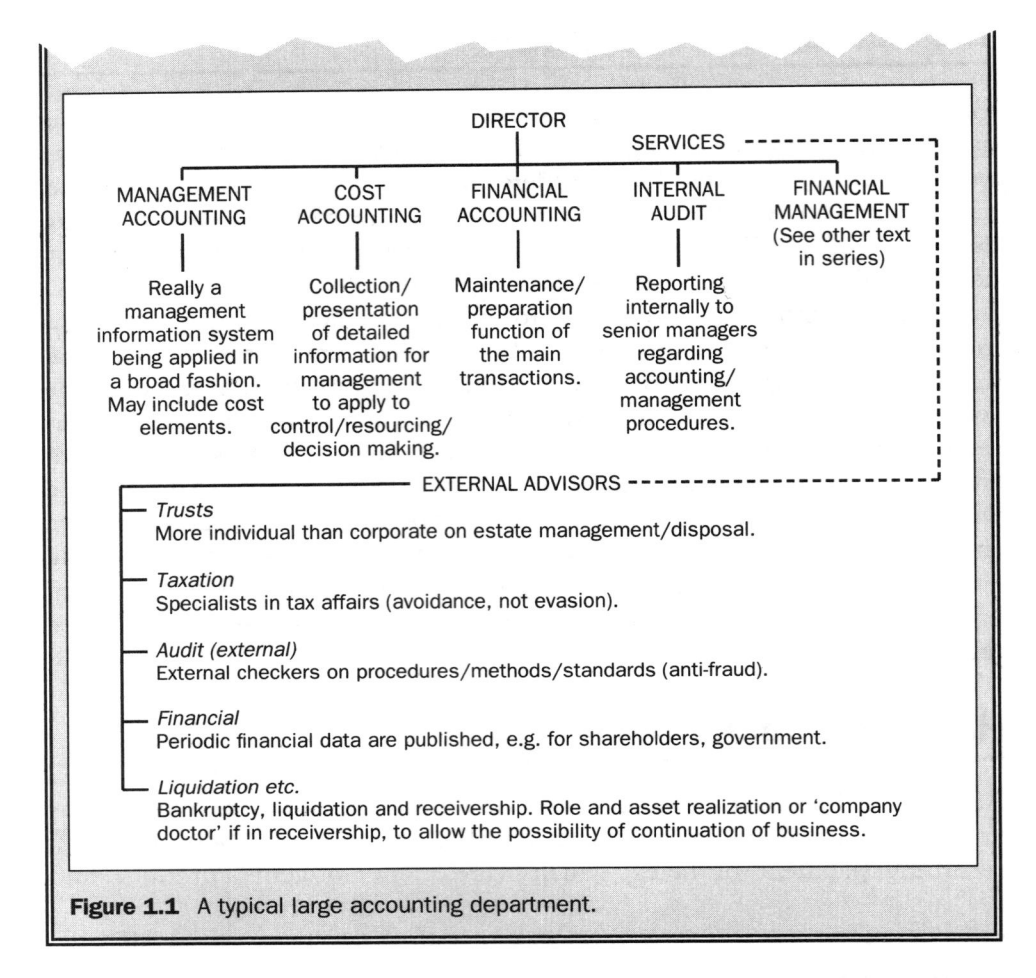

livestock. It is not easy to make comparisons or to convert grain into sheep and sheep into cows. A common medium of exchange was needed to express the value of each different type of item against a constant currency. The medium of exchange adopted by most societies was gold, and gold coinage became known as money.

The origins of modern accounting in the UK can be traced back to the Middle Ages. Landowners of the large estates set up after the Norman conquest were often absent from their estates or it was impossible for them to control all their properties. Stewards were appointed to look after the estates and they would have to 'account' for the property left in their charge. The assets held at the end of the time period should have been equal to those held at the start, plus any incomings and less any outgoings. Discrepancies meant inefficient 'accounting' or perhaps dishonesty. This was the basis of accounting for many years and today we still talk about the 'stewardship function' of accounting, where the managers of a business account for their stewardship to the owners.

INTRODUCTION: THE CONTEXT OF ACCOUNTING

The method of recording transactions in the Middle Ages was to keep a tally (a simple listing) of items. During the Middle Ages a new system of recording was introduced and spread, having gained popularity with Italian merchants who traded widely throughout Europe at that time. The method was known as double entry bookkeeping and this is still the foundation of the recording of financial transactions in business today.

Until the industrial revolution in the UK most businesses (with the exception of large estates) were small and family run. They did not need to produce accounts for 'stewardship' purposes. They still kept accounts, however, in order to keep the score and to allow the owner or manager to know how well the business was doing.

The demands of the industrial revolution called for new forms of business organization. Individuals were unable to fund entire projects on their own. This was particularly true in the case of railways. Enormous sums of money were required to finance new ventures. The need for finance saw the creation of joint stock companies, where there was more than one owner and each had a shareholding in the company. Not all the shareholders could or wanted to partake in the management of the business. Professional managers were appointed, resulting in the separation of ownership and management in the same way as seen on estates. In the same way that stewards had reported, managers now had to account for their 'stewardship' of the business to its owners. It was at this time that legislation that related to accounts first appeared, although the requirements were fairly scant.

To encourage investment, legislation was introduced allowing these new forms of companies to have limited liability. This means that should a company run into trouble, a shareholder would not have to put any money into the company beyond that initially agreed. This was important in attracting investors to put their money into new ventures. For the first time the financial risk of a company failing fell on people other than the owners. People (creditors) who supplied materials or services faced the possibility of not getting paid if the company ran out of cash. They could not go to investors to ask for the shortfall. Further legislation was introduced giving greater protection to investors.

Early legislation gave little guidance on the preparation of the accounts. Books were required to be regularly balanced, and 'full and fair' balance sheets were to be produced, signed by the directors and audited (checked and verified) by one or more shareholders. An accountant could be employed to assist in the audit, but there was no requirement for one to be present. The accounting profession was in its infancy and there were few accounting concepts. As business became more complicated and an annual audit became compulsory a profession began to take shape, much along the lines of the legal profession. It developed consensus opinions on the treatment of transactions and established best practices. During the twentieth century the profession has had a significant impact on further legislation.

Accounting regulation in the UK has largely been a reactive process, usually responding to scandals. Accounting continued to emphasize the 'stewardship' role into the twentieth century. The introduction of a requirement to produce a profit and loss account marked the beginning of a move towards meeting the needs of investors and other users of information. A famous case in 1931 brought to the fore the changing emphasis. The Royal Mail Steam Packet Company had for a number of years built up reserves in its accounts (it had under-declared profits, keeping some back 'for a rainy day'). When it ran into a difficult trading period the reserves were released, so it appeared still to be making a profit. The company collapsed and an outcry ensued. The auditors were sued for aiding and abetting the falsification of accounts, but no laws had been broken so the case failed. Shareholders were thought to have been only interested in dividends received and the value of shares. It was seen from this case that investors wanted information to help them forecast the future of the company and to enable a judgement to be made on the financial effectiveness of management. It was following this case that a committee was set up to look at accounting legislation. The result was the comprehensive Companies Act of 1948, which still provides the basis of much of today's accounting legislation.

Another major development occurred in 1967 and concerned the takeover of Associated English Industries by the General Electric Company. During the takeover battle AEI announced forecast profits for the year of £10 million, which made the takeover that much more difficult and expensive. Following the takeover accounts were prepared which showed a loss of £4.5 million. Of the £14.5 million difference £5 million could be attributed to matters of fact. The remainder was the result of the different accounting treatments chosen by the two companies. There was nothing illegal about the choice of treatments, as the law did not state in detail how particular items were to be treated. The extent of the problem was now appreciated and something had to be done. The government indicated that it would intervene unless the accounting profession took steps to restore public confidence. The result was the setting up of a committee of the major accounting bodies in the UK to decide on best practice in accounting. Self-regulation has remained a feature of accounting in the UK despite pressure from the European Community to have more accounting regulation codified into law. The current framework of accounting regulation will be looked at in more detail in the next section.

Most of this section has been concerned with companies. Of course, there are other types of business organization, such as sole traders and partnerships. These have not been affected by the accounting legislation, but their accounts are remarkably similar to those of companies. This is because the accounting profession is a body of expertise. Most businesses are run by people good at a particular line of business and not necessarily at accounting. They employ accountants who have trained in the profession and are aware of best practices, and naturally employ them when preparing any accounts. One of the major reasons businesses other than companies prepare accounts is for the assessment of income tax. The Inland Revenue has its own rules for the calculation of taxation, but prefers to see proper accounts as an indication that proper records have been kept.

Who Are the Users of Accounts?

In the development of UK accounting we can see that at different times emphasis has been placed on different groups of people and their perceived needs. Who are the people who want information from accounts today? What information are they looking for? It is crucial to understand this before deciding what information should be produced. The groups of people and their interests in a company are outlined below.

Investors and owners

This group includes both current investors and potential investors. Traditionally investors have been individuals who hold small holdings of shares. Increasingly people are relying on various institutions to make investments on their behalf; for example, pension funds and unit trusts. Professional fund managers may be more knowledgeable users than small investors but basically they are interested in the same information. They require information that will help them decide when to buy and sell shares, whether to buy more shares if the company decides it wants to raise more finance and how to vote at general meetings. Their particular concern is for information that impacts on the future price of shares. They will also want information which is comparable with that produced by other companies, as this allows them to make comparisons and to identify the best investments. They want information about dividend payments, as these make up their income. They want to assess the ability of current management to run the company efficiently and honestly.

Lenders

Lenders are the non-equity providers of finance for a company. Sometimes loans are secured; that is, if the company is unable to make payments the lenders take possession of some of the company's assets and sell them (in the same way that building societies can repossess your home if you don't keep up with your mortgage payments). Long-term providers of loan finance are usually called debenture or bond holders in the UK (stock holders in the USA). Long-term lenders will be interested in the liquidity of the company, the ability to meet payments. In addition they are concerned with the longer-term prospects as it may be several years before they are due to have their capital repaid. Short-term lenders are principally concerned with a company's liquidity and the company's ability to repay capital and interest in a short time.

Creditors

Creditors supply short-term finance to a company by supplying goods or services and accepting a delay in payment. Like short-term lenders they will be largely concerned with short-term liquidity.

Business contact groups

Customers have an interest in a company in that they want to have a stable supply of goods or services. Suppliers want to be sure of having a market, even if they do not extend credit. They want information that will allow them to assess the prospects of the company and its ability to meet commitments and contractual arrangements.

Employees

Current and potential employees of the company will be interested in assessing the prospects for long-term employment. They may also want to assess the ability of the company to pay increased wages. Past employees have an interest when they are dependent on the company's pension plan.

Analysts and advisors

These are people who make their living by advising or informing other people about a company, such as financial journalists and stockbrokers. Their concerns will be the same as those of the people they hope to advise.

Rivals

Competitors will wish to identify and exploit potential opportunities for their own benefit. Some may be able to anticipate the future actions of a company from financial data. An increase in plant and machinery might signify an increase in the quality of products or reduced costs. Some may be looking to take over other companies. Where the takeover complements current activities, information will be required on the assets owned (and outstanding liabilities) and on profitability, in order to judge what price to offer. Where the takeover is designed to remove a competitor or to take advantage of an undervaluation, information is required to assess the value of the business in terms of market price against the realizable value of assets.

The government

Central and local tax authorities will want information on earnings so that they can assess the amount of tax to be paid. Other government departments will need information for the collection of statistics on the economy. This information is far-ranging and in great detail. It is probably not required by any other user.

The general public

Companies can have a substantial impact on a region or on the environment. Individual members of the general public and pressure groups who are affected by the actions of the company will want information. The information required depends on the nature of their concern. Where a company is a large employer in an area the concern will be with the prospects for continued or expanded employment.

Management

These are the people who are being assessed for efficiency by the shareholders and they are responsible for acting in the interests of the shareholders. They are responsible for the preparation of information that is given to shareholders and they will be concerned that this shows them in the best possible light. In order to operate efficiently they need large amounts of detailed information, which is used for score keeping, decision making, planning and control.

Different groups have different access to information. Management can have access to all the information they require provided it is cheaply available. Other groups have the backing of law in demanding information. Government agencies can go into a company and closely examine all information. To supply all the information required by all interest groups may not be in the best interests of the company. Rivals may act upon this information to the detriment of other users. Information that is made available to shareholders becomes easily available to other groups, including rivals. There is a limit to the amount of financial information that should be provided.

Accounting Today

Accounting is about providing the economic information required for people to make decisions. As we have seen, the people wanting information are diverse and have different needs. Accounting is subdivided into two main, separate yet related, areas: providing information to those outside the organization and providing information to people who manage the organization. The former is known as financial accounting, the latter as management accounting. There are many differences between the two sorts of accounting but the major difference is in detail of information and availability. There are no restrictions on the information that can be given to managers (provided it is not too costly to collect the information). There are no rules laid down about what information should be used and how often it should be available. It is for management to decide. The issue is whether it helps the manager to become more effective. A related but wider issue is the whole contribution of management accountancy to organizational effectiveness. Please refer to Activity AM1.1.

ACTIVITY AM1.1

THE LIMITS OF ACCOUNTING

Activity code
- ✓ Self-development
- ✓ Teamwork
- ☐ Communications
- ☐ Numeracy/IT
- ✓ Decisions

To a great extent accounting is applied information management for control, planning and decision-making purposes, either within the organization or for interested parties outside the enterprise. The language is money. In itself this language may be *the* acid test of efficiency and wider effectiveness but other factors are also to the fore in such measurement, from new product development to the quality of labour relations. Kaplan[1] notes some other factors that need to be taken into account in this evaluation of alternative plans and options; Campbell[2] argues for a whole range of effectiveness measures, including accounting.

Task
Your role is to group Campbell's categories, listed below, into main categories, to compare their relative importance and to weigh the importance of accounting compared to the other measures of effectiveness in the organization.

Category	Link/ classification	Classification rank in importance	Comparison with accounting

1 Overall effectiveness
2 Productivity
3 Efficiency

Category	Link/ classification	Classification rank in importance	Comparison with accounting
4 Profit			
5 Quality			
6 Accidents			
7 Growth			
8 Absenteeism			
9 Turnover			
10 Job satisfaction			
11 Motivation			
12 Morale			
13 Control			
14 Conflict/cohesion			
15 Flexibility/adaptation			
16 Planning/goal setting			
17 Goal consensus			
18 Internalization of organizational goals			
19 Role and norm congruence			
20 Managerial interpersonal skills			
21 Managerial task skills			
22 Information management and communication			
23 Readiness			
24 Utilization of environment			
25 Evaluations by external entities			
26 Stability			
27 Value of human resources			
28 Participation and shared influence			
29 Training and development emphasis			
30 Achievement emphasis			

Sources:
1. Adapted from Kaplan, 'The evaluation of management accounting'
2. Campbell, 'On the nature of organizational effectiveness'

To return to the basic question of information, we find that there are restrictions on the information available to those outside the organization. As seen in the previous section, the objectives of user groups are sometimes contradictory. Although it might be good to provide all the information that anyone might want, the information could be used to the detriment of shareholders. The minimum amount of information that can be given is set down in company law. The law to some extent also stipulates the presentation of the information. Legal requirements are largely intended to protect the shareholders and creditors of the organization. In addition to the law the accounting profession has developed standards that are followed in the preparation of accounts. The aim of financial accounting is to give a 'true and fair' view of the company's position and performance.

A 'true and fair' view is not necessarily the same as a 'true and correct' view. The 'true and fair' view is supposed to give a view of the true economic situation. A 'true and correct' view means that certain procedures have been followed properly, but something might still be hidden. Closely connected with financial accounting is the audit. This is where an independent person ascertains how far accounts do provide a 'true and fair' view. Situations have occurred where audited accounts have been found not to represent a 'true and fair' view when a company has failed or a scandal has resulted. Auditors are not supposed to look into every single transaction, as they would be taking on the jobs of the company's accountants and directors and the cost of the audit would be excessive. Samples of transactions are looked at and judgements are formed from these samples. It may be argued that an auditor is negligent in missing a fraudulent transaction. The wish to avoid a legal judgement on what constitutes negligence may be the reason why so many cases are settled out of court.

The Job of an Accountant

To become an accountant in the UK you must be admitted to membership of one of the professional institutes. There are several institutes, some representing quite different aspects of accounting. Someone who describes himself or herself as an accountant is probably a member of one of the following:

Institute of Chartered Accountants in England and Wales (ICAEW)
Institute of Chartered Accountants in Scotland (ICAS)
Institute of Chartered Accountants in Ireland (ICAI)
Chartered Association of Certified Accountants (ACCA)
Chartered Institute of Management Accountants (CIMA)
Chartered Institute of Public Finance and Accountancy (CIPFA)

There are two levels of membership. Associates are those who have passed the professional examinations of the institute and fulfil the requirements for practical experience. Associate members are entitled to add some letters after their name; for example, in the ICAEW, they would be ACA. Fellows are those who have gained substantial practical experience. Fellows are also entitled to add letters after their name; for example, in CIMA they could be FCMA. Note that all the institutes are chartered; that is, they have a royal charter. Someone who describes herself as a chartered accountant will be a member of one of the first three institutes on the list.

There are differences between the institutes. Sometimes these are minor, reflecting differences in training requirements or company law and taxation in England, Scotland and Ireland. Two of the institutes listed are fundamentally different from the others. CIMA is particularly concerned with accounting for use by managers. CIPFA is particularly concerned with accounting in the public sector; that is, central and local government and nationalized (and the newly privatized) industries. The remaining institutes are largely concerned with accounting as a means of providing information to those outside an organization. To perform an audit on a company you must have a practising certificate from one of these four institutes. Although there are differences between the institutes their interests do overlap and there is significant cooperation between them. There are some people who think the institutes should amalgamate but there are others who think that the existence of more than one institute adds to the debate on important issues.

Now tackle Activity AM1.2.

The Regulatory Framework

Regulation of accounting is essential for a healthy financial market. Without regulation investors could not be confident in the accounts and companies would not be able to attract finance. In the UK regulation comes from three major sources, as demonstrated in figure 1.2.

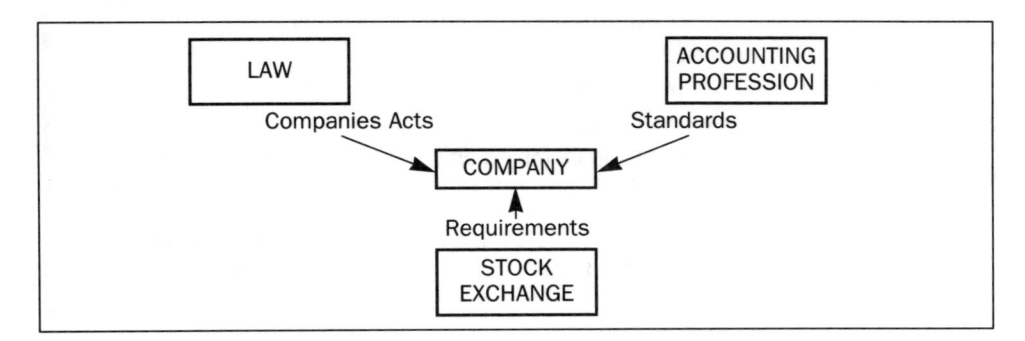

Figure 1.2 The regulatory framework.

ACTIVITY AM1.2

A MANAGEMENT ACCOUNTANT: JOB AND PERSON PROFILES

Activity code
- ✓ Self-development
- ✓ Teamwork
- ☐ Communications
- ☐ Numeracy/IT
- ✓ Decisions

There are two tasks to be completed:

Task 1
You have to outline the role and duties of a management accountant. This should be derived from the specification below but should really involve an extrapolation of information from this unit.

Task 2
You then derive a candidate profile for this job by using a seven point plan. A fuller discussion of this plan and selection can be seen in a sister book of this series,[1] but brief details are attached. You should assume that there is a vacancy for this position.

Company details
The management accountant reports to the financial director, who also acts as the financial accountant for the firm. From time to time, the management accountant may have to conduct financial accounting tasks as well in his or her capacity as deputy.

The company is in the business of coin-operated machines. It buys juke boxes, video games, pool tables and amusement machines, and rents them out to brewers and to independent public houses. Subcontractors install, maintain and collect cash from these machines. Currently some 8000 public houses are being 'serviced'.

Financially the company objectives revolve around:

1. Rent – an average of machine rental per week of £60.
2. The number of machines that can be rented out. Some are very popular but most have a limited timespan of 9 months only (this equates to an average uptake of 1.3 machines per outlet).
3. Income per machine. 'Earnings' fluctuate but on average the machines take about £400 per week. The retailer gets a 50 per cent cut and the remainder goes to the company.

INTRODUCTION: THE CONTEXT OF ACCOUNTING

4 Downtime must be limited. Servicing and repairs, as well as poor stockholding, particularly of popular machines, mean an average loss of machine usage (i.e. 1.3 machines) of 4 weeks. Rental and earnings are thus reduced.

The job holder has one administrative assistant who prepares and collates information. The role of the job holder is to provide a full management accounting service to line management and to participate in the achievement of the company's business plans and objectives.

Task 1
Job objective:

Duties (1–10):
1
2
3
4
5
6
7
8
9
10
Others, e.g.
11 Financial
12 Internal audit

Task 2
From these duties, extrapolate your views of the ideal candidate for this position using the plan below (basic definitions of the plan are attached).

Work experience (type, nature, function, industry etc.)

Training (level, skills, knowledge etc.)

Education (level and type)

Personal (motivation, adaptiveness etc.)

Plans (expectations related to job prospects)

Source: See Anderson, *Effective Personnel Management*, for a detailed commentary on the selection plan

Not all businesses are affected by all three sources of regulation. Only the very largest companies quoted on the stock exchange need worry about complying with their requirements. The full extent of regulation will only apply to businesses that are companies. The larger the company the more regulations there are to be complied with.

The Companies Acts

The present law is set out in two acts: the Companies Acts of 1985 and 1989. These acts relate to all aspects of company regulation and not just accounting. The accounting regulations require that:

- accounting records are kept which are adequate to show and explain the company's transactions, and from which final accounts can be prepared;
- the following statements are prepared and published on an annual basis – a profit and loss account, a balance sheet, and a directors' report;
- the accounts should provide a 'true and fair' view of the company's performance and position;
- the shareholders appoint qualified auditors to conduct an independent review of the company's accounting records and published accounts, to ensure compliance with the statutory requirements.

The Companies Acts are primarily aimed at providing a 'true and fair' view of a company's position and performance in a given period. They lay down the minimum amount of information that must be disclosed and sometimes give formats for its presentation. They do not expand upon what is meant by a 'true and fair' view. They do not even specify what accounting records should be kept. The reason for this is the strength of the accounting profession. When drawing legislation the government has been content to allow the profession to take the lead. In fact, the profession has been relied upon to interpret the legislation once it is on the statute books.

A 'true and fair' view, as has been mentioned, is not the same as a 'correct' view. In the treatment of many accounting items there is no one 'correct' method. Accounting requires the exercise of judgement. A 'true and fair' view is one that complies with generally accepted practices. The reliance on the profession to interpret and to be flexible is the main feature of UK accounting that differs from practice seen in continental Europe. Traditionally company law in the UK has provided a bare framework, with the accounting profession filling in the gaps. Membership of the European Community has meant some changes in the UK. The Companies Act of 1981 for the first time incorporated a European Community directive. This gave formats for the presentation of accounting statements and specified that five accounting principles must be followed in giving a 'true and fair' view.

One reason for this reliance on the accounting profession for regulation is the need for flexibility. For many transactions there is no one right treatment for every situation. Each company is different. If the accounts are to reflect the individual character of the business then the directors must be left free to choose the appropriate accounting treatment. Another reason is that the profession can respond far more quickly than laws can be enacted. Accountants have produced their own accounting standards identifying best practice. Although the law does not insist that accounting standards be followed, the general interpretation is that if they are not, the accounts will not be showing a 'true and fair' view.

The accounting profession

The accounting profession enjoys a monopoly in being able to audit the accounts of companies. The justification for this and for the profession's position in guiding and interpreting company law comes from the control exercised by the institutes over their members and the set of conventions used by accountants in their work. However, these conventions in themselves became insufficient for dealing with the complexities posed by large businesses. As demonstrated by the GEC takeover of AEI, a wide number of possible methods existed for the treatment of transactions.

Further guidance was needed to promote best and acceptable practice. The ICAEW had issued recommendations since 1942 but these were only applicable to its own members. It was not until the beginning of the 1970s that all the major professional institutes began to cooperate on issuing statements that were applicable to all of their memberships. The Accounting Standards Committee was formed and by its dissolution in 1990 had issued 25 Statements of Standard Accounting Practice (SSAPs). It has now been replaced by the Accounting Standards Board, which issues Financial Reporting Standards. A full list of the Standards issued by the accounting profession is given in Box AM1.2. In addition to these are Statements of Recommended Practice (SORPs), which relate to accounting issues affecting particular industries or business sectors.

As can be seen from Box AM1.2 the standards have been subject to many revisions, withdrawals and replacements over the years. Some have been revised to reflect changes in company law. Others have had to be changed because of more serious flaws. Problems with standards led to the replacement of the Accounting Standards Committee by the current structure. The previous structure had been criticized for failing to take into account the opinions of non-accountants, taking too long in developing standards, requiring complete consensus from the professional bodies for adoption of standards and having insufficient power in ensuring compliance. The current structure is administered through a number of committees.

22 EFFECTIVE ACCOUNTING MANAGEMENT

BOX AM1.2

Standards

Standard	Title	Date issued or revised (R)
SSAP 1	Accounting for Associated Companies	R 1982
SSAP 2	Disclosure of Accounting Policies	1971
SSAP 3	Earnings Per Share	R 1974
SSAP 4	The Accounting Treatment of Government Grants	R 1990
SSAP 5	Accounting for Value Added Tax	1974
SSAP 6	Extraordinary Items and Prior Year Adjustments	Withdrawn
SSAP 7	Accounting for Changes in the Purchasing Power of Money	Withdrawn
SSAP 8	The Treatment of Taxation under the Imputation System in the Accounts of Companies	R 1977
SSAP 9		R 1988
SSAP10	Stocks and Long-term Contracts	Withdrawn
SSAP11	Statement of Sources and Applications of Funds	Withdrawn
SSAP12	Accounting for Deferred Taxation	R 1987
SSAP13	Accounting for Depreciation	R 1989
SSAP14	Accounting for Research and Development	1978
SSAP15	Group Accounts	R 1985
SSAP16	Accounting for Deferred Taxation	Withdrawn
SSAP17	Current Cost Accounting	1980
SSAP18	Accounting for Post Balance Sheet Events	1980
SSAP19	Accounting for Contingencies	1981
SSAP20	Accounting for Investment Properties	1983
SSAP21	Foreign Currency Translation	1984
SSAP22	Accounting for Leases and Hire Purchase Agreements	R 1989
SSAP23	Accounting for Goodwill	1985
SSAP24	Accounting for Acquisitions and Mergers	1988
SSAP25	Accounting for Pension Costs	1990
FRS 1	Segmental Reporting	1991
FRS 2	Cash Flow Statements	1992
FRS 3	Reporting Financial Performance	1993
FRS 4	Capital Instruments	1994
FRS 5	Reporting the Substance of Transactions	1994

Financial Reporting Council (FRC) This takes overall responsibility for the direction, funding and public relations of standard setting. It consists of 26 members drawn from the accounting profession and managers in both the public and private sector.

Accounting Standards Board (ASB) This body is responsible for the technical task of developing financial reporting standards. It consists of 12 qualified accountants.

Urgent Issues Task Force (UITF) This is an offshoot of the ASB. It aims to respond in a timely manner to issues as they arise. It produces abstracts that come into effect after a month of publication.

Financial Reporting Review Panel This monitors the financial reporting practices of large companies. The panel (or the Secretary of State for Trade and Industry) can take a company to court for failing to comply with a standard (resulting in a failure to show a 'true and fair' view).

The stock exchange

Some requirements apply only to the relatively few but very large companies listed on the stock exchange. Their intention is to give more information to one group of users, investors. They extend the requirements of legislation and standards; for example, they require that interim (6 months) accounts are published. Any company not complying with the requirements can have trading in its shares suspended, so this is a very powerful sanction.

Please refer to Box AM1.3.

BOX AM1.3

Creative accounting – at an end?

The accounting profession is guided by standards but 'creative' accounting has been an aspect of accounting that can hardly be called professional. From the end of June 1993 in the UK a new standard (FRS3 – Reporting Financial Performance) puts some beef into cleaning up the situation on company reporting.

The main aspects include:

- the separation of *acquisitions* and *disposals* from the *results of continuing operations*;
- highlighting *profits* from property sales and disposal of business;
- showing any reorganization costs *before calculating pre-tax profits*;
- the near abolition of '*extraordinary items*', which had suffered from much creativity as they were excluded from the earnings per share (EPS) calculation;
- the EPS calculation will be based on *net profits available to ordinary shareholders after all deductions*.

However, the 'creative' flair of those who cheat is difficult to legislate against, and no doubt other doors are ajar, from asset valuations to the cost of goodwill.

24 EFFECTIVE ACCOUNTING MANAGEMENT

Measuring Wealth and Profit

The major financial statements, the balance sheet and the profit and loss account, try to show the financial position of the company at a particular moment in time and the profit earned during a period. How are they related? Quite simply, if you measure wealth at one point in time and then measure it again at some later point, an increase in wealth is profit and a decrease is a loss. The profit and loss account shows how this increase or decrease has come about.

Crucial to the calculation of profit is the measurement of wealth. Before going on to look at any accounting statement we will spend some time looking at measurement of wealth. We will start with a simple example.

WORKED EXAMPLE

On 1 May 1993 Sid has £2000 in cash and owns nothing else but the clothes he stands in. On that day he takes a lease on a beach bar on a tropical resort island. By 30 April 1994 he has £150 in cash, £500 of stock, furniture and fittings that had cost £1500 when purchased on 1 May 1993, and personal clothing and belongings worth £600.

Let's begin by listing the value of Sid's possessions at the two dates.

Wealth	1 May 1993	30 April 1994
Cash	2000	150
Stock	0	500
Furniture	0	1500
Personal	0	600
Total	2000	2750

At the end of the year the value of the possessions has risen. We can say that Sid has made a profit in the period because he has more now than he did a year ago. A profit and loss account for Sid would show the value of all the sales made during the year less all the expenses that had been incurred, and might look as follows.

Sales		20000
Expenses		
Drink purchased and sold	−13700	
Food consumed	−5550	−19250
Profit		750

The result, the profit, is the same as the change in the value of the possessions. The actual amount of cash spent on purchasing drinks would be higher than shown in the profit and loss account. At the end of the year £500 is held in stock, so £14 200 in total would have been spent. Only the cost of items that have been used up is *written off* (included) in the profit

INTRODUCTION: THE CONTEXT OF ACCOUNTING

and loss account. Assets are still in use, so the cost of their purchase does not appear in the profit and loss account.

Note that profit is not the same as cash. The opening cash plus the cash from sales have been used to purchase assets as well as the expenses found in the profit and loss account.

A question that you might have raised when looking at this example is why the furniture and fittings are valued at their cost at the beginning of the year. It is a crucial question and one that is the cause of much debate. There are a number of alternatives.

Historic cost

This is the original cost of the asset. The advantage of using the historic cost is that it can be verified easily from the invoice or receipt. The disadvantage is that it is not a current value, it is out of date. Some assets, such as property, may have increased in value in that someone may be willing to pay more for the property than you did. Other assets, such as furniture and fittings, may have decreased in value. Furniture and fittings would be subject to quite a bit of wear and tear over a year and no longer worth their purchase value.

Historic cost less depreciation

Depreciation is the term given to the fall in value of an asset. It takes into account wear and tear. There are different ways of estimating depreciation (see Unit Two) but they all attempt to find a current value for the asset. In the above example perhaps the furniture and fittings are expected to last for five years. The depreciation could be spread equally over those five years at £300 per year. The valuation of the asset becomes £1500 − £300 = £1200. The listing of assets becomes:

Wealth	1 May	30 April
Cash	2000	150
Stock	0	500
Furniture	0	1200
Personal	0	600
Total	2000	2450

The profit is reduced to £450 because part of the asset has been used up and part of cost has been written off in the profit and loss account.

Sales		20000
Expenses		
Drink purchased	−13700	
Food consumed	− 5550	
Depreciation	− 300	−19550
Profit		450

This method has the advantage that the initial cost is verifiable, and it takes into account the loss in value through wear and tear. It does not, however, address the problem of an increase in value. The amount of the depreciation is also a subjective judgement and not verifiable.

Net realizable value

This is the amount that would be received if an asset was sold less any selling expenses, such as commission. This gives a valuation that is up to date and shows the true worth of the asset. The disadvantage is that it is not always easy to establish unless there is an active second-hand market. This means that a subjective judgement has to be made. One person's valuation might be very different from another's. As any reduction from the original cost will be written off, profitability is also affected. Another problem with this method is that the second-hand value might be minimal and bear no comparison to the value of the asset in the business.

Replacement cost

This is the amount that would have to be expended to find an exact replacement for the asset. It takes into account the value to the business and is up to date. The problem is in establishing the cost of an exact replacement, with the same degree of wear and tear, which again calls for a subjective judgement to be made.

Economic value

This is the value of all the future profits that result from owning the asset. If you were deprived of the asset you would be deprived of those profits, so they would be the worth of the asset. This is a very different view of worth from the other approaches. The problem is that it is extremely subjective, based on estimates of future profits.

The simple worked example above shows just one of the contentious points that can arise in accounting. Which is the correct valuation? They all are to different people. There are many such issues and different people have different opinions. Different people will produce different balance sheets and profit and loss accounts. There is a need to standardize practices and define the rules of the accounting game.

Boundary Rules

There are concepts that are fundamental to accounting. These can be called concepts, postulates or conventions. Some people like to draw distinctions between them. We will treat this as purely semantics and use only the term 'concepts'. They are the boundary rules that have been developed over many years and are accepted by all accountants.

INTRODUCTION: THE CONTEXT OF ACCOUNTING

They are intended to add to the lack of bias in accounting and keep accounts objective.

The separate entity concept. This means that a business is treated separately from the person or persons that own it. This idea comes from the legal recognition of a company as an artificial person separate from its owner. It means the company can sue and be sued, and can enter into contracts just as a person can. The consequence for accounting is that personal finances and transactions need to be separated from those of the business. In the example we used above all personal transactions should be separated from the business transactions. The personal transactions are treated as *drawings*, money removed from the business.

The money measurement concept. Accounts will only show things that can be measured in monetary terms. This is a matter of practicality and objectivity. Having a good morale among the workforce might be extremely important to a business, but how do you put a monetary value on it, especially when it could be wiped out by a single event?

The going concern concept. The assumption here is that a business will continue to trade beyond the time the accounts are drawn up. This means that items held for resale but not yet sold are assumed to be sold in the next year.

The realization concept. Profits are never anticipated until they happen. Sales revenue is not counted until a sale is made. Stock that is bought in is valued at its cost until sold. It may be that it can be sold at a higher price, but until it is sold it stays at its cost value.

The accruals concept. Sales are accounted for in the period they are earned and not when the money is received. In the same way, costs are accounted for in the period in which they are incurred and not when the payment is made. The delay between the transaction taking place and cash changing hands creates debtors and creditors. Where an invoice has not been received an estimate should be made of the costs.

The matching concept. The revenues from a sale and the costs incurred in making the sale should be accounted for in the same period. This will often mean making accruals for costs that have not yet been invoiced.

The consistency concept. The accounting treatment for like items should be the same. The treatment should also remain the same from year to year, to aid comparability. Should a company change its accounting treatment in any way it should alert people to this fact and explain the reason behind the change.

The prudence concept. A cautious approach is taken in the preparation of accounts, so as not to inflate values and profits. This means that revenue is never anticipated. In the valuation of assets one must always err on the side of caution. If values fall adjustment is always downwards, but if they rise valuation is left at the original cost.

The materiality concept. Where amounts are small and including them in the accounts would not add to the ability of people to make decisions, then they may be ignored. It would not be worth the time and effort for someone to count and value all the stationery people have in their desks.

The objectivity concept. Accounts should be based on fact and not opinion. They should be free from bias and capable of verification.

The historic cost concept. Assets should be valued at their historic cost. One advantage of this is that the value is verifiable. The cost concept is supportive of the objectivity concept.

The duality concept. Every transaction has two effects on the accounts, one positive and one negative. For example, when purchasing an asset you gain an asset but you lose some cash.

The stable monetary unit concept. It is assumed that the monetary unit in which the accounts are expressed is constant over time. This means that inflation is ignored. This concept obviously does not apply in all countries of the world.

Some of these rules are conflicting, such as prudence and historic cost. If you purchase some stock at £2 and the price then falls to £1, what should it be valued at? The historic cost concept says £2 and the prudence concept says £1. Where such conflicts arise the prudence concept takes precedence. Exceptions can be made to these rules (e.g. revaluation of properties), but only when a professional valuer is involved, not just following the opinion of the directors.

These are the rules of the game. It is now time to look and see what is the aim of the game. The result that is sought is the production of financial statements that give a 'true and fair' view of the position of an entity.

The Financial Statements

The Companies Acts contain formats for the presentation of the balance sheet and the profit and loss account. There are a number of different formats, which do not look much like published accounts: for a start they contain no numbers. The comparative figures from the previous year would also be shown in the actual accounts. If a company has no items under a heading, it does not have to be shown, so when you look at accounts in practice you will find that they do not contain all these items. A company may choose to use any of these formats, although in the UK the first format shown for each statement is the one most often found in use.

Many companies in the UK have a group structure. That is, there is a parent company which owns and controls other companies. Where more than 50 per cent of the share capital is owned or controlled by the parent these are called subsidiaries. Where more than 20 per cent but fewer than 50 per cent of the shares are owned they are called associates. In an investment fewer than 20 per cent of the shares are held. The parent companies can be very small in themselves and reporting on just the parent may be meaningless. The Companies Acts require that consolidated accounts are published for groups. That is, financial statements are

INTRODUCTION: THE CONTEXT OF ACCOUNTING

prepared as if the group were one single company. When looking at the published accounts for many large groups in the UK you will see statements for both the group and the parent company alongside each other.

An example of a balance sheet for a company that does not have a group structure is shown in Box AM1.4.

BOX AM1.4

Balance sheet

	£ million	£ million	£ million
Fixed assets			
Intangible assets:			
Development costs		21	
Tangible assets:			
Land and buildings	440		
Plant and machinery	157		
Fixtures, fittings, tools and equipment	34	631	652
Current assets			
Stocks:			
Raw materials	23		
Work-in-progress	6		
Finished goods	42	71	
Debtors:			
Trade debtors	56		
Prepayments and accrued income	21	77	
Cash at bank and in hand		8	
		156	
Creditors: amounts falling due within one year			
Trade creditors	40		
Other creditors	20		
Accruals and deferred income	16	76	
Net current assets			80
Total assets less current liabilities			732
Creditors: amounts falling due after more than one year (all sources)		22	22
			710
Capital and reserves			
Called-up share capital			400
Share premium account			49
General reserve			50
Profit and loss account			211
			710

In the statement in Box AM1.4 there are three columns in which numbers appear. This is an attempt to clarify the presentation of the statement so that items which are being added together can more clearly be seen. The approach taken is to put all items to be added into one column, and when they are to be added the final item is underlined. The total does not usually appear in that column but in the next one to the right. Look at fixed assets, for example. The total of the three figures for tangible assets is given in the second column. This total is added to the intangible assets to give an overall total for fixed assets, which appears in the third column.

Note that in the statement there are no minus signs. But the net current assets have been calculated by taking creditors' amounts falling within one year away from current assets. To overcome confusion some accounts will show numbers to be taken away in parentheses, for example (76).

In practice you may not see this amount of detail in the balance sheet. It is common practice to include notes to the accounts. These will be found just after the accounts and will generally contain much more detail than is required or can be shown clearly on one statement. For example, fixed assets may be shown as one figure, but the notes will show the different categories of assets and details of new acquisitions, disposals and any changes in value.

Short explanations of the terms found in the statement are given below.

Fixed assets: items held by the company that are of a long-term nature. Generally if an asset is expected to be held for more than one year it will be classified as a fixed asset.

Intangible assets: items that cannot physically be accounted for. These are the major exceptions to the basic accounting concepts. Historic cost is not observed because these items are not acquired. Objectivity is not observed because they are subjective valuations. One example that might be found is research and development costs, where the costs of developing new products are valued in the balance sheet and are written off over the life of the product. Other items are the valuations of brand names and goodwill. There are accounting standards for each of these items, which lay down acceptable practice.

Tangible assets: assets that are physical. They are shown on the balance sheet at their new book value; that is, historic cost less an allowance (called depreciation) for use. An exception to the historic cost rule is allowed in relation to land and buildings. As their value has historically increased in the UK it is possible to revalue these assets. Remembering the duality rule, the gain is the increase in asset value but what is the other side of the transaction? It involves no cash transaction. No profit has been made as the gain has not been realized. The accounting treatment is the creation of a revaluation reserve, which can be found under the capital and reserves section of the balance sheet.

Current assets: assets held that the company will benefit from within a short time frame, usually one year.

Stocks: items held to be sold at a later stage. A retailer will only hold stock for resale. A manufacturer might hold three different types of stocks, and the value for each will differ:

- raw materials – items that have been bought in but have not yet been processed;
- work-in-progress – items that are in the process of being converted into final products, whose cost will be that of the raw materials bought in plus the production costs incurred in getting the items to the partly completed state;
- finished goods – items that have been fully processed and are awaiting resale, whose value will comprise raw materials and production costs incurred in bringing the items to their fully finished state.

There is an accounting standard that deals with how to value stocks.

Debtors: monies owed to a company. These can be the value of credit extended to customers who have already received goods or services, and will also include accrued income, that is income earned but not yet invoiced to the customer. Prepaid bills are included in this category, because money has been paid in advance for services not yet received. If those services are not received the money will have to be refunded.

Cash at bank and in hand: any cash available to the company, whether it is held in cash or is in a bank account. If a company has more than one bank account and there is money in one but not the other, the balance of the one with money will be shown here. An overdrawn account will appear under the section of the balance sheet called 'creditors: due within one year'.

Creditors: amounts falling due within one year (sometimes called current liabilities). These are any amounts due to other people where the repayment is due in the short term.

- Trade creditors – money due to the suppliers of goods and services, where invoices have been received but have not yet been paid.
- Other creditors – anyone else owed money, including tax authorities, employees and shareholders when dividends have been proposed but not yet paid. Bank overdrafts would also be shown here. If a long-term loan is to be repaid within the next 12 months then the amount will be shown under this section.
- Accruals and deferred income – accruals are where invoices have not yet been received but goods or services have been supplied. Deferred income is where a customer has paid in advance for goods or services that have not yet been supplied.

Net current assets: the difference between current assets and creditors: amounts due within one year. This is sometimes referred to as *working capital*.

Creditors: amounts falling due after more than one year. These are the long-term commitments to outside parties. They include debenture loans and any future charges, such as to a pension fund.

Capital and reserves: how the company has been financed by the owners of the business, the shareholders. The total value is not how much the company is worth now, merely how assets have been financed.

Called-up share capital: the value of shares in issue. When a company is formed the directors will decide how many shares it will have and the value of each, called the face value or sometimes at par. They do not have to issue them all. Initially some will be issued and the business gets under way. At a later stage when more capital is required some of the remaining shares can be issued. The called-up share capital is how much has been paid by shareholders in obtaining the shares. It is possible that some or all of the shareholders have not paid in full for the share. For example, in the privatization of nationalized industries in the UK payments for shares were made in instalments.

Share premium account: the extra monies paid by shareholders for the purchase of shares. The directors decide on the value when the company is formed. After several years of operation the value of shares will probably have risen to several times the original value. The company would be unwise to issue new shares at their face value when it could get more. The extra paid above the face value is the share premium.

General reserve: as the name suggests a reserve is any amount put aside for a particular purpose. When profits are earned they are not all distributed to shareholders in the form of dividends. Some are reinvested in the business. Some companies will show the reinvested profits under the profit and loss account. Others will transfer funds from the profit and loss account into a general reserve. If a loss is made in a year dividends can still be paid as long as there is a positive balance in the profit and loss reserve. Transferring amounts to another reserve makes them a little less accessible. A revaluation reserve may also be found in this section of the balance sheet. This shows the increase in value of assets not yet realized, and is not distributable as dividends to shareholders.

Profit and loss account: the value of profits retained in the business for reinvestment in assets. More details about what happens to change the balance during a year will be found in the profit and loss statement, which is published alongside the Balance Sheet. Please refer to Box AM1.5. Brief explanations of the terms used in this statement are given below.

Turnover: the revenue earned from making sales, excluding sales taxes such as VAT. The terms turnover, sales and revenue are synonymous in this text. Turnover does not have to be cash collected: sales that have been made on credit are included.

Cost of sales: the cost of making items sold into the state where they are ready for sale. This includes the cost of bought-in materials and, where applicable (in a manufacturing company), production costs.

Gross profit: the profit made on trading in the items the company sells.

BOX AM1.5

The profit and loss statement

	£ million	£ million
Turnover		415
Cost of sales		216
Gross profit		199
Distribution costs	63	
Administrative expenses	35	98
		101
Interest payable and similar charges		25
		76
Tax on profit or loss on ordinary activities		27
Profit or loss on ordinary activities after taxation		47
	89	
Extraordinary income	29	
Extraordinary charges	60	
Extraordinary profit or loss	10	50
Tax on extraordinary profit or loss		97
Profit or loss for the financial year		
		184
Retained profit brought forward from last year		281
	50	
Transfer to general reserve	20	70
Proposed dividend on ordinary shares		211
Retained profit carried forward		

Distribution costs: all costs of delivering items to their point of sale and costs of making sales. Advertising costs incurred to promote products are included under this heading.

Administrative expenses: basically all operating costs not included elsewhere. The cost of departments like accounts and personnel will be included under this heading.

Interest payable and similar charges: interest due on short-term and long-term loans.

Tax on profit or loss on ordinary activities: tax is paid on the taxable profit earned. Taxable profit is hardly ever the same as accounting profit. The Inland Revenue has special rules as to what is an allowable expense; for example, entertainment is not an allowable expense unless it is for an overseas customer. Specified amounts (capital allowances) can be written off in each year when fixed assets are purchased. The exact amount of tax to be paid is agreed with the Inland Revenue after the year end. An estimate is made at the year end and deducted in the profit and loss account to show how much profit will be left for shareholders. If the estimate proves to be wrong, it is corrected in the following year.

Extraordinary items: income less charges less tax. These are items that are not part of the normal activities of the company. To include them in the profit and loss account would distort the picture. An example would be where a company sells off part of its operations to another company. It will receive payment for the sale and there may be some associated expenses, like redundancy. This will result in a profit that is a one-off and will not occur again in the future. To include it with the rest of the profit and loss account might lead people to think operations had improved and might influence their decisions. There has been much debate over what is a extraordinary item and companies have taken advantage of this to show results in their favour. A Financial Reporting Standard has recently been issued which makes very few events extraordinary. Few companies will show this item in future.

Retained profit brought forward from last year: the total profit kept back in previous years. This gives a total which could all be distributed to shareholders as dividends.

Transfer to general reserve: putting amounts aside into balance sheet reserves (see 'reserves' in the balance sheet).

Proposed dividend on ordinary shares: how much the directors will recommend for distribution as dividends to the shareholders. The shareholders can vote at the annual general meeting if they wish to accept or reject this recommendation.

Retained profit carried forward: the amount carried forward to future years.

Please complete Activity AM1.3.

INTRODUCTION: THE CONTEXT OF ACCOUNTING

ACTIVITY AM1.3

TERMINOLOGY

Activity code
- ✓ Self-development
- ✓ Teamwork
- ✓ Communications
- ☐ Numeracy/IT
- ✓ Decisions

Task

Without consulting the text define the following terms in your own words. You can then cross-reference by checking the text.
- Intangible assets
- Tangible assets
- Stocks
- Trade debtors
- Other creditors
- Accruals
- Deferred income
- Working capital
- Distribution costs
- Extraordinary income
- Administrative expenses

Conclusion

We have set the scene for *Effective Accounting Management*. A context has been given and the nitty gritty aspects of an accountant's task have been described. Wealth and profit are clearly critical areas. In addition the main financial statements have been introduced. The next unit looks to the derivation of these financial statements, and prepares the ground for the accounting principles and techniques surrounding these statements (the concluding unit analyses these statements in depth).

Note
1 D. Schulke, Managing Director of Perstella, Wimborne, Dorset, commenting on the accountancy profession.

Unit Two

Recording Financial Information

Learning Objectives

After completing this unit you should be able to:
- understand the principles of double entry bookkeeping;
- post transactions and make journal entries to accounts;
- balance accounts and draw up a trial balance at the end of an accounting period;
- understand the alternative approaches that can be taken to making year end adjustments;
- calculate the year end adjustments;
- draw up the final accounts for different organization types;
- apply the generic skills.

Contents

Overview

Accounting Records

- ▶ Double entry bookkeeping
- ▶ Computerized bookkeeping

The Trial Balance

Period End Adjustments – Overview

Preparing Final Accounts

Period End Adjustments – Detail

- ▶ Stocks and cost of sales
- ▶ Depreciation
  Straight line depreciation
  Reducing balance depreciation
- ▶ Gain or loss on disposal
- ▶ Accruals and prepayments
- ▶ Bad debts and other provisions

Financial Statements

- ▶ The sole trader
- ▶ Partnerships
- ▶ Companies

Conclusion

Unit Two

> " Without liability much poor audit work is concealed by growth ensuring that audit deficiencies do not come to light."
>
> *Sikka et al., 'After Maxwell and BCCI ...'* [1]

Overview

There is a system of recording accounting information that is used throughout the world, with the possible exception of the former communist countries. This system is known as double entry bookkeeping. It has been in use since the Middle Ages and it spread with the movement of Italian merchants as they traded. It is this system that is the cause of most people's fear of the whole accounting subject. They do not understand how it works and to compound the problem it is full of confusing terminology. What is a debit, a credit, a ledger?

It is not actually necessary to understand double entry bookkeeping to be able to use accounting information, in the same way that it is not necessary to understand how the internal combustion engine works to be able to use a motor car. It is possible to skip the entire section on double entry bookkeeping and still be able to use the accounting information. We hope you will not.

This unit begins with a section on double entry bookkeeping. The next section goes on to look at some of the adjustments that need to be made at the end of an accounting period. It is not necessary to master double entry bookkeeping to appreciate this section. By reading it, it is hoped that you will be able to participate in the discussion of such items, which inevitably arises at financial year ends. Next we turn to the preparation of the accounts. We cover the trial balance, final accounts and period end adjustments. These sections cannot be 'skipped'. The unit concludes by looking at the different formats of financial statements of different types of business organization.

Accounting Records

Double entry bookkeeping

The Companies Acts require that companies keep proper books but do not specify what constitutes proper books. For a small company with few transactions a cash book may prove to be sufficient as long as it enables an accountant to be able to produce final accounts. More complex companies are not going to be able to cope with such a simple system. The VAT authorities are certainly going to want to see that more adequate records are kept.

Today computers are in widespread use, keeping records and producing final accounts. A computer will speed up the processing of information and keep very accurate records but they can be kept adequately with a manual system. *Double entry bookkeeping* is the name given to this manual recording system. It is also the technique upon which computerized accounting is based.

The system is based upon the duality concept; that is, every transaction has two aspects. For each of the two aspects an entry is made in the books. Each entry will be made in a different *account*. An account is a record of all entries of a particular type, for example all the entries that affect cash at bank. In a manual bookkeeping system each account will be kept in a book, usually called the *ledger*. Individual accounts are called T accounts, because of the shape drawn on the page when the account is divided into two, as shown in the example here.

Cash at bank

Opening balance	1000	Payment	125
Receipt	200	Closing balance	1075
	1200		1200

This might be the kind of record you would design yourself. It is clear. It shows you how much cash you have in the bank at the start of the period. Receipts are listed down one side (which increase the amount in the bank). On the other side are listed all payments (which reduce the amount in the bank). At the end of the month, if you add up both sides of the account one is usually larger than the other. In this example the left hand side totals £1200 and the right £125. The difference between the two is how much is left in the account at the end of the period (£1200 − £125 = £1075). Calculating the closing balance on the account is called *balancing the account*. The closing balance will obviously be the opening balance in the next period. Opening balances are *brought down* to the other side of the page, ready for the next period's transactions to be listed.

Cash at bank

Opening balance (P1)	1000	Payment (P1)	125
Receipt (P1)	200	Closing balance (P1)	1075
	1200		1200
Opening balance (P2)	1075	Payment (P2)	250
Receipt (P2)	400	Closing balance (P2)	1225
	1475		1475

Every time a transaction is made that involves cash at the bank one entry will be made in this account. A second entry is made in another account, this time on the opposite side of the page. For example, suppose the payments in each period are for goods bought from a supplier and the receipts are the amount paid by a customer for those goods. The entries in the other accounts would be:

Sales

Closing balance (P1)	200	Cash (P1)	200
	200		200
		Opening balance (P2)	200
Closing balance (P2)	600	Cash (P2)	400
	600		600

Purchases

Cash (P1)	125	Closing balance (P1)	125
	125		125
Opening balance (P2)	125		
Cash (P2)	250	Closing balance (P2)	375
	375		375

The name given to the act of putting entries into accounts is *posting*. When an entry is posted to one account is has been cross-referenced to the account where the other entry is made. This helps us to know where to look for the other side of the entry. Where there are few transactions it is sufficient merely to use the name of the other account as a cross reference. Where there are a lot of transactions it is going to become increasingly

42 EFFECTIVE ACCOUNTING MANAGEMENT

difficult to keep track. Additional information then needs to be recorded. Each transaction is given a unique reference number (sometimes called a folio number). All sales might be given a reference number like S1234, where the S makes it recognizable as a sales transaction. The reference number is also used to file the documentation relating to the transaction. Take, for example, the case where a sale is made to a customer. An invoice is prepared and sent to the customer, with details of the goods received and the amount to be paid. The sales reference number will normally also be the invoice number. A copy of the invoice is then filed away in case it should be required in future.

In the sales and purchases accounts, entries hardly ever go in more than one side, the only time being when refunds are given or received. So far it has been fairly simple, but what about more complex situations?

WORKED EXAMPLE

In period 3 a sale of £300 is made on credit. £200 in cash is paid later in the period, but the remaining £100 is not paid until the next period.

We need to see this as three separate transactions, each with two aspects:

1 A sale is made and a debtor (someone who owes us money) comes into existence.
2 Cash is received and the amount owed by the debtor is reduced.
3 The remaining cash is received, reducing the amount owed by the debtor to zero.

An extra account is now needed to deal with the debtor. The entries in the accounts for these transactions will be:

Sales

		Opening balance (P3)		600
Closing balance (P3)	900	Debtor (P3)		300
	900			900
Closing balance (P4)	900	Opening balance (P4)		900
	900			900

Debtors

		Cash (P3)		200
Sales (P3)	300	Closing balance (P3)		100
	300			300
Opening balance (P4)	100	Cash (P4)		100
		Closing balance (P4)		0
	100			100

Cash at bank

Opening balance (P3)	1225		
Debtor (P3)	200	Closing balance (P3)	1425
	1425		1425
Opening balance (P4)	1425		
Debtor (P4)	100	Closing balance (P4)	1525
	1525		1525

Looking at the debtors account we can keep track of how much is owed to us. We can keep as many accounts as we want to. We may want to keep a separate account for every single debtor. This is a sensible move when there are lots of customers buying on credit. We can keep track of who exactly owes money. Sometimes the volume of sales is so great that a completely different book needs to be kept. This is called the *sales ledger*. The *sales day book* is the name sometimes given to the record of the left hand side entries in the sales account. Similarly, *purchase ledgers* and *purchase day books* are kept to record transactions relating to the purchase of goods and services from suppliers.

You will have noticed from the example that for every transaction one entry is made on the left hand side of an account and one on the right hand side. There are special names given to these entries: the one on the left hand side is called a *debit* and the one on the right hand side a *credit*. One of the most confusing things for people new to bookkeeping is how to decide which account should get the debit and which should get the credit. This is a matter of practice, and once you get used to the idea it comes fairly naturally. To start with, it is worth having an *aide-mémoire*. Please refer to Box AM2.1.

BOX AM2.1

Debits and credits – *aide-mémoire*

Transaction type	Debit	Credit
Assets, e.g. cash at bank	increase	decrease
Liabilities, e.g. creditors	decrease	increase
Income	refund given	sale
Expenditure	incurred	refund received

For any transaction think about the two aspects involved. For example, you buy some goods on credit, which you plan to sell in the future. The two aspects of this transaction are: (1) an increase in an asset (you now hold some stock) and (2) an increase in a liability (you now owe some money to the supplier). Looking at Box AM2.1 we see that an increase in an asset is a debit and an increase in a liability is a credit. We now know that we want to debit the stock account, that is put the entry on the left hand side of the stock account, and credit the creditors account, that is put the entry on the right hand side of the creditors account.

You may be wondering why it is that when you receive your bank statement everything is in reverse to this. When you pay some money into your account it is credited. When money goes out it is a debit. When you are overdrawn it is shown as a debit balance. Our cash at bank account shows a debit balance yet there is money in the account. Why is this? The reason is that the bank sends a statement of its dealings with you, not your dealings with it. When you have money in your account, they owe you money – a credit. When you are overdrawn, you owe them money – a debit. This can be confusing when you are learning how to do bookkeeping, as most of our prior experience with debits and credits is with a bank account. Just remember when you are keeping accounts yourself to do things the opposite way to the bank.

WORKED EXAMPLE: JOE BUILDER

A short example shows the accounts that are needed and the transactions that have to be recorded for a sole trader just starting up a business.

Date	Reference	Transaction
1 May	JB1	Joe opens a bank account with £5000 which he invests in his own building business.
2 May	JB2	Building plant costing £2500 was purchased, paid for by cheque.
2 May	JB3	Building materials costing £2000 were purchased on credit from A. Supplier.
9 May	JB4	Drew money from bank to pay wages of £550 to labourers.
16 May	JB5	Drew money from bank to pay wages of £600 to labourers.
23 May	JB6	Drew money from bank to pay wages of £500 to labourers.
30 May	JB7	Drew money from bank to pay wages of £450 to labourers.

RECORDING FINANCIAL INFORMATION

Date	Reference	Transaction
31 May	JB8	A. Customer is invoiced for £7500 for work completed during the month.
31 May	JB9	£5000 paid into the bank received from A. Customer as payment 'on account'.
31 May	JB10	A cheque for £1500 is sent to A. Supplier 'on account' for the materials supplied.

Before making any entries to accounts let us just think about the two aspects of each transaction and whether they are debits or credits.

Reference	Debit	Credit
JB1	£5000 cash put into bank account.	£5000 owner's capital, owed by the business to the owner.
JB2	£2500, a fixed asset is purchased.	£2500 reduction to cash at bank.
JB3	£2000 stock of materials is acquired.	£2000 owed to creditor.
JB4	£550 wages incurred.	£550 cash at bank reduced.
JB5	£600 wages incurred.	£600 cash at bank reduced.
JB6	£500 wages incurred.	£500 cash at bank reduced.
JB7	£450 wages incurred.	£450 cash at bank reduced.
JB8	£7500 debt becomes due from the customer.	£7500 income is earned.
JB9	£5000 increase to cash at bank.	£5000 reduction in amount owed by debtor.
JB10	£1500 reduction of amount owed to creditor.	£1500 decrease in cash at bank.

The T accounts with transactions entered and balanced for Joe Builder will be:

Owner's capital

Closing balance	5000	1 May	JB1	5000
	5000			5000

Cash at bank

1 May	JB1	5000	2 May	JB2		2500
31 May	JB9	5000	9 May	JB4		550
			16 May	JB5		600
			23 May	JB6		500
			30 May	JB7		450
			31 May	JB10		1500
			Closing balance			3900
		10000				10000

Fixed asset – building plant

2 May	JB2	2500	Closing balance		2500
		2500			2500

Stock – building materials

2 May	JB3	2000	Closing balance		2000
		2000			2000

Creditor – A. Supplier

31 May	JB10	1500	2 May	JB3	2000
Closing balance		500			
		2000			2000

Expenditure – wages

9 May	JB4	550			
16 May	JB5	600			
23 May	JB6	500			
30 May	JB7	450	Closing balance		2100
		2100			2100

Sales

Closing balance		7500	30 May	JB8	7500
		7500			7500

Debtor – A. Customer

30 May	JB8	7500	31 May	JB9	5000
			Closing balance		2500
		7500			7500

These accounts are randomly ordered, the first being the first one we needed to use. In practice they tend to be ordered in such a way that people can easily find the accounts. As already mentioned, the sales and purchase ledgers may be separate from the rest of the ledger. The accounts that relate to income and expenditure can also be separated into what is sometimes known as the *nominal ledger*. The ledger where the remainder of the accounts will be found is called the *general ledger*.

Computerized bookkeeping

All computerized bookkeeping packages are based on the principles of double entry. Transactions are entered in exactly the same way, with one entry as a debit and one as a credit. There are two noticeable differences in using a computerized system. First, the words debit and credit are rarely used. Debit values are shown as positive values, credit values are shown as negatives. The second noticeable difference is the organization of the accounts. Before doing anything with a computerized system you must first set up the accounts that are to be used. A *chart of accounts* will tell you the names of the accounts and their account numbers. A feature of a computerized system is that accounts are recognized by their numbers. Accounts for similar items are grouped together. An extract from a typical example of a chart of accounts is:

Account number	Account name
1---	Sales
11--	Sales of product ABC
1101	Sales of product ABC in region 1
1102	Sales of product ABC in region 2
1103	Sales of product ABC in region 3
12--	Sales of product DEF
1201	Sales of product DEF in region 1
1202	Sales of product DEF in region 2
1203	Sales of Product DEF in region 3
.	.
.	.

With a computerized system there may be thousands of accounts and there can be as many digits in the account numbers as desired. In this extract we are only looking at a small section of the sales accounts.

A separate account is used for sales of every product in every region. When all the accounts beginning with 1 are added together we will find the total sales for the company. When all accounts with 11 as the first two digits are added together we find the total sales for product ABC.

The great thing about a computerized system is its data-handling ability. Computerized systems can produce management accounts as well as financial accounts. If the sales manager from region 1 wants to know the value of sales of all products in the region, all we need to do is to get the computer to add together all the accounts where the first and fourth digits are 1.

Many people who work in large companies will be familiar with a chart of accounts. The accounts department might ask where expenditure should be coded after an order is placed or when an invoice arrives for payment. What they want you to do is identify which account you would like to see the debit entry placed in. Each department of a company will have several accounts so that different types of expenditure can be separated.

The Trial Balance

Before the production of final accounts there is an intermediate stage. It is a necessary stage as it helps us check that the accounts have been prepared correctly. To produce the trial balance we need to carry down all the individual closing balances from the accounts. When balancing the account we have already done the calculation, ready to use the answer as the opening balance in the next month. In the trial balance the balance from the account is always shown on the side it will begin the next month. All the accounts are listed by name and the balance is put into either the debit column or the credit column, whichever is applicable.

JOE BUILDER – TRIAL BALANCE

Account name	Debit	Credit
Owner's capital		5000
Cash at bank	3900	
Fixed asset – building plant	2500	
Stock	2000	
Creditor – A. Supplier		500
Expenditure – wages	2100	
Sales		7500
Debtor – A. Customer	2500	
	13000	13000

Note that the totals of the debits and the credits are the same; that is, they balance. This is why this statement is called the trial balance. It is the desired result and shows that for each debit entry a credit entry was made. If a mistake had been made it would not balance. For example, if in the entries for transaction reference JB2 the credit entry in the cash at bank account was correctly entered (£2500) but £2600 was entered in error as the debit entry in the Fixed asset – building plant account, the trial balance would have been:

Account name	Debit	Credit
Owner's capital		5000
Cash at bank	3900	
Fixed asset – building plant	2600	
Stock	2000	
Creditor – A. Supplier		500
Expenditure – wages	2100	
Sales		7500
Debtor – A. Customer	2500	
	13100	13000

Here the trial balance does not balance, so we know that an error has been made somewhere. We would have to check each account and transaction until the error was found and corrected. An advantage of a computerized system is that there are checks that make sure that you don't enter different values for the debit and the credit.

Please tackle Activity AM2.1.

ACTIVITY AM2.1

KEN COLLEGE

Activity code
- ✓ Self-development
- ✓ Teamwork
- ☐ Communications
- ✓ Numeracy/IT
- ✓ Decisions

Jim Mo is the Principal of Ken College in Bath. The college is a new venture started by Jim with financial backing from an old friend. Jim's background is in financial management and consultancy. British by birth and Kenyan by adoption, Jim has a Euro-African vision of business.

His early working life revolved around financial consultancy, audit and management for large partnerships based in London and Nairobi. Involvement in small and medium-sized businesses in financial appraisal, investment analysis and capital funding projects occurred in this ten-year period. In addition, he had experience of management consultancy, particularly training. The years were getting by and he was reasonably comfortable as a professional accountant, but he yearned for the financial independence of being his own man.

The skills and expertise of a financial accountant are easily transferable, so he started his own firm. At first he looked at an import–export agency between Kenya and the UK but lack of capital inhibited such a programme getting off the ground. There was some success, but the mainstay of the income came from financial management. Even then, the big audit firms had a stranglehold on the compulsory company audits and managed to have the profitable spin-offs in other financial consultancy owing to their presence in the market. Indeed, some of their financial services could be seen as loss leaders or at least were easily absorbed into the enormous audit fees. Competition was tough – very tough.

On a flight back from Africa during this tough period, he flicked through a business magazine and found an interesting article. Here, competition was not bad; quite the reverse as it could lead to great success since energy and commitment were required to get above your rivals. He was refreshed in mind and reflected further.

He was certainly envious of those large accountancy firms and he realized that their size inhibited innovation. However, his one-man band could not compete on the same stage as a centre of excellence because of resource constraints. It was excellent – clients had encouraged him to, but he could

RECORDING FINANCIAL INFORMATION

never compete in international finance with these big boys without institutional backing, or without an international reputation, acquired from writing innovative work in the fashion of American business guru Professor Porter. The writing would have to wait but the institutional backing could not. He would act on his return.

Jim, an active, fast-thinking man, decided to look around for some institutional backing for his financial consultancy. He had a competitive edge with his unique experience, contacts, knowledge of developing countries and external funding to these countries, particularly in Africa. He tried to get some pump-prime funding but to no avail. He was shrewd enough not to go to the high street banks, with their rates of interest which verged on usury in some cases.

'Perhaps the idea itself is flawed', he reflected. 'Let's look at the facts. Unique knowledge and experience of Africa, UK and financial management, coupled with a vision of enterprise.' 'Correct', said his friend, Ala. 'But you are taking a production-oriented view. It is not just what you can do; this must be tailored to what the marketplace wants. Indeed, the market dictates and your strengths must dovetail into these opportunities. Forget "minimization of weaknesses" which many texts advise – go for your strengths related to an opportunity.' 'Mm,' Jim concurred. The issue was opportunity.

Needs must, so Jim continued with financial consulting, and did some part-time teaching at a private college. He was a natural teacher with good communications skills, a pleasant manner and a rapport with the students, underpinned by practical exposure to finance and accounting at a senior level.

During a financial exercise his thoughts moved back to some earlier ideas that had occurred to him on the way into town by underground train. 'I teach two separate groups of some fifty students. That's a hundred in all, each of whom pays fees of around £5000. Now they do about ten subjects including mine – so that's around £500 per subject per student and there are a hundred students. That makes quite an attractive sum (£50000). They pay me £21 per hour for four hours' work, which is £84, and no extra for marking – although they allow me a one-hour tutorial per week, so that makes £105. Call it £100 per week for thirty weeks. That is £3000. So six students pay my salary. Apart from the fixed costs of the building and the variable costs of administration and advertising etc., the mark-up here must be colossal. More importantly, these overseas students – often from Africa – end up paying full fees for a qualification which is at best only partly recognized in the UK and in their own country. It's not on.'

Armed with a sense of indignation, a need for money and a desire for fairness, Jim now knew where he was going. A fellow African businessman, a friend of a friend, agreed to put some capital into the project, which both saw as viable.

Jim's first step was to go back to finance. The professions surely needed some college to prepare their respective students. Market research showed this to be the case, but arguably the market was saturated with such specialist colleges. Professor Porter was right, thought Jim, but the playing field at

52 EFFECTIVE ACCOUNTING MANAGEMENT

the beginning of the game needs to be a little more level. His exposure to the private business college was the way forward. It would include both finance and business. Good premises were obtained in a reasonably well-to-do part of Bath where students from abroad could come to learn both finance and business studies.

After three months Jim jotted down some figures. He is an accountant but his entrepreneurial activities have been dominant of late. He would get one of the account clerks to do the trial balance and he would take it further.

The 'key facts' of the business for the first three months were as follows:

- Cash at outset £100 000;
- £65 000 paid into the bank;
- rent/government property tax came to £3000 per month (£9000 paid 'up front' with no premium);
- all of the manuals bought on credit at £8000 for resale;
- office 'stores' and day to day college 'stores' came to £5000 – bought by cash;
- all of the manuals sold on credit to Tassco for £12 000 (60 days credit);
- incoming student fees for period came to £25 000 (either cash or cheque – no credit);
- incoming company fees for period came to £19 000;
- drawings were £22 000.

Task
Bring these figures to trial balance.

Trial balance (summary)

	Debit	Credit
Bank		
Capital		
Cash		
Drawings		
Office/college expenses		
Books/manual expenses (resale)		
Books/manual expenses (non resale)		
Other purchases		
Trade creditors		
Trade debtors		
Sales (student) fees		
(company) fees		
Opening/closing 'stock'		

Period End Adjustments – Overview

All the transactions that we have made entries for, thus far, have been made from the *records of prime entry*. That is, each transaction is entered from an original source document, whether an invoice, payment advice or other documentary back up. There are a number of entries that have to be made to accounts that are not entered from the records of prime entry. These are called *journals*. These journals are necessary to make entries that alter the accounts or make corrections to improperly posted entries. They are called journals because details relating to the alteration were traditionally kept in a journal (diary).

What are the alterations that need to be made to the accounts? We will look at the major ones in more detail in the next section. For now we will use the Joe Builder example and make just one adjustment, for stock. Building materials costing £2000 had been put into stock early in the month. It is reasonable to assume that at least some of this will have been used up during the month. This means the balance now being shown in the stock account will not be the value of the physical stock left. Suppose that at the end of the period £1800 of the building materials had been used up and only £200 worth remained in stock. A journal entry would have to be made to take £1800 from the stock account. Where will the other half of the entry go? It becomes an expense and another account will be needed. The journal reference given to this adjustment is J100. The entries to the accounts and the trial balance become:

Stock – building materials

2 May	JB3	2000	31 May	J100	1800
		2000	Closing balance		200
					2000

Expenditure – building materials

31 May	J100	1800	Closing balance	1800
		1800		1800

JOE BUILDER – FINAL TRIAL BALANCE

Account name	Debit	Credit
Owner's capital		5000
Cash at bank	3900	
Fixed asset – building plant	2500	
Stock	200	
Creditor – A. Supplier		500
Expenditure – wages	2100	
Expenditure – building materials	1800	
Sales		7500
Debtor – A. Customer	2500	
	13000	13000

Preparing Final Accounts

Once the final trial balance has been prepared, incorporating any period end adjustments, the final accounts can be drawn up. We shall look at this briefly at the moment, returning to the subject at the end of this unit.

The first statement that should be prepared is the profit and loss account. It is prepared first, as the balance from the profit and loss account goes into the balance sheet. To begin with let us just list the accounts that we expect to see in a profit and loss account, along with their debit or credit balances. These will be all the accounts that are related to sales or expenses.

Account name	Debit	Credit
Expenditure – wages	2100	
Expenditure – building materials	1800	
Sales		7500
	3900	7500

Note that the total for the accounts with credit balances is higher than that for accounts with debit balances. The difference between the two is the profit that has been made during the period (£7500 – £3900 = £3600). We need to balance the profit and loss account in the same way as all the other accounts, the result being:

RECORDING FINANCIAL INFORMATION

Account name	Debit	Credit
Expenditure – wages	2100	
Expenditure – building materials	1800	
Sales		7500
Closing balance	3600	
	7500	7500

The closing balance of the profit and loss account is now added to the list of remaining accounts. Together, these accounts make up the balance sheet.

Account name	Debit	Credit
Owner's capital		5000
Cash at bank	3900	
Fixed asset – building plant	2500	
Stock	200	
Creditor – A. Supplier		500
Debtor – A. Customer	2500	
Profit and loss		3600
	9100	9100

The two main financial statements have now been completed, but not in a format that is easy to understand or that complies with the formats required by the Companies Acts. Sole traders and partnerships do not have to use the Companies Acts formats, and may use any format they choose. Whatever format is chosen, it is just a question of rearranging the figures calculated above.

JOE BUILDER – PROFIT AND LOSS ACCOUNT FOR THE MONTH ENDED 31 MAY

Sales		7500
Less: expenses		
Building materials	1800	
Wages	2100	3900
Profit in the period		3600

JOE BUILDER – BALANCE SHEET AS AT 31 MAY

Fixed assets

Building plant		2500

Current assets

Stock	200	
Debtors	2500	
Cash at bank	3900	
	6600	

Creditors: amounts falling due within one year

Trade creditors	500	
Net current assets		6100
		8600

Capital and reserves

Owner's capital		5000
Profit and loss		3600
		8600

Period End Adjustments – Detail

In this section accounting period end adjustments are looked at in some detail. By no means all the accounting adjustments are looked at here. The major ones, which will be found in most companies' accounts, are covered.

Stocks and cost of sales

Making a period end adjustment for stocks is very important. Stocks have two impacts on the financial statements. The first is a value shown in the balance sheet. The second is the value of used stocks, which becomes an expense in the profit and loss account. At the end of the previous section we saw an adjustment for stocks being demonstrated for Joe Builder. Of the £2000 originally spent on materials, £1800 was used up and became an expense in the profit and loss account, and £200 remained in stock for future use, this value appearing as a current asset in the balance sheet.

Let us assume that in the following month £2500 is spent on more building materials and that by the end of the month the stock left over is valued at £400. What is the value of materials used that should be included in the profit and loss account? The calculation could be made in a T account but for the benefit of those who have struggled we shall abandon the double entry format from now on.

RECORDING FINANCIAL INFORMATION

	£
Opening stock	200
Add: purchases	2500
Total of materials available for use	2700
Less: closing stock	400
Materials used	2300

Many businesses are in a situation where no accurate records are kept of the value of stock sold. Imagine a grocer's shop. Unless there is an electronic scanner at the cashdesk, it will be a tremendous task to keep track of the value of all items sold. What happens is at the end of an accounting period the stock is counted and valued. Records of the value of purchases are always kept, because suppliers send invoices and want to be paid. They use this method to find out the value of goods that have been sold.

Businesses that do keep accurate records may sometimes find a discrepancy between the stock counted and valued at the period end and the amount they think has been used. For example, a market trader starts the day with ten coats, which had cost £5 each. During the day six are sold but at the end of the day just three are left.

Opening stock (10 × £5)	50
Purchases	0
	50
Less: closing stock (3 × £5)	15
Stock sold (7 × £5)	35

We suspect that we all know what has happened here: someone has stolen a coat during the day. Instead of four coats being left there are only three. How much should appear in the profit and loss account, the £35 calculated above or £30, which is six coats at £5 each? The answer is £35. We may want to show two separate amounts in the profit and loss account, £30 cost of sales and £5 stock loss, but the total must be £35. It is important that the balance sheet shows the correct stock valuation. Any discrepancy has to be written off to the profit and loss account in the period in which the loss occurred.

So far we have just looked at stock that is bought in for resale. Unfortunately there are a lot of complications that relate to the valuation of stock values. As we noted in unit one, there can be three categories of stocks in a manufacturing company: raw materials, work-in-progress and finished goods. The value of each element has to be calculated. The cost of stocks used also has to be calculated for each of these categories. The calculations for raw materials will be as shown above. The valuation of the other types of stock is much more complicated.

58 EFFECTIVE ACCOUNTING MANAGEMENT

The value of finished goods in a manufacturing company will include all costs of production. These include raw materials used, but also the employment costs of people working in the production process and all other costs (known as overheads), such as machinery used, supervisors' salaries, rent, rates, heat and light in the factory.

WORKED EXAMPLE

In a month a company buys 1000 components for £10 000. During the month it pays production workers £5000 and incurs overheads of £7500. During the month all components are transformed into the final product, some are sold and at the end of the month 200 units remain in stock. What is the value of the stock and what is the value of the goods sold?

The first stage is to find out how much it costs to produce one unit of the final product:

Raw materials – components	£10000	
Labour	£5000	
Overheads	£7500	
Total costs	£22500	(a)
Number of units produced	1000	
Cost per unit	£22.50	
Value of closing stock:		
200 × £22.50	£4500	(b)
Value of goods sold:		
Opening stock	£0	
Production costs	£22500	(a) above
	£22500	
Less: closing stock	£4500	(b) above
	18000	

You will see this calculation in the profit and loss accounts for many companies. Others will just show the end result. The valuation of stock is the subject of Statement of Standard Accounting Practice 9. It covers the valuation of work-in-progress as well as finished goods. The process for valuing work-in-progress is similar to that for finished goods but is that much more complicated because an estimate needs to be made about how complete the products are. This is not discussed here: those wishing to know more about this subject are referred to specialist costing texts.[2]

Depreciation

In Unit One we noted that assets do not retain their value for their entire lives. Depreciation is the name given to the fall in value. It is calculated in each accounting period to give a cumulative total over the life of the asset. Depreciation is deducted from the cost of the asset to give the net book value (NBV) of the asset. The depreciation calculated in an accounting period becomes an expense to be written off in the profit and loss account for that period. There are a number of methods of calculating depreciation, and the two most popular are described in this section. First we need to think about what value we are depreciating.

When accounts are prepared on an historic cost basis, the value will be the historic cost.[3] In addition, all the costs associated with delivering and getting the asset into a working condition should be included. Also to be considered is the *residual value* of the asset; that is, how much it is expected to be sold for at the end of its use. There may be no residual value where there is no second hand market for an asset. Where there is, the residual value to be used should be the expected receipt from sale less any costs of making the sale, such as commission payable and removal cost.

Straight line depreciation

This method spreads depreciation equally over the life of an asset. The amount charged to the profit and loss account is the same for all periods.

WORKED EXAMPLE

A company buys a machine for use in the production process at a cost of £700 000 including delivery and installation. It is expected to be used for five years. At the end of this time it will be sold at its second hand value, which is estimated to be £100 000 after selling costs (called the residual value).

There is a formula that can be used to find the depreciation charge. This can be done to find either the annual or the monthly charge:

$$\frac{\text{Original cost} - \text{residual value}}{\text{Useful life}}$$

$$\frac{£700\,000 - £100\,000}{5} = £120\,000 \text{ per year}$$

Table 2.1 shows what happens to the net book value of this asset over the five-year period when straight line depreciation is used. Plotting the net book value for each year on a graph shows us how straight line depreciation gets its name (see figure 2.1).

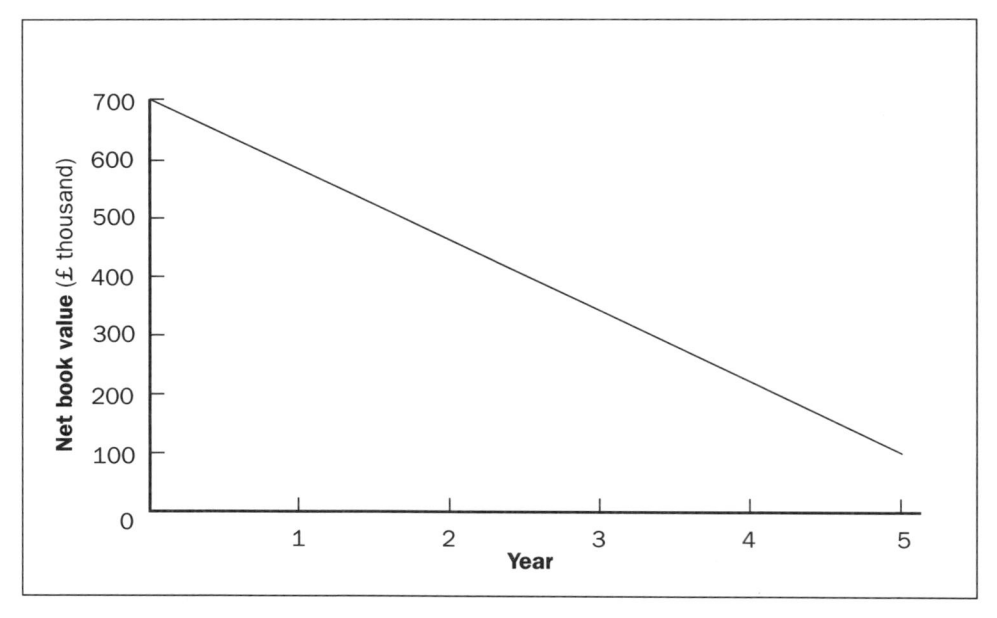

Figure 2.1 Straight line depreciation.

Table 2.1 Straight line depreciation

	Year 1	Year 2	Year 3	Year 4	Year 5
Historic cost	700 000	700 000	700 000	700 000	700 000
Depreciation					
Opening balance	0	120 000	240 000	360 000	480 000
In period	120 000	120 000	120 000	120 000	120 000
Accumulated	120 000	240 000	360 000	480 000	600 000
Net book value	580 000	460 000	340 000	220 000	100 000

Reducing balance depreciation

This method of depreciation recognizes that an asset does not fall in value equally over its life, but that the biggest fall comes in the early stages of the asset life. If you have ever bought a new motor vehicle you will know that this is true. The biggest fall in value is as you drive it off the forecourt. After this falls in value are more gradual.

To find the annual depreciation charge under this method the net book value at the start of the year is multiplied by a depreciation rate. Before doing this we need to calculate what the depreciation rate is. To do this there is a formula:

Depreciation rate $= 1 - \sqrt[n]{\dfrac{\text{residual value}}{\text{historic cost}}}$

Where n is the useful life in years. In the same worked example as used above:

Depreciation rate $= 1 - \sqrt[5]{\dfrac{100\,000}{700\,000}}$

$= 1 - 0.6776$

$= 0.3224$ or 32.24 per cent

Depreciation in year 1 = Opening net book value × Depreciation rate

$= 700\,000 \times 0.3224$

$= 225\,680$

Closing net book value = Opening net book value − Annual depreciation

$= 700\,000 - 225\,680$

$= 474\,320$

Table 2.2 shows what happens to the net book value of this asset over the five-year period when reducing balance depreciation is used. When the net book value for each year is plotted on a graph we get an idea of why this method is called the reducing balance method (see figure 2.2).

Table 2.2 Reducing balance depreciation

	Year 1	Year 2	Year 3	Year 4	Year 5
Historic cost	700 000	700 000	700 000	700 000	700 000
Depreciation					
Opening balance	0	225 680	378 600	482 215	552 425
In period	225 680	152 920	103 615	70 210	47 575
Accumulated	225 680	378 600	482 215	552 425	600 000
Net book value	474 320	321 400	217 785	147 575	100 000

Note that with the reducing balance method the value falls more quickly than with the straight line method. The principle of duality tells us that this has an effect elsewhere. The effect is on the amount of the depreciation expenses that is written off in the profit and loss account. The expenses will be higher in early years with the reducing balance method than with the straight line method. The principle of consistency means that companies cannot switch between the different methods, from year to year, to end up with the lower expense in the profit and loss account.

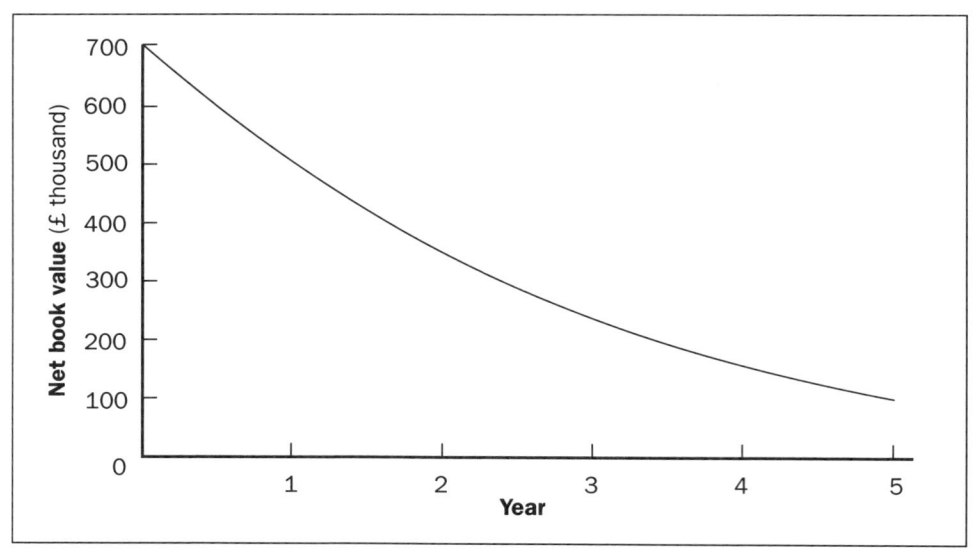

Figure 2.2 Reducing balance depreciation.

Gain or loss on disposal

What happens if an asset is disposed of before the end of its expected useful life? First, its net book value will no longer appear on the balance sheet. An adjustment may also have to be made where the proceeds from the sale are not equal to the net book value. This is best demonstrated by an example. Assume in the case above that the machine is only kept until the end of the third year, and is sold for £300 000 net of selling costs. Where straight line depreciation was used:

Historic cost	700 000
Cumulative depreciation	300 000
Net book value	400 000
Disposal value	300 000

In this case the net book value is higher than the disposal value. The depreciation charge has not been high enough in the three years, so the asset is overvalued. The difference between the net book value and the disposal value will have to be written off to the profit and loss account in the period in which the asset is disposed of. This adjustment is called a loss on disposal.

If the reducing balance method was used:

Historic cost	700 000
Cumulative depreciation	482 215
Net book value	217 785
Disposal value	300 000

In this case the disposal value is higher than the net book value. Too much depreciation has been charged in previous years. An adjustment also needs to be made in the profit and loss account in the period in which the sale occurs. This time the adjustment is for a profit on disposal of £82 215.

There is almost always a profit or loss resulting from the disposal of assets. It is difficult when buying a new asset to predict accurately what the residual value will be. It is important to choose a method of depreciation that, as far as possible, does not result in overvaluations of the assets in the company's account.

Accruals and prepayments

Sometimes at an accounting period end we will not have received invoices and bills for some of the goods and services supplied. Just because we do not have the invoices the costs should not be ignored. They have been received and we are liable for their payment, even if we don't know exactly how much yet. At the accounting period end estimates of the costs are made and are *accrued* in the accounts. This means that a debit entry is made to the expense account and a credit entry is made to an accruals account. The expense is therefore included in the profit and loss account and the accrual is shown in the balance sheet under 'liabilities: amounts falling due within one year'.

For example, a business employs an advertising agency to run an advertising campaign. The adverts are to be shown over a two-month period, at the end of which the agency will bill the company for all the adverts. The total cost of the campaign is expected to be £500 000. The business has its financial year end at the end of the first month. Approximately 40 per cent of the adverts have been shown at this stage. No costs have been accounted for at this stage as an invoice has not been received and no payment has been made. An accrual needs to be made. The best estimate is that £200 000 (40 per cent of the expected cost) has been incurred. An accrual is made so that the profit and loss account will show advertising costs for the period. When the invoice eventually arrives it will be entered in the purchase ledger like any other invoice. The value of the invoice is £500 000 and advertising expenses will show this as having been expended. But £200 000 was accounted for in the last period, so only the remaining £300 000 should be shown in the new period. Once the actual bill is received the accrual is released; that is, the accounting entries made at the end of the last period are reversed. The amount shown for advertising will be £500 000 less £200 000.

Some expenses are continuously accrued. Take, for example, charges for utilities, such as electricity. These are always billed in arrears, depending on how much electricity has been accrued.

The accounting department will make the accounting period end adjustments for accruals, but does not estimate them. It is for each departmental manager to estimate the value of goods and services supplied but not yet billed. Most managers will at some time be asked to do this activity by the accounts department, but usually only at financial year ends.

Accrued income is treated in a similar fashion to accrued expenses. It is income not yet accounted for. If the advertising agency had its financial period end at the end of the first month, it would have to accrue for the £200 000 work not billed. When it prepares its invoice for the full amount, it will release the accrued income.

Prepaid expenses are the opposite to accrued expenses. They are costs that have been paid in advance of the receipt of goods or services. Local authority taxes are usually billed to businesses and paid for in advance for an entire year. If the financial year end of a business does not coincide with the end of the billing period there will be some expenses paid in advance. The total amount is not charged to the profit and loss account, but is reduced by the amount prepaid. The prepayment is then shown under current assets in the balance sheet.

Prepaid income is the opposite of accrued income. It is a payment made in advance for which goods or services have to be supplied in the future. Prepaid income should not be shown as income in the profit and loss account of the period in which it is received. It should be held in an account until such time as the work is done, and then it can be counted as income.

Bad debts and other provisions

It would be a very unusual state of affairs if a business was to be paid in full by its debtors. One of the problems of limited liability is that you can supply goods and services on credit, and if the customer runs into trouble you may never get paid for them. When you are certain that you will not get paid, the debt should be written off. That is, it becomes an expense in the profit and loss account and debtors are reduced by the amount written off.

Many companies make a *provision for bad debts*. This anticipates that some of the debt may not be collected. A provision is like writing off a debt. It reduces debtors so that the amount shown in the balance sheet is not more than can be expected to be collected. It also means that profits are reduced immediately rather than in the future. Provisions can be *specific*; that is, a particular customer is identified as being likely not to pay. Provisions may also be *general*; that is, no particular customer is identified but it is assumed that a small percentage of customers will not pay.

Here is an example. A company has debtors at its year end of £120 000. Of this amount £12 000 is owed by one customer who is known to be in financial difficulties. The company wishes to make a general provision against other debtors of 2 per cent.

Total debtors	120 000
Specific debtor	12 000
Other debtors	108 000

General provision = 108 000 × 2 per cent = 2160

Total bad debt provision = 2160 + 12 000 = 14 160

Debtors as shown in balance sheet = 120 000 − 14 160

The bad debt provision is treated as an expense of this period in the profit and loss account. What happens in the future if the £12 000 is recovered from the customer who was in difficulties? Cash is received and the £12 000 is added back to the profit and loss account in the period when it is received.

The bad debt provision may need to be updated every year. It remains at the same amount unless amounts are added to it or taken away. In the above example the following year end debtors (excluding specific debtors) may be £140 000. A general provision of 2 per cent is equal to £2800. The existing provision is for £2160 so it needs to be increased by £640. Only the increased amount is charged to the profit and loss account in the second period.

Some companies calculate their general provision by looking at outstanding debt very closely. For debt that is not overdue the provision might be 1 per cent; for debt more than 30 days late the provision might be 2 per cent; for debt more than 60 days late, 3 per cent and so on.

A provision is an amount deducted from profit to provide for expenses that are not known accurately at the time the accounts are prepared. If legal action is being brought against a company it might make a provision against legal costs and claims. This is acting prudently, recognizing the possible costs as soon as possible.

Financial Statements

There are three basic types of business organizations in the UK. The presentation of financial statements can differ for each.

A *sole trader* is someone who owns his or her own business. He or she provides the finance for the business (perhaps with the help of a bank loan or overdraft) and all the profit belongs to him or her. There is no requirement for a sole trader to publish accounts. However, there are two people who will want to see the accounts of the business: the bank manager, if the bank is being asked to provide finance, and the Inland Revenue. The Inland Revenue will want to see the accounts to assess the business for income tax, but does not require accounts to be prepared in any particular format, so this is entirely down to the discretion of the owner or his or her accountant.

66 EFFECTIVE ACCOUNTING MANAGEMENT

A *partnership* is where two or more people own the business. Usually when a partnership is set up an agreement is struck between the partners as to the payment of wages, payment of interest on loans to the business and distribution of profits (if no partnership agreement exists and there is a dispute the courts will assume that profits are to be shared equally). As with the sole trader, the bank manager and the Inland Revenue will be interested in the results of the company. In addition, the partners will want to be able to see the distribution of profit between themselves. Special formats of financial statements display this information.

A *company* is a separate legal body from the shareholders and in addition it may have limited liability. The people who will be interested in seeing the financial results of a company are listed in Unit One. As already seen, the format for the presentation of accounts is specified in law. For internal management purposes the statements can be in any format; it is only for external publication that the company law formats are required.

This section will look at the format of financial statements for the three types of business organization. An example will be used, which is essentially the same in all three cases except for the distribution of profits.

The sole trader

Sole traders may pay wages and salaries to people employed by the business but not to themselves. Any payments (in cash or in goods) to the sole trader are termed *drawings*. The profit and loss account and the balance sheet will show drawings separately from other expenses of the business.

WORKED EXAMPLE

Green Stores is a retail business that buys in stock in bulk for resale to the general public. It is owned by a sole trader and the trial balance of the year ended on 31 December 199X has been drawn up with all year end adjustments made.

	Debit £ 000	Credit £ 000
Sales accounts		
Sales		725
Expenses accounts		
Depreciation – store fittings	25	
Depreciation – van	5	
Heat and light	18	
Cost of sales	350	
Insurance	12	

	Debit	Credit
Interest paid	12	
Miscellaneous	9	
Rent and rates	126	
Van expenses	3	
Wages – store	54	
Wages – administration	13	
Asset accounts		
Cash at bank	33	
Debtors	2	
Prepayments	8	
Stocks	200	
Store fittings – cost	250	
Store fittings – accumulated depreciation		100
Van – cost	15	
Van – accumulated depreciation		10
Liabilities accounts		
Accruals		7
Bank loan		120
Other creditors		6
Trade creditors		72
Capital accounts		
Drawings	24	
Owner's equity brought forward		119
	1157	1157

Stock at the end of the previous year was also £200 000; therefore purchases and cost of sales are identical. The business is partly financed by a long-term fixed interest (at 10 per cent) bank loan, which is repayable in 13 years' time.

As the financial statements do not need to be published the owner may use any format. For them to be of use to the owner probably as much detail as possible is required. The statements produced might look as follows.

PROFIT AND LOSS ACCOUNT FOR GREEN STORES
FOR THE PERIOD ENDING 31 DECEMBER 199X

	£ 000	£ 000
Sales		725
Cost of sales		350
Gross profit		375
Less: expenses		
Depreciation – store fittings	25	
Depreciation – van	5	
Heat and light	18	
Insurance	12	
Miscellaneous	9	
Rent and rates	126	
Van expenses	3	
Wages – store	54	
Wages – administration	13	265
Profit before interest		110
Interest paid		12
Profit after interest		98

GREEN STORES BALANCE SHEET AS AT 31 DECEMBER 199X

	£ 000	£ 000
Fixed assets		
Stores fittings		150
Van		5
		155
Current assets		
Cash at bank	33	
Debtors and prepayments	10	
Stocks	200	
	243	
Liabilities: amounts falling due within one year		
Trade creditors and accruals	79	
Other creditors	6	
	85	
Net current assets		158
		313

Liabilities: amounts falling due after one year

Bank loan		120
		193

Owner's capital

Balance at beginning of the year		119
Add: profit in period	98	
Less: drawings in the year	24	74
Balance carried forward at the end of the year		193

Points to note here are:

- In the profit and loss account no provision has been made for taxation. The Inland Revenue will want to see the accounts to help it assess income tax. Income tax is paid by the owner and not the business. Therefore taxation is not shown in the accounts of the business.
- The 'bottom' part of the balance sheet deals with changes in the amounts owed by the business to its owner (owner's equity). During the year profits have been earned, which increase the amount owed to the owner. During the year some drawings have been taken out of the business, which decrease the amount owed to the owner. Profit less drawings is therefore the change in the owner's equity.

Partnerships

A partnership is essentially the same as a sole trader's business. The difference is that profits are shared between partners. The accounts have to reflect how much is owed by the company to each of the partners. There are also legal requirements regarding debt etc., which need not concern us in this context.

WORKED EXAMPLE

Green Stores is used again, but this time it is owned by two partners, Jim and Sue. The trial balance after year end adjustments is:

	Debit	Credit
	£ 000	£ 000
Sales accounts		
Sales		725
Expenses accounts		
Depreciation – store fittings	25	
Depreciation – van	5	
Heat and light	18	
Cost of sales	350	
Insurance	12	
Interest paid – Jim	5	

	Debit	Credit
	£ 000	£ 000
Interest paid – Sue	7	
Miscellaneous	9	
Rent and rates	126	
Van expenses	3	
Wages – Jim	8	
Wages – Sue	6	
Wages – others	40	
Wages – administration	13	
Asset accounts		
Cash at bank	33	
Debtors	2	
Prepayments	8	
Stocks	200	
Store fittings – cost	250	
Store fittings – accumulated depreciation		100
Van – cost	15	
Van – accumulated depreciation		10
Liabilities accounts		
Accruals		7
Loan – from Jim		50
Loan – from Sue		70
Other creditors		6
Trade creditors		72
Capital accounts		
Drawings – Jim	11	
Drawings – Sue	13	
Owners' equity brought forward		
Jim		62
Sue		57
	1158	1158

RECORDING FINANCIAL INFORMATION

The following have been agreed under the partnership agreement:

- Jim is to be paid a salary of £7000 and Sue is to be paid a salary of £5000. Both have taken this amount in full during the year.
- Each partner is to be paid interest of 10 per cent on loans made to the business. Both Jim and Sue have loaned the business money and the capital is due to be repaid in 13 years' time.
- Each partner is to share equally in the profits of the business, after the deduction of salaries and interest, as outlined above.

Now, please tackle Activity AM2.2. The format is given, the data are given above but need to be restructured, and a profit and loss account and balance sheet should be delivered.

ACTIVITY AM2.2

THE GREEN STORES PARTNERSHIP

Activity code
- ✓ Self-development
- ✓ Teamwork
- ✓ Communications
- ✓ Numeracy/IT
- ✓ Decisions

PROFIT AND LOSS ACCOUNT FOR GREEN STORES PARTNERSHIP
FOR THE PERIOD ENDING 31 DECEMBER 199X

£ 000   £ 000

Sales
Cost of sales
Gross profit
Less: expenses
Depreciation – store fittings
Depreciation – van
Heat and light
Insurance
Miscellaneous
Rent and rates
Van expenses

72   EFFECTIVE ACCOUNTING MANAGEMENT

	£ 000	£ 000
Wages – other		
Wages – administration		
Profit before appropriations	————	————
Salaries:		
Jim		
Sue	————	————
Interest payable:		
Jim		
Sue	————	————
Profit after interest		————
Residual Profit:		
Jim (50 per cent)		
Sue (50 per cent)	————	————
		————

GREEN STORES PARTNERSHIP BALANCE SHEET AS AT 31 DECEMBER 199X

	£ 000	£ 000
Fixed assets		
Stores fittings		
Van		————
Current assets		
Cash at bank		
Debtors and prepayments		
Stocks	————	
Liabilities: amounts falling due within one year		
Trade creditors and accruals		
Other creditors	————	
Net current assets		————
		————

RECORDING FINANCIAL INFORMATION

> **Owners' capital**   Jim   Sue   Total
>   £ 000   £ 000   £ 000
>
> Capital
> Current account:
> Balance at beginning of year
> Add: profit in period
> Less: drawings in year   _____   _____
> Balance carried forward at end of year _____   _____   _____
>   _____
>
> Points to note here are:
>
> - No provision has been made for taxation, for the same reason as for the sole trader.
> - In the profit and loss account net profit is calculated on all transactions, excluding those involving the partners. Deductions are then made for those items in line with the terms of the partnership agreement. The profit after those items have been deducted is called the *residual profit*. It is allocated to each partner in the proportion agreed.
> - The 'bottom' part of the balance sheet deals with changes in the amounts owed by the business to each of its owners. First, there is the *capital account*, which shows how much is outstanding on the loans from each partner. Then there is the *current account*, which details the entitlement of each owner to profits. It is not necessary to split these two accounts.

Companies

Companies are very much different from sole traders and partnerships in a number of respects. Companies are subject to corporation tax, so we shall see taxation in these accounts for the first time. Distributions to owners are made as *dividends*. These may be paid during the year, in which case they are called *interim dividends*. It is usual to pay most of the dividend a few months after the end of the year (when the amount of profit earned is known). *Proposed dividends* are shown in the profit and loss accounts even though they have not yet been approved. They are also shown in the balance sheet as a liability that will become due within one year.

WORKED EXAMPLE

The same example is used, but this time Green Stores Ltd is a limited company. The trial balance with year end adjustments made is as follows:

	Debit	Credit
	£ 000	£ 000
Sales accounts		
Sales		725

	Debit £ 000	Credit £ 000
Expenses accounts		
Depreciation – store fittings	25	
Depreciation – van	5	
Heat and light	18	
Cost of sales	350	
Insurance	12	
Interest paid	12	
Miscellaneous	9	
Rent and rates	126	
Taxation	30	
Van expenses	3	
Wages – store	54	
Wages – administration	13	
Assets accounts		
Cash at bank	33	
Debtors	2	
Prepayments	8	
Stocks	200	
Store fittings – cost	250	
Store fittings – accumulated depreciation		100
Van – cost	15	
Van – accumulated depreciation		10
Liabilities accounts		
Accruals		7
Bank loan		120
Proposed dividend		18
Provision for taxation		30
Other creditors		6
Trade creditors		72
Share capital and reserve accounts		
Dividends paid	24	
Dividends proposed	18	
Share capital		60
Retained profit brought forward		59
	1207	1207

RECORDING FINANCIAL INFORMATION

As the financial statements are to be published they will take one of the formats allowed under the Companies Acts.

Please tackle Activity AM2.3, using the above data and the format contained in the activity. Both the profit and loss account and the balance sheet are required.

ACTIVITY AM2.3

GREEN STORES LIMITED

Activity code
- ✓ Self-development
- ✓ Teamwork
- ✓ Communications
- ✓ Numeracy/IT
- ✓ Decisions

PROFIT AND LOSS ACCOUNT FOR GREEN STORES LTD
FOR THE PERIOD ENDING 31 DECEMBER 199X

	£ 000	£ 000
Sales		
Cost of sales		_____
Gross profit		
Distribution		
Administration	_____	_____
Profit before interest		
Interest paid		_____
Profit after interest		_____
Taxation provision		_____
Profit after tax		
Dividends:		
Paid		
Proposed	_____	_____
Retained profit for the period		
Retained profit brought forward		_____
Retained profit carried forward		_____

GREEN STORES LTD BALANCE SHEET AS AT 31 DECEMBER 199X

	£ 000	£ 000
Fixed assets		
Stores fittings		
Van		_____
Current assets		
Cash at bank		
Debtors and prepayments		
Stocks	_____	
Liabilities: amounts falling due within one year		
Trade creditors and accruals		
Other creditors	_____	
	_____	
Net current assets		_____
Liabilities: amounts falling due after one year		
Bank loan		_____
		_____
Share capital and reserves		
Share capital		
Retained profit carried forward		_____
		_____

A point to note here is that some costs have been split into distribution and administration, depending on what the expense was incurred for. In the profit and loss account distribution is made up of:

Depreciation – van	5
Van expenses	3
Wages – store	54
Depreciation – store fittings	25
Heat and light	15
Insurance	10
Rent and rates	100
	212

Administration is made up of:

Miscellaneous	9
Rent and rates	26
Heat and light	3
Insurance	2
Wages – administration	13
	53

Please tackle Activity AM2.4. The company in the activity operates in a retail environment.

ACTIVITY AM2.4

PRINCIPLES OF THE PROFIT AND LOSS ACCOUNT – RETAIL EXAMPLE

Activity code
- ✓ Self-development
- ☐ Teamwork
- ✓ Communications
- ☐ Numeracy/IT
- ✓ Decisions

Ten 'principles' contained in a retail profit and loss account are given here. Explain the meaning of these 'principles' and make comments on the implications of the ten principles (seven in effect).

Principle	Commentary
1 Company name	1 ⎫
2 Trading, profit and loss account	2 ⎬ Self-explanatory
3 For year ending 'x'	3 ⎭
4 Sales	4
5 Less cost of goods sold	5
6 Opening stock	6
7 Purchases	7
8 Less closing stock	8
9 Gross profit	9
10 Less expenses	10

Conclusion

In this unit we have covered the essential ingredients of the accounting task as far as recording information is concerned. We have started with basic documentation and gone through to more complex financial statements covering the main types of organizations. We started with profit as a key concept in Unit One and continued this theme in this unit. Now we must turn to the other half of the equation, costs.

Notes

1. Sikka et al., commentating in the *Guardian* on recent judgements that auditors do not have a 'duty of care' to individual shareholders.
2. See, for example, Drury, *Management and Cost Accounting*.
3. Depreciation can also be calculated with other valuation bases. With current cost accounting, depreciation will be the fall in current value from one period to the next. It is not discussed here because the historic cost convention is the one in widespread use in the UK.

Unit Three

Costs and Their Classifications

Learning Objectives

After completing this unit you should be able to:

- understand the different ways in which costs are grouped together and why cost information has to be presented in this way;
- recognize the behaviour patterns of costs at different levels of activity;
- understand the different costing techniques used in different companies to find product costs;
- understand the different ways of allocating overheads to products;
- apply the generic skills.

Contents

Overview

Cost Classification

▶ Manufacturing and non-manufacturing costs

▶ Direct and indirect costs

▶ Breaking down costs

Cost Behaviour Patterns

▶ Variable costs

▶ Fixed costs

▶ Semi-variable costs

▶ Semi-fixed (step) costs

Cost Accumulation

▶ Product costing

▶ Job production

▶ Contract production

▶ Batch production

▶ Process production

Recording Costs

▶ Direct material costs

   Purchase order

   Goods received note (GRN)

   Material requisition

   Stock records

   Stock ledger account

▶ Stock taking

- Stock pricing
- Labour costs
- Expenses

Overheads

- Predetermined overhead rates
- Blanket (or factory-wide) rates
- Multiple rates
- Activity-based costing

Unit Three

" To invert a saying of Oscar Wilde, it is important not only to know the value of something, but to know its cost as well. "

Overview

We cannot talk meaningfully about profit unless we consider costs. Profit equals revenue less costs. Revenues are sometimes outside the control of managers but costs are certainly something that managers can exercise some influence over. Logically we might think that if costs are kept low then profits will be higher. However, this may not be correct. If costs are kept to a minimum, for example by not advertising or by producing low quality goods, revenues will be lost and profits will be lower.

Before we are able to decide on the optimal level of costs it is necessary to understand the costs that are incurred in business. The purpose of this unit is to look at some of the many costs and to see how they are accounted for.

Cost behaviour patterns provide a useful mechanism for categorizing costs and this is forwarded in the book. We then look at various methods of cost accumulation depending upon the type of production process. The detailed recording of costs completes this unit.

Cost Classification

In accounting, the term classification is used to describe the grouping together of costs. We have already seen one example when looking at the profit and loss account. For publication purposes all the individual types of expenses were not shown. They were grouped together and summarized under particular headings. This is an example of cost classification, but this is only one example, and there are other ways in which costs can be grouped together.

While the classifications used for financial reporting are useful for providing information to people outside the organization, they are unlikely to be useful to managers. They are too summarized and some costs may be under the wrong headings. A facilities manager wants to know how much is being spent on rent, rates, heat, etc. He or she wants to know this in total, across the whole company. He or she is not interested in which departments occupy which buildings or where the costs have been recorded. The financial accounting information is no good to him or her.

Fortunately, computerized accounting systems make it very easy to analyse historic cost information in many different ways.

Managers may want information about what is going to happen in the future. The information provided by the financial accounting system is unlikely to be useful for this and other ways of classification are needed. This section looks at some of the ways in which costs can be grouped together.

Manufacturing and non-manufacturing costs

One important way of classifying cost comes from financial accounting and company law. This defines what can be included under the heading 'cost of goods sold'. In financial reporting it is important to find the cost of stocks held at the end of the period. According to the matching principle the cost of a product does not become an expense in the profit and loss account until it is sold. It is valued as a current asset in the balance sheet until sold.

The law is strict about what can be included in the cost of the product. Only the costs of production can be included. For a manufacturing company all the costs associated with the manufacturing process may be included. For a non-manufacturing company only the bought-in cost may be included. Any non-manufacturing costs, e.g. wages paid to sales staff, appear elsewhere in the profit and loss account and must be deducted in the period in which they are incurred. This distinction is made so that stock can be valued at the cost of getting it to its saleable condition. Distribution or selling costs should not be included, as the product has not yet been distributed or sold.

Please refer to Activity AM3.1.

Direct and indirect costs

This classification is very important when one is trying to establish the cost of a product or providing a service. As can be implied from the term, direct costs are those which can be directly identified with a product or service. If in the manufacture of a table we can see that 10 kg of a wood is used and the cost of the wood is £20 then this is a direct cost. If in providing a training programme a lecturer is employed for one day and the cost of employment is £200 then that is also a direct cost.

Direct costs are the costs of things that can easily be identified and traced to individual products or services. Direct costs can be made up of three elements:

- Direct materials – the cost of items that can physically be seen to be going into a product.
- Direct labour – the cost of employing a person for the time he or she spends working on a product or providing the service.
- Direct expenses – any other expenses that are incurred specifically to enable the manufacture of a product or to provide a service. Subcontracted work is an example of such a cost.

COSTS AND THEIR CLASSIFICATIONS

ACTIVITY AM3.1

DEBATE ON ADVERTISING COSTS

Activity code
- ☐ Self-development
- ☐ Teamwork
- ✓ Communications
- ☐ Numeracy/IT
- ☐ Decisions

Task
Examine the proposal below for a debate or discussion.[1]

> Advertising is a cost of the period and of the goods sold in a given period. It is not a cost set against future sales.

Source:
1 You may wish to consult Anderson and Kleiner, *Effective Marketing Communications*

Any cost that cannot be directly traced to a product or service is an indirect cost, more commonly known as an overhead. All selling, distribution and administration costs are treated as indirect costs for financial reporting purposes, as they are not incurred in the production of goods.

In the manufacturing process there are costs that cannot be traced directly to products. Indirect materials may be purchased for use in servicing the machines that process products. They are indirectly incurred for the benefit of the product. There are other materials that could be traced to individual products, but it would be too time-consuming to do so as their cost would be insignificant; for example, the cost of screws used to hold a table together.

Indirect labour costs are also likely to be incurred. These are the costs of employing any person in the factory who does not work directly on production. They can be found in a non-production department; for example, in the stores room or in a maintenance department. They may also work in a production department; for example supervisors, who oversee the work of others.

Indirect production expenses are all other costs incurred in manufacturing a product. They include the cost of heat and light for the building and any other facility costs.

A product can incur some costs that are direct (for example, carriage) but that are not manufacturing costs and, for stock valuation, could not be included as part of the product cost (quite rightly, as the stock has not yet

86 EFFECTIVE ACCOUNTING MANAGEMENT

been sold and distribution costs will not yet have been incurred). For decision-making purposes managers may want to know what the full cost of a product is, including the non-manufacturing costs. A company that uses the financial accounting information as the product cost is giving the wrong information to managers.

Breaking down costs

Please tackle Activity AM3.2, which consolidates this section.

ACTIVITY AM3.2

BREAKING DOWN COSTS

Activity code
- ✓ Self-development
- ☐ Teamwork
- ✓ Communications
- ✓ Numeracy/IT
- ✓ Decisions

Task
Summarize the cost breakdown in the following example, *under appropriate headings*.

'My business costs some £15000 in indirect costs, another £6000 for administration, labour is some £10000 and materials another £20000. I'm also concerned about my selling and distribution costs, which cost me £9000, and the expenses of the manufacturing process cost me another £5000.'

Cost Behaviour Patterns

The costs incurred by a company increase at different rates in relation to varying levels of activity. These patterns can be illustrated using graphs. Some costs will increase with activity while others remain constant. This section looks at these various patterns. It is important to be able to recognize these patterns for two reasons. One is so that we can predict what will happen to costs in the future when decisions are made. The second reason is that understanding the underlying patterns can help us to identify costs that managers should be able to control.

Variable costs

These are the costs that increase in direct proportion to an activity. Take, for example, the cost of raw materials going into a product. The cost is

COSTS AND THEIR CLASSIFICATIONS

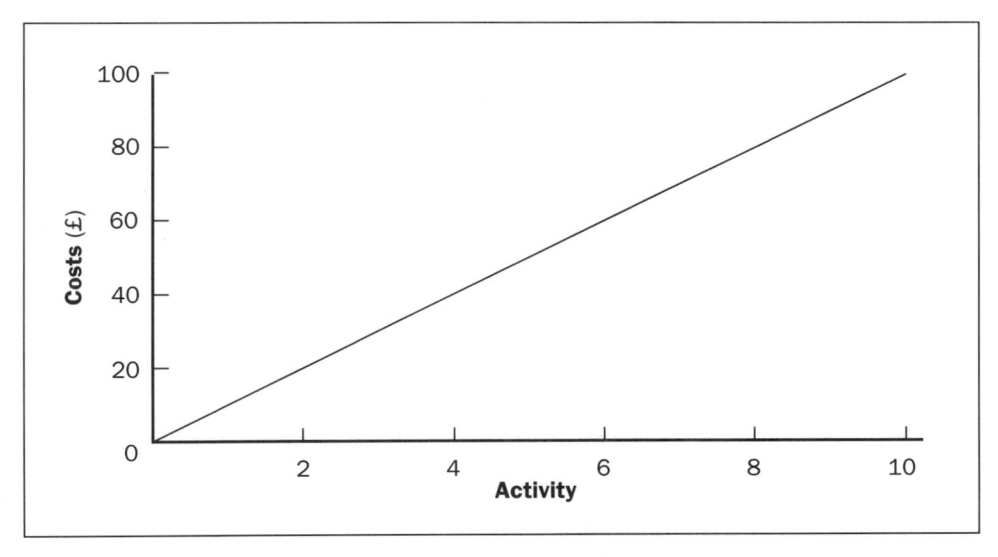

Figure 3.1 Variable costs.

£1 per unit. The total cost for one unit of production is £1, for two units £2, for 100 units £100. Displaying this on a graph, we can see that the pattern formed is of a straight line (figure 3.1). The vertical axis displays the total costs incurred, the horizontal axis the number of units produced. There are many costs that display this pattern. Labour used to be thought of as a variable cost, but modern employment contracts mean that employees are not hired only as needed.[1] Only piecework labour can be said truly to display a variable cost pattern.

Variable costs for the most part will be *direct* costs. That is, as they increase with each unit the cost can be directly attributed to that unit. Some costs are variable to some activity but not to the number of units produced (or services provided). These costs are not direct even though they are variable.

Fixed costs

At the other extreme from variable costs are fixed costs. *These remain the same regardless of the level of activity* (figure 3.2). The rent paid for a factory is the same regardless of the level of activity inside the factory.

Fixed costs are in reality only observed in the short term. Rents are usually fixed for a period but then are subject to review in the light of inflation and economic conditions. Increases in fixed costs are not the result of changes in activity. Thus fixed costs are very difficult to attribute directly to individual products or services. Without renting a factory you would be unable to make the product, but the rent has not increased as a result of making the product: therefore it is an indirect cost.

88 EFFECTIVE ACCOUNTING MANAGEMENT

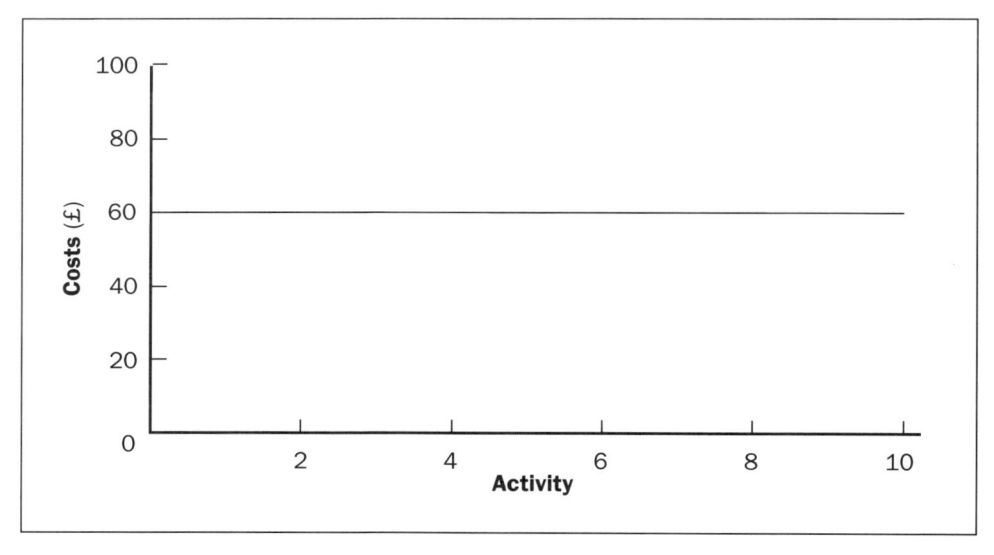

Figure 3.2 Fixed costs.

Semi-variable costs

These costs are a combination of variable and fixed costs. There is a fixed sum to be paid even when there is no activity. As the activity increases the cost increases proportionately. Most bills for utilities display such a behaviour pattern. For example, in a telephone bill there is a charge for the line and equipment rental and then there is a charge for each call made. The variable element of the cost can be directly attributed to products or services, but the fixed element cannot. See figure 3.3.

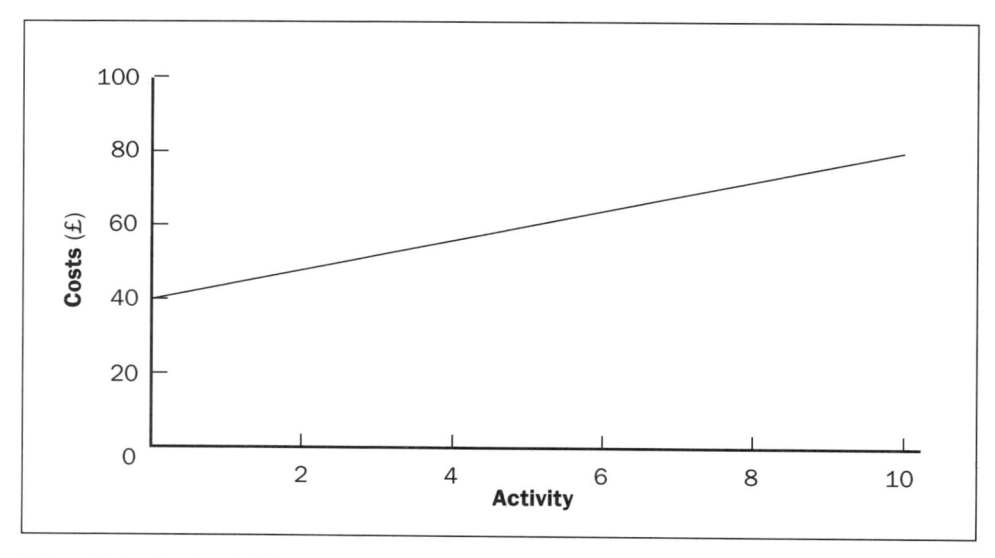

Figure 3.3 Semi-variable costs.

Semi-fixed (step) costs

These are similar to fixed costs, but they increase in steps (figure 3.4). The costs of hiring machinery typically display this behaviour pattern. Initially just one machine is needed. As activity increases the machine becomes fully utilized. Then a second machine is needed, at double the cost, and perhaps a third or a fourth. Many costs today display this pattern. Direct labour costs are in reality a bit of a mix between a step cost and a variable cost. Workers are not hired just as needed: they tend to be taken on permanently, with a fixed wage. If activity increases beyond their working hours, then they may be paid overtime (at a premium). Eventually, if activity continues to increase, the worker will not be able to cope and another worker must be hired.

Please tackle Activity AM3.3.

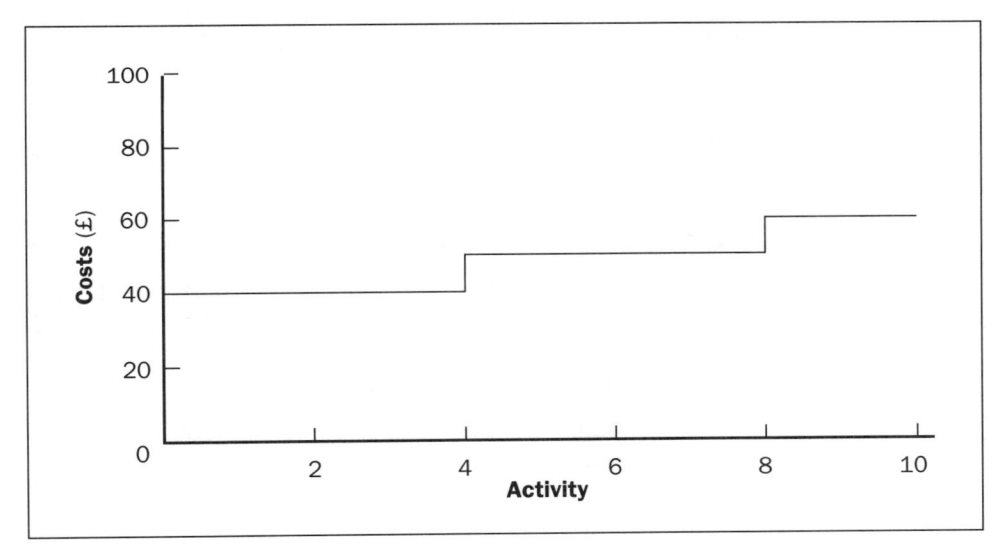

Figure 3.4 Step costs.

Cost Accumulation

Product costing

Companies in manufacturing and service industries will want to know the cost of their products. Cost is often used as the basis for setting prices. Many decisions are made on the basis of product profitability. To calculate profitability, costs are required. While noting that product costing in a service industry is as important as in a manufacturing industry, this section focuses on manufacturing. This is because of the complexities of

ACTIVITY AM3.3

SMALL ENGINEERING LIMITED

Activity code
- ☐ Self-development
- ☑ Teamwork
- ☐ Communications
- ☑ Numeracy/IT
- ☑ Decisions

The directors of Small Engineering Ltd decided to examine all costs incurred in the running of their firm. They have asked the training officer to go into such an analysis of costs for the training department.

The training officer approached the accountant and was told that it had not been the practice in the past to establish the costs of training. The policy had been to 'lose' training costs in departmental budgets. The accountant provided the following information.

Total costs for the firm in the year ended 31 December 199X

Personnel costs	£2 168 950 (training school £21 250; training department £8000; craft apprentices in training £72 700; operative trainees in training £20 500; clerical trainees in training £42 200)
Insurance	£20 750 (other departments £15 000; training department £5750)
Depreciation	£890 700 (training department £8500; school £18 000)
Materials	£101 000 (training department £2500; school £2500)
Purchasing and selling costs	£40 000 (not related to training)
Fees	£8300 (training department £1400)
Building costs	£115 000 (training department £10 000; school £60 000)
Transport and travel	£30 000 (training department £5000)
Administration costs	£100 000 (training department £38 000; school £2500)

Some 15 per cent of the training school costs could be allocated to the trainee operatives. Little use was made of the school by the administrative

COSTS AND THEIR CLASSIFICATIONS

> and clerical trainees. The craft apprentices used the facilities almost as much as the operative trainees.
>
> The costs needed to be split among the different types of trainee. It seemed fair to use a ratio of 5:4:1 for trainee operatives, craftspeople and administrators/clerks.
>
> Last year's trainee numbers, which would be similar to this year's, were:
>
> Operatives   25
>
> Craftspeople   105
>
> Administrators/clerks   15
>
> Average trainee costs (national), according to state figures, were:
>
> Operatives   £8000
>
> Craftspeople   £7000
>
> Administrators/clerks   £6000
>
> The salaries or wages of trainees account for 60 per cent of costs
>
> Analyse the specific training costs and allocate them under a 'training head' as opposed to general company costs, to give the costs incurred by the training department.
>
> *Source:* The basic idea for this activity comes from a former tutor, J. Jocelyn.

manufacturing and not because it is seen as more important. The techniques described here apply equally to the service sector.

For a manufacturing company the costs must be found for each of the individual products, so that stock can be valued and profit can be calculated. Where a company has just one standardized product this may be fairly easy. When several products are made within a shared factory facility it can become a very complex task to trace costs down to individual products.

There is no one method of calculating product costs for all circumstances because of the different nature of the manufacturing processes found in companies. Some manufacture standard products; that is, identical units all with the same inputs and with the same costs. Others may work on very large one-off projects; for example, a construction company working on long-term projects such as building hospitals or motorways. Methods of product costing have been developed for the different types of industry. These methods of production and costing techniques are outlined below.

Job production

This occurs where each and every product is different (or at least a substantial number of products are different). The product may even be

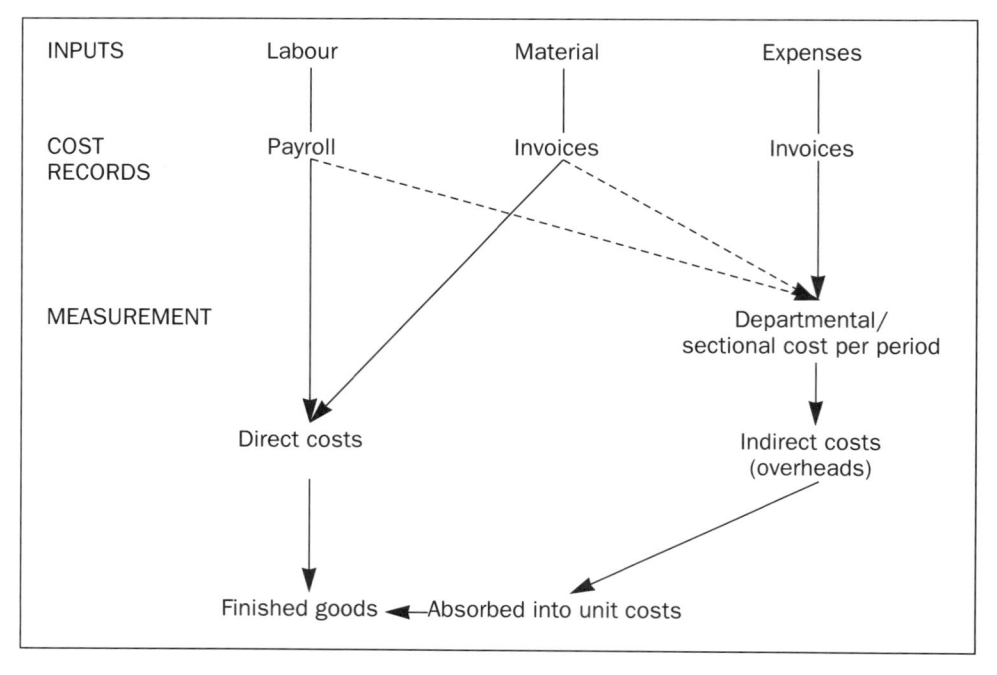

Figure 3.5 Job costing.

manufactured to the customer's own specifications. An example of job production is an engineering workshop that produces machines for use by a wide variety of other manufacturers with a wide variety of products. The costing technique used in such an environment is known as *job costing*. Very often in a job environment the price charged to customers is determined by adding a profit margin to the cost. It is doubly important in such cases that the costs of a job are accurately determined. All costs, as far as is possible, have to be traced directly to the job. This can be a very time-consuming job and is normally carried out by a specialized costing section of the accounts department. Please refer to figure 3.5.

The costs incurred on the job are recorded on a job sheet, and will include the following elements.

- Direct materials: the quantities of raw materials and components used and their costs. The physical quantities are provided from the materials requisition document, and the costing section of the accounts department will determine the appropriate cost (see the section on materials later in this unit).
- Direct labour: the time spent by production workers in manufacturing the product and the cost of employing the workers. The time spent on each job is recorded on a job card or a time sheet. The costing department determines the appropriate cost of this time from the payroll records (see the section on labour later in this unit).
- Direct expenses: any expenses incurred solely to enable completion of the job; for example, subcontracted work. Information on the cost of such work comes directly from the supplier's invoice.

BOX AM3.1

Job sheet – example

JOB SHEET		Job no	
Customer			
	Quantity	Rate	Total
DIRECT MATERIALS			
Store rec. no.			
ZZ63	2 kg	£16.00	£32.00
IP20	1	£20.00	£20.00
DIRECT LABOUR			
Employee	3 hours	£7.30	£21.90
OVERHEADS			
TOTAL LABOUR HOURS	3 hours	£10.00	£30.00
TOTAL COST			£103.90
Job complete date			
Date passed to costing			
Date entered to general ledger...			

- Overheads: the cost of facilities and activities without which the product could never have been manufactured, but where exact usage and cost cannot be determined. An allocation of the overheads costs has to be made to jobs, in approximate proportion to the demands made on facilities. Suitable bases for allocation are determined by the costing department (see the section on overheads later in this unit). In Box AM3.1, overheads are charged on labour hours.

Contract production

This is similar to job production, with each product being different, but here production is on a large scale and/or takes a long time to complete. Construction companies fall under this heading. The method of costing used in such circumstances is known as *contract costing*. There is a Statement of Standard Accounting Practice (SSAP 9) that specifically deals with problems of contract costing. The technique is very similar to job costing and in some respects it is easier to trace many costs directly to the contract, because a manager devotes all of his or her time to the contract, and not between a variety of jobs. The problems of contract costing are often related to the time span involved. Should profit only be taken at the end of the contract? If profit should be taken during the life, how much? How should progress payments be dealt with? Please tackle Activity AM3.4.

ACTIVITY AM3.4

DOMSEC

Activity code
- ✓ Self-development
- ✓ Teamwork
- ✓ Communications
- ✓ Numeracy/IT
- ✓ Decisions

There is an adage that nothing succeeds like success, and it applied to Domsec. The firm went from strength to strength. The success rested on meeting the growing needs of the marketplace and the expertise of Ted 'Plodder' Harvey and 'Boots' Smith. The company name itself was a bit of a misnomer as the work involved safety and security in both domestic and industrial settings, and involved both consultancy advice and the fitting of a range of security and safety devices.

In a sense, there were really two operating units, the security firm with its emphasis on the domestic market and the safety firm with its orientation on the business-to-business or industrial market. The domestic security market to date could be termed 'low tech'. There were no closed circuit TVs or access controls, no video entry systems or security grilles or doors. They would put in window bars if the customer demanded it but 'Boots' was against the concept on safety grounds. So it was not state-of-the-art electronic detection. Nor did it involve highly trained 'officers' or dog handlers to protect property or people. It was on a basic level: door spy-holes, intercoms, bolts, snibs and digital locking systems whereby the homeowners could punch in their number. But even this digital system had been quite a recent innovation. The industrial security market had demanded greater technical specialization and manpower, so the company to date had majored on the new building, refurbishment and security-conscious owner market segments.

The health and safety part of the business was co-ordinated by 'Boots'. The firm provided 'any safety piece of equipment', or so it boasted. It manufactured nothing as a deliberate policy but it provided safety shoes, goggles, gloves, breathing apparatus, protective uniforms and suits, and so on. In

COSTS AND THEIR CLASSIFICATIONS

addition, the firm provided guidance on safety to the industrial users and consultancy-cum-training skills for representatives. It also crossed over to the other 'division' in giving advice on such things as fire alarms to domestic users but this advice had largely become routine, apart from in the initial sales pitch for large construction contracts.

'I've just been reading this article on domestic security. Since the Tories came to power in 1979, the burglary rate has risen some 163 per cent: that's one every 24 seconds. The 1992 British Crime Survey reckons that the true figure is near to 1 365 000 burglaries per annum – more than double the official figure. Blame the recession, the Tories or deviants but it is a marketing opportunity for us', said Ted, the ex-policeman. 'We should look to the domestic security market.'

'Mm, all these locks on doors are all very well, but labour is expensive and there's the equipment and the van etc. I'm not sure that the financial return is there', responded Boots. 'We'll need to do a very detailed job costing to see if it's a starter. I'll get Mary, my PA, to pull some figures together.'

- Labour cost per operative
    1. £7.00 per hour
       40 hours   =
    2. Overtime at time and one-half rates
       £10.50 per hour
       5 hours   =
    Weekly cost per operative   =
    Monthly cost per operative   =
    (assume 13 x 4 weeks) per annum
    Employees' costs (£50)
    (insurance etc.) per week   =
- Lease of vehicle
  (maintenance contract)
  Small van rental scheme over
  3 years: £170 per month   =
- Fuel/insurance/Road Tax
  Fuel: London only
        = £100 per month
      plus non-London
        = £30 per month
      Insurance (group/vehicle)
        = £360 p.a.
      Car Tax 1 (per annum)
        = £125
      Equipment (per annum)
        = £180
- Tools/equipment for installation
  Initial start-up £250
  Ongoing   £36 per week   =
- Overhead transfer charge
  of (per month) £100
              Total   =

- Material for ten customers
  1. Assume locks/bolts for all
     £60 per customer
  2. Additional window locks and door locks
     £100 per customer
  3. Alarm system in addition
     £150 per customer
  4. New lighting arrangements
     £220 per customer

  Most, 80 per cent, will go for options 1 and 2: allow
  20 per cent for alarm
  10 per cent for lighting
  = £197 per average customer

Task
Work out the validity of this project given the job costs and customer numbers per operator.

Batch production

This is where products are manufactured in a batch but, when completed, can be separated into individual products. Brewing is an example of such an industry, with beer being produced in large quantities and then placed into barrels for resale. Many modern manufacturing operations have batch production, where perhaps 1000 units of a particular product are made before machines are turned over to the production of a run of 500 units of a different (but similar) product; for example, tennis racquets then squash racquets. The method of costing used in such circumstances is known as *batch costing*. It has some similarities with job costing in that the costs of direct materials, direct labour and direct expenses are traced and overheads are allocated to the batch. An average cost per unit is found by dividing the total cost of the batch by the number of units in the batch.

Process production

This is where there is a continuous flow of items being processed with no discernible end point. This is at the other end of the scale from job production. If production was stopped at a particular moment there would be products at different stages of completion, some just started and others nearly finished. The method of costing used here is known as *process costing* (see figure 3.6). In some respects the task of finding product costs is easier than with job costing because a process comprises a single department. Costs can be traced to the department and then total costs for a period can be divided by the total output for a period to give an average cost per unit.

In practice there are a number of problems with process costing. These particularly relate to: how to value incomplete units still in the process at

COSTS AND THEIR CLASSIFICATIONS

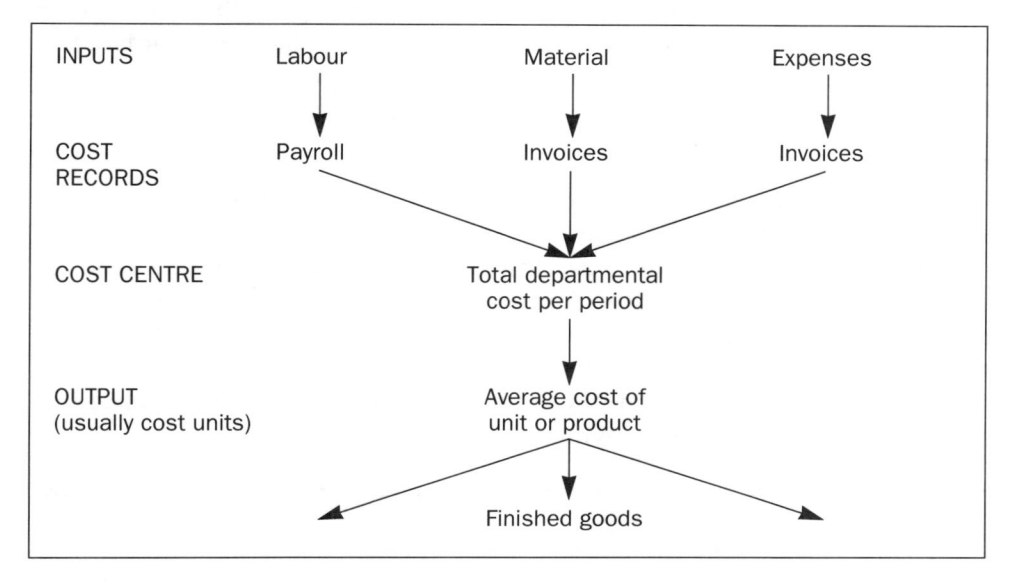

```
INPUTS          Labour           Material          Expenses
                  │                 │                 │
                  ▼                 ▼                 ▼
COST            Payroll          Invoices          Invoices
RECORDS            ╲                │                ╱
                    ╲               ▼               ╱
COST CENTRE          Total departmental cost per period
                              │
                              ▼
OUTPUT               Average cost of
(usually cost units)  unit or product
                              │
                              ▼
                       Finished goods
```

Figure 3.6 Process costing.

the end of the financial period; how to deal with losses in production; by-products of the main process; and joint products resulting from the same process.

Recording Costs

Whichever method of product costing is used, there will be material, labour, direct and indirect expenses to be included. How these are recorded and controlled is the subject of this section.

Direct material costs

These consist of the cost of materials, components or raw materials going into a product. To be able accurately to find the materials costs for any product, good stock and store records must be kept. This is not only to provide product costs but also to control stocks and to pay suppliers. The typical procedure for accounting for stock involves a number of stages of documentation.

Purchase order
This gives authority to the supplier to provide materials. A formal order ensures that the supplier will get payment and should also set the price for the materials. Often this function is carried out by a specialist purchasing department, which can negotiate the best prices and terms with suppliers. A purchase order will only be raised after a purchase requisition is raised by a

production department or the stores department. A copy of the order will be sent to the stores department to confirm that the goods have been ordered. A copy also needs to be sent to the accounts department to alert them to the fact that a supplier will want to be paid at some point in the future.

Goods received note (GRN)
This details the items received in a delivery, and should match up with the supplier's delivery note. The quantity delivered should always be checked against the delivery note because this document will be the basis of the supplier's invoice. The GRN forms the basis for updating the store's records. A typical GRN is shown in Box AM3.2. Copies should be sent to the purchasing department so that the order can be closed, and also to the account department so that the supplier's invoice can be checked for accuracy when it arrives for payment.

BOX AM3.2

Goods received note – example

GOODS RECEIVED NOTE   No. ....

Supplier ....   Date ....

Delivery note ....

Description	Order no.	Quantity
Received by	Comments	

Material requisition
This details the items sent on to the factory floor for use in production. For costing purposes this will contain details of the job or the department to which the materials have been issued. The costing department will use this information to find the cost of direct materials to include for a job, a batch or a process. The stores records can then be updated to take account of the issue. Box AM3.3 gives an example of the format.

COSTS AND THEIR CLASSIFICATIONS

> **BOX AM3.3**
>
> ## Material requisition – example
>
> MATERIAL REQUISITION   No. ....
>
> Charge to
>
> Authorized by
>
> | Description | Code | Quantity | Price | Value |
> |---|---|---|---|---|
> | | | | | |
>
> Issued by .... Issue date ....
>
> Stock record updated ....
>
> Passed to costing ....
>
> Date charged to job/department ....

Stock records
These should detail how many units of each item are held in stock. Typically, manual stock records are kept on stock cards, an example of which is shown in Box AM3.4.

Stock ledger account
The cost of items held in stock needs to be recorded. The accounts are usually the responsibility of the costing department and are often separate from the stock records kept by the stores department (with periodic reconciliation between the two records being required). This is because of complications of stock pricing (see the section on stock pricing in this unit). A typical stock ledger account is shown in Box AM3.5.

The keeping of all records relating to materials is an ideal application for computerization. Computerization allows for the easy matching up of all stages of ordering, receipt, payment and issue. It also avoids much of the duplication that goes on. Computerized systems are based on good manual procedures and will contain the same data as found on a manual system.

100 EFFECTIVE ACCOUNTING MANAGEMENT

BOX AM3.4

Stock record card – example

STOCK RECORD   Description ....

Code ....   Location ....

Date	Receipts		Issues		Quantity in stock
	GRN no.	Quantity	Req. no.	Quantity	

Ordering level ....   Ordering quantity ....

BOX AM3.5

Stores ledger account – example

STORES LEDGER ACCOUNT   Material code no. ....

Date	Receipts			Issues			Balance £
	Ref.	Qty	Price £	Ref.	Qty	Price £	

Stock taking

At the end of the financial year all stock should be counted and valued. The physical stock-take and its subsequent valuation will be observed by an auditor, who is interested in verifying the value for stock used in the balance sheet. The stock count identifies discrepancies between physical quantities and the stock records. Stock may be stolen or damaged and the stock count allows these items to be written off. To reduce the opportunities for theft many companies have more frequent stock checks.

Stock pricing

Problems of pricing stock arise when items arrive at different points in time and different prices are paid. There are a number of methods for dealing with this, and these will be demonstrated using the following example, for component XYZ.

At the start of January there is no stock, then two deliveries are made with different costs per unit. Some of the components are used in manufacture during the month. What is the value of the components used and what is the value of the components left in stock at the end of the month?

Date	Transaction	Quantity	Cost per unit
1 January	receipt	500	£2.00
14 January	receipt	300	£2.50
23 January	issue	600	

FIFO (first in first out). This method is based on the assumption that stock received first will be issued first; that is, in chronological order. Stock that is left at the end of a period is valued at the price of the last units to be received.

Materials issued to production
500 units at £2.00 each   1000
100 units at £2.50 each   250
                                     1250

Materials in stock at period end
200 units at £2.50   500

LIFO (last in first out). This method prices issues at the cost of the latest receipts. Closing stock is valued using earlier prices. In times of rising prices production is valued at the current replacement cost, but stocks may be undervalued. This method is not approved by the UK accounting profession for use in financial reporting (SSAP 9).

Materials issued to production
300 units at £2.50 each   750
300 units at £2.00 each   600
                            1350

Materials in stock at period end
200 units at £2.00   400

AVCO (average cost). With this method no assumption is made about the order of issue. All items and their costs are pooled together. This method is preferred in industries where prices fluctuate both up and down; for example, raw materials such as tin or oil.

Units	Cost per unit	Total
500	2.00	1000
300	2.50	750
800	2.1875*	1750

* £1750 divided by 800 units

Materials issued to production
600 units at £2.1875 each   1312.50
Materials in stock at period end
200 units at £2.1875   437.50

The three methods of stock pricing give three different results in this example. There are two effects of the differences: the production costs in a period are lowest with LIFO and highest with FIFO, thus increasing or decreasing current profit; and closing stocks have the highest value in the balance sheet with LIFO and lowest with FIFO.

Value of	Production cost	Closing stock
LIFO	1250.00	500.00
FIFO	1350.00	400.00
AVCO	1312.50	437.50

The method used is left to the choice of the individual company, depending on its individual circumstances. A company dealing with materials where the price is volatile is likely to choose AVCO. Where prices are fairly stable or rising slowly over time the LIFO method is likely to be selected. The LIFO method is unlikely to be used in the United Kingdom because of the disapproval of the accounting profession and the Inland Revenue.

Labour costs

There was a time when the major cost of producing an item was the direct labour. With modern manufacturing techniques it has become a far smaller proportion of total costs. In a modern manufacturing firm, using modern technology and working practices, the direct labour costs may be as low as 2–3 per cent of the total costs of production. Yet many companies still have sophisticated systems for accounting for labour costs. This comes from a perhaps outdated philosophy of trying to control labour to make sure that workers did not take advantage of the company.[2] This was particularly true when hourly paid staff were used. Today many workers are on permanent contracts and are in effect salaried. The need to record costs for control purposes has become less important.

There are industries in which direct labour is still an important input to the manufacturing process and the costs form an important part of the product costs. This section looks at the full process in which costs are traced to products.

The start of the payment process for all employees is in the personnel department when a contract of employment is drawn up. This states the rate and method by which employees are to be paid. The main methods of payment are as follows.[3]

- Salary: a fixed annual amount is paid (normally monthly) regardless of the number of hours worked.
- Hourly rate (or daily rate): the employee is paid for time in attendance at the job place. The hourly rate is determined by the contract up to a predetermined number of hours, say 40 hours per week. Should the employee work beyond this time he or she receives overtime, which is often paid at a premium.
- Piecework: payment is made according to how much work is completed, regardless of the time taken. Outwork, where people work from their own homes, is the most common form of piecework found today. The cost of such work is really a direct expense and not direct labour.
- Combinations of the above: perhaps an hourly rate plus a bonus for the amount produced.

Once the contractual aspects of employment are agreed it becomes the responsibility of the payroll section of the accounts department to see that employees receive payments that are due to them. This section also has the responsibility of making payroll deductions; for example, payments due to tax authorities. From a company's point of view the salary or wage is not the only cost of employment. For example, in the United Kingdom employers pay National Insurance contributions. These additional costs of employment also need to be taken into account.

The payroll department relies on input from other departments to make the correct payments. The personnel department needs to communicate the starting or finishing dates of employment and to provide details of changes in rates. It also relies on individual supervisors and managers to inform it of attendance (either directly or indirectly via the Personnel Department). Payroll costs are charged to the department in which the employee works, thus enabling the supervisor to see how much has been spent and to be able to exercise control over these costs.

In production departments, information about attendance serves a secondary role. It is used to determine the labour element of the cost of products. The information required for payroll purposes does not need to be very detailed: a record of time in attendance is adequate. For product costing purposes, particularly in a job costing environment, greater detail is required. For example, exact details of how much time employees have spent working on products will be necessary.

Many companies will use a time recording system that can be used by both the payroll department and the costing department. Time sheets serve such a purpose. Each worker puts in the details about hours worked on various jobs and activities. This is approved by the departmental supervisor before being passed on to the payroll and costing departments.

Some companies will use a time clock or similar device to record time in attendance. This level of information is insufficient for a job costing environment, where the amount of time spent on various jobs needs to be known. In these circumstances a time sheet or a job card will be used to provide the extra information. With a job sheet, the paperwork is attached to the work as it makes its way through the production process. The job sheet is used in addition to the time recording system used for payroll. Each worker who works on the job will record the time spent. The card then passes on to the next worker. Material use is also recorded on the card. When the job is completed (or at the year end if work-in-progress needs to be valued) the card is passed to the costing department.

In a process environment employees are assigned to particular departments, which are themselves processes. Therefore there is no need to analyse time other than at departmental level.

Expenses

Of increasing importance in modern manufacturing industry are the costs that are not incurred on material and labour. Direct expenses can be an important element when subcontractors are used, but in all industries indirect expenses, or overheads, are major items. The procedures employed for processing payments are the same for direct and indirect expenses, although their treatment in costing will differ.

Before any expenses are incurred a purchase request should be approved and raised. The purchasing department will then find the best price from suppliers at the required quality level. A purchase order will be raised, stating the price to be paid for the goods or service, and becomes a firm commitment between the company and the supplier. As goods are delivered, goods received notes are issued and matched to the purchase order. Following delivery, an invoice is received by the bought ledger department of the accounts department. It is checked against the purchase order for prices and the goods delivery note for quantity. If quantity and price are correct the invoice will be paid without reference back to the person authorizing the expenditure. Where there is a significant difference the invoice will have to be approved for payment by the originator of the order. Where a service has been supplied, goods received notes obviously cannot be raised. In this case all invoices will have to go to the person authorizing the expenditure to ensure that the service has been delivered. When the purchase request is raised the person raising the request will give details of what the expense is being incurred for. If it is for work on a particular job then information will be given so that the costing department can allocate the cost to the job. If the expense is for a department then the costing department will know which department should be allocated.

Overheads

These are all the costs incurred by a company that have not been analysed as direct materials, labour or expenses. They have been incurred in order to benefit all products and cannot be traced directly to individual products. Overheads include the following.

- Indirect materials: materials purchased for use in the factory but not going into actual products; for example, materials used by the maintenance department.
- Indirect labour: the cost of employing people not actually working on products. These can be people employed in a production department, such as a supervisor. They can also be people working in non-production departments that provide a service to the production departments, such as production scheduling, maintenance and store departments, and can include the cost of non-productive time where direct labour is unable to work directly on products.
- Indirect expenses: all other costs in departments, including general facility costs such as rent, occupancy taxes, heat and lighting.

To value stock some of these costs have to be allocated to the individual products. It is worth mentioning at this point that there are two methods of allocating overheads. *Absorption costing* includes all overheads and is sometimes known as full costing. *Variable costing* only allocates variable costs to products, treating any fixed cost as a period cost to be deducted, for profit calculation, within the period incurred. There is an active debate in accountancy as to which is the better technique. This debate is discussed in Unit Six. For financial reporting purposes, absorption costing must be used. The procedure for calculating the fully absorbed cost of a product is first demonstrated. The variable cost method is then shown and compared.

Overheads are allocated to products using a four-stage process as shown in figure 3.7.

106 EFFECTIVE ACCOUNTING MANAGEMENT

```
┌─────────────────────────────────┐
│ Allocate and apportion costs to │
│          departments            │
└─────────────────────────────────┘
                │
                ▼
┌─────────────────────────────────┐
│  Reallocate service department  │
│ costs to production departments │
└─────────────────────────────────┘
                │
                ▼
┌─────────────────────────────────┐
│   Calculate overhead absorption │
│              rate               │
└─────────────────────────────────┘
                │
                ▼
┌─────────────────────────────────┐
│   Charge overheads to products  │
└─────────────────────────────────┘
```

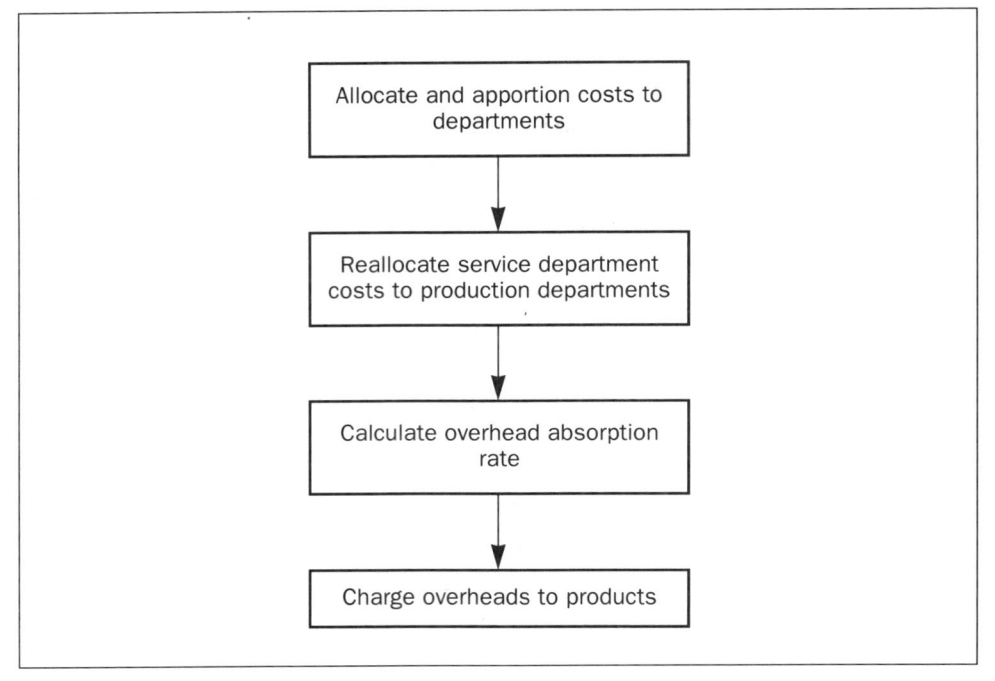

Figure 3.7 The overhead allocation process.

1 *Allocate and apportion costs to departments.* Costs are allocated to the departments responsible for their incursion. Indirect material costs can be traced to departments according to who raises the stock requisition. Indirect labour costs are allocated to departments by the payroll department, according to the physical location of people. Invoices for indirect expenses are coded to the relevant department responsible for ordering the items. There are some expenses that are incurred for the benefit of more than one department. In such cases the costs must be apportioned to departments, using a reasonable method of allocation. For general facility costs the most usual basis is the floor space occupied. A department that occupies 20 per cent of the floor space receives 20 per cent of the facility costs.

2 *Reallocate service department costs to production departments.* The object of absorption costing is to get all costs to products, but products do not directly receive any of the services provided by service departments. It is the production departments that use their services. Costs can be allocated to products in the production departments. The costs of the service departments are therefore transferred to those production departments. This is achieved by looking at the use made of the service departments by the production departments. The suitable basis for reallocating the costs requires careful consideration. An equitable base needs to be found if managers are in any way held responsible for the allocated costs (see Unit

Five). If one department makes 80 per cent of the store requisitions then is it reasonable for that department to receive 80 per cent of the costs of the stores department? It will be only if each stores requisition generates the same amount of work. The basis of allocation is often subject to dispute from production managers and in practice common sense must prevail.

3 Calculate overhead absorption rate. Once all the costs have been transferred to the production departments a suitable basis needs to be found for transferring those costs to the products. If a standard identical product is made in a department then the overheads can be shared out equally between the products. In a job production environment the products are not standard. They make different demands on the production department. One job might take 200 hours to complete, another just five hours. Would it be fair to allocate the same amount of overhead to each job? It would not be fair if the company was to base its pricing policy on cost. It would end up underpricing the first job and overpricing the second. There are a number of alternative ways of allocating overheads according to the demands made by different products or jobs. The assumption is that there is one measure in each department that reflects the demands placed upon the resources of the department by each product. See Box AM3.6. Historically the most commonly used method has been direct labour hours. As modern manufacturing becomes more machine intensive the machine hour basis has become more popular. The rate chosen should reflect the activity of that department.

BOX AM3.6

Calculating overhead recovery rates

1. Direct labour hours $= \dfrac{\text{Total overheads}}{\text{Total direct labour hours}}$

2. Direct labour cost (per cent) $= \dfrac{\text{Total overheads}}{\text{Total direct labour costs}} \times 100$

3. Machine hours $= \dfrac{\text{Total overheads}}{\text{Total machine hours}}$

4. Prime cost (per cent) $= \dfrac{\text{Total overheads}}{\text{Total prime costs}} \times 100$

5. Direct material cost (per cent) $= \dfrac{\text{Total overheads}}{\text{Total direct material costs}} \times 100$

6. Per product $= \dfrac{\text{Total overheads}}{\text{Total number of products}}$

4 *Charge overheads to products.* Finally, overheads can be charged to the products according to the demands placed on the production department. For example, if the overhead rate is £10 per direct labour hour and a product takes two direct labour hours to be manufactured, then the amount of overhead allocated will be £20. The overhead is added to the direct costs of the product to arrive at the fully absorbed cost of production. This is the value of the product while it is held as stock and the cost of goods when sold.

Predetermined overhead rates

A predetermined overhead rate is one that is worked out in advance based on estimated overheads and estimated activity during the year. In a job production environment a company will not want to wait until the end of the financial year to calculate the correct overhead rate. It will require a rate that can be applied to jobs as they come in during the year.

Where a predetermined overhead rate is used an adjustment will have to be made at the end of the year if the estimates turn out in retrospect to have been wrong. The cause of the difference can be that expenditure was different from that estimated, or that activity was incorrectly estimated. Whatever the cause, the treatment is the same.

Where the amount of overhead absorbed by products at the end of the year is more than the overheads actually incurred there is an over-absorption. Too much has been accounted for in the profit and loss account. An adjustment needs to be made to reduce costs by the amount over-absorbed. If the reverse happens, the adjustment needs to increase costs by the amount of the under-absorbed.

Blanket (or factory-wide) rates

Some companies use a single overhead rate, which is applied to products without regard to the demands made on the resources of particular production departments. This avoids having to find suitable bases for allocating costs to all departments, then reallocating to production departments and then having to apply overheads in each department. The problem with using a blanket rate is that it does not reflect the use of resources by products and therefore the product costs are likely to be inaccurate. However, all allocation is to some extent arbitrary and it could be argued that this method is no more inaccurate than the four-step method outlined above.

Multiple rates

There is a movement towards trying to find more accurate product costs, particularly when pricing or product profitability decision are involved. One criticism of the procedure outlined above applies to step 3, where one overhead rate is used. This assumes that costs in the department vary with the measure; for example, if machine hours are the base, costs are incurred to support the machines. It may be that only part of the costs varies with machine hours. Some may vary with direct labour hours, for example supervision. Some might vary with materials used, for example the reallocated stores department costs. More accurate product costs will be obtained when more than one rate is used, reflecting machine hours, direct labour hours and materials used.

Activity-based costing

In the 1980s some companies became dissatisfied with how overheads were being allocated. For the most part they were still using direct labour hours as the basis for making allocations to products. This was despite the fact that there were very few direct labour hours being worked and that the overheads being allocated were many times greater than the costs of labour. Rather than simply moving to a different basis of allocation, they developed a new and more complex method. This has come to be known as activity-based costing.

Overhead costs are incurred for many different reasons. They are incurred in providing engineering services, maintenance, stock handling and many other activities. Activity-based costing identifies the cost of all activities being carried out. It then finds a suitable base for allocating those costs to products. It can be extremely complex to implement. It is claimed by those in favour of the technique that it produces more accurate product costs. It is still the subject of debate and this book makes no attempt to make a judgement on the technique.

In the next unit we are going to start applying much of this costing information through budgets for management control and planning purposes. Before we move to this area, consolidate your understanding by completing Activities AM3.5 and AM3.6.

Notes
1   Despite this, the movement towards 'flexibility' is now proceeding unabated (see Anderson, *Effective Labour Relations*), and labour costs may become more variable as a result.
2   This fetish for control is enlarged upon in Anderson, *Effective Labour Relations*.
3   See Anderson, *Effective Personnel Management*, for a fuller discussion of payment systems.

110 EFFECTIVE ACCOUNTING MANAGEMENT

ACTIVITY AM3.5

DEFINITIONS AND EXAMPLES

Activity code
- ✓ Self-development
- ☐ Teamwork
- ✓ Communications
- ☐ Numeracy/IT
- ✓ Decisions

Task

Define the following terms, giving an example of their use. Do not consult the book at this stage. Check your answers against the text *when you have finished*.

Terms	Definition	Example
Manufacturing costs		
Direct costs		
Indirect costs		
Variable costs		
Fixed costs		
Semi-variable costs		
Step costs		
Job costing		
Process costing		
Goods received note		
Stock records		
LIFO		
FIFO		
AVCO		
Expenses		
Absorption costing		
Variable costing		

ACTIVITY AM3.6

THE PAPER MILL

Activity code
- ✓ Self-development
- ☐ Teamwork
- ✓ Communications
- ✓ Numeracy/IT
- ✓ Decisions

The company
The company in question is an independent manufacturer of paper and board, based in Donside, Aberdeenshire. The paper is not high quality and is used for the packaging industry. The board, or chipboard, is predominantly used for the building industry. The firm employs some 400 people on a continuous shift system (6 a.m. – 2 p.m., 2 p.m. – 10 p.m. and 10 p.m. – 6 a.m.) and works all year round, apart from the three weeks maintenance closure in July which coincides with the main vacation of the nearby town. It is an old plant, founded in the late eighteenth century, but with considerable modern machinery recently imported from Germany. There are two board machines and two paper machines with approximately 100 employees to each. In addition, there is a staff white-collar administrative and commercial group of ninety-two.

The market
Although it is well established, the board market is quite fickle, as it is dependent primarily on the building industry – itself a good indicator of the economic wellbeing of the country. The packaging industry is less fickle and is expanding, although there is competition from the plastics industry. However, from milk cartons to chocolate eggs, the company has a growing presence in this market sphere.

Production
Production is a continuous flow process with the raw materials (which are increasing in cost) being mixed at the wet end of the machine and appearing at the dry end as almost the finished product. Printing and coating as necessary are done in the finishing department. Breakages of paper flow through the machines are quite frequent.

Finance
The company is still family owned but increasingly it has opened up to take professional managers in to run the firm. It is highly profitable and much of the money has been ploughed back over the last ten years (at least) to buy more modern machinery. This has trebled the potential output, although the

112 EFFECTIVE ACCOUNTING MANAGEMENT

plant is running at only 68 per cent capacity. There are no cash-flow problems, although an over-reliance on the building industry in the past has caused difficulties, particularly over the winter months owing to the construction slump then. Reserves and borrowing power are strong.

Organization structure and personnel
Figure 3.8 below shows the structure. The rest of the employees are employed in production, catering, finishing and as 'outside' staff. There is an external security firm (400 people).

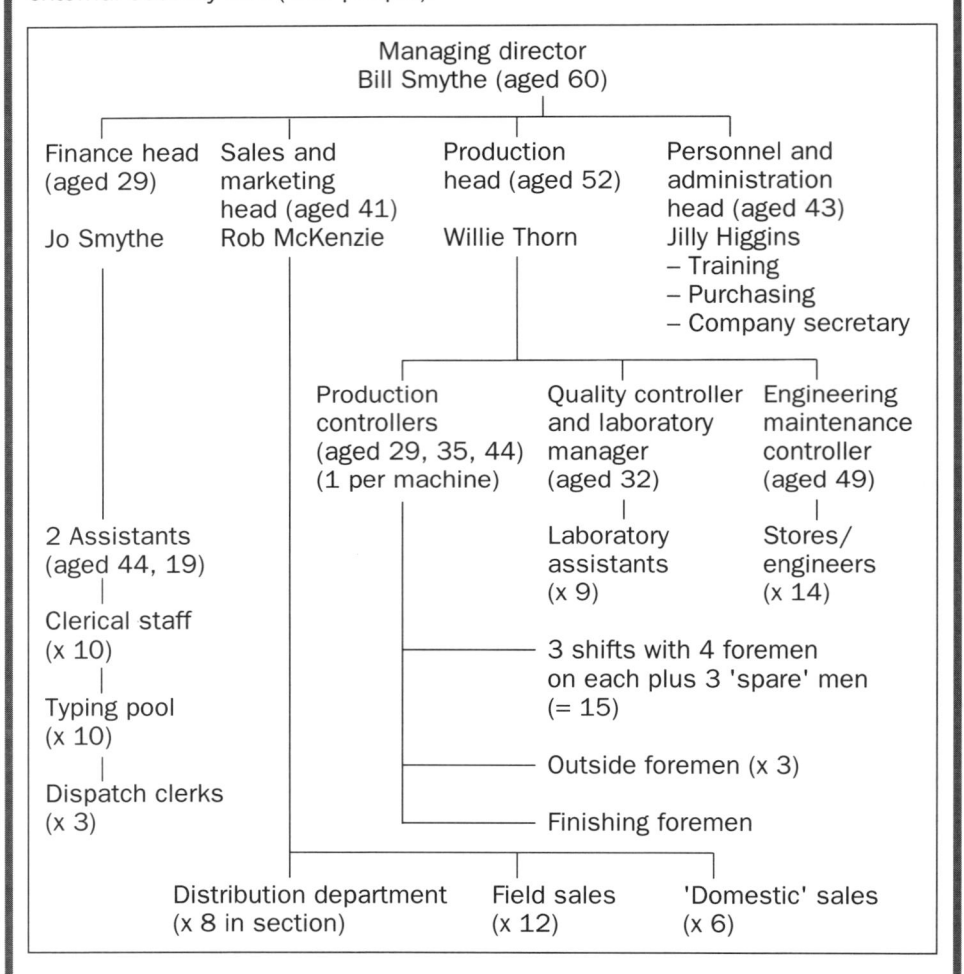

```
                           Managing director
                           Bill Smythe (aged 60)
        ┌──────────────┬──────────────┬──────────────┐
Finance head    Sales and       Production      Personnel and
(aged 29)       marketing       head (aged 52)  administration
                head (aged 41)                  head (aged 43)
Jo Smythe       Rob McKenzie    Willie Thorn    Jilly Higgins
                                                 – Training
                                                 – Purchasing
                                                 – Company secretary

                        ┌───────────────┬──────────────────┬──────────────┐
                        Production      Quality controller  Engineering
                        controllers     and laboratory      maintenance
                        (aged 29, 35, 44) manager           controller
                        (1 per machine) (aged 32)           (aged 49)
2 Assistants                            │                   │
(aged 44, 19)                           Laboratory          Stores/
│                                       assistants          engineers
Clerical staff                          (x 9)               (x 14)
(x 10)
│                       ─────────── 3 shifts with 4 foremen
Typing pool                         on each plus 3 'spare' men
(x 10)                              (= 15)
│
Dispatch clerks         ─────────── Outside foremen (x 3)
(x 3)
                        ─────────── Finishing foremen

              Distribution department   Field sales   'Domestic' sales
              (x 8 in section)          (x 12)        (x 6)
```

Figure 3.8 Organization structure and personnel.

Bill Smythe, the MD of the paper mill, noted that the market for board and paper was not particularly healthy. 'In the past our finances have been very solid indeed, based on a buoyant marketplace, particularly in the construction sector, which influences our board plant. I'm concerned that the accounting housekeeping in the past has been a little too ... shall we say, liberal – if not sloppy.

COSTS AND THEIR CLASSIFICATIONS

'Take, for example, Willie's maintenance section with its staff of some 15 people including the controller', continued Bill. 'There is no real control over costs – everything is "lost" in the departments – it can't be right. Some allocation or method must be used to sort it out. Jo from finance and Willie from production get together on this one.'

The work in the accounts section was delegated to a more junior member of staff. One of the part-qualified assistants handled the report, but he was rushed off his feet at the time doing the quarterly returns. The information given to Willie in the production department looked like the following.

Labour	■ £15 000 p.a. on average for the technicians (×10) and £12 000 p.a. for the semi-skilled stores and maintenance men (×4). £22 000 for the manager. Employer costs of some 50 per cent of this sum are on top of this total salary bill.
	■ £60 000 for administrative support.
	■ Two apprentices at college (£14 000 in total) in addition to the fixed establishment of engineers.
	■ Part salary of the production head ($\frac{1}{3}$ allocated to maintenance) = £12 500.
Materials for company	■ Stock, components, cleansing cream, oils, tools etc. come to £200 000.
	■ Stocks of goods (replacement for production) = £3 002 000.
External income	■ Maintenance courses for local industry result in some incoming fees of £8 200 but costs come to £5 200.
Insurance	■ Buildings £120 000. Supplies £100 000. Some £8000 should be allocated to your maintenance department.
Building costs	■ These are down to you: the new annexe costs £100 000.
Transport/travel	■ £2000 plus trainees expenses/training sessions on new technology = £12 000, all down to your department.
Admin.	■ Of a total of £1 520 321 your allowance is £500 000 as there is much work involved in ordering/stocking and preparing jobs.

The production head almost burst a blood vessel. 'I've never seen anything like this in my life. This is a support function for the business. Everyone benefits from our work and the more people in the department the more work we seem to do. What's all this "administration" stuff? Perhaps we should change our time? Yes, their 40 hours can be seen as 30 actual working hours per person × 46 weeks (excluding holidays etc. and allowing for sickness etc.) to give us the full wage cost and the overheads for our department.' The Secretary nodded. 'Either way, we'll need to get these costs sorted out before proper allocation can be made, let alone a decent charge out rate.' 'Finally, watch out for revenue and capital differences.'

Tasks
1. Revamp these figures into a coherent form for the manager.
2. Classify the costs under appropriate heads.
3. Optional: could a charge out policy work, and if so, how?

Unit Four

Budgeting for Planning and Control

Learning Objectives

After completing this unit you should be able to:

- understand the uses of budgets within organizations;
- understand the planning and control cycle within an organization;
- appreciate the conflicting use of budgeting information and be aware of the influence of budgets on human behaviour;
- understand the budgeting process and be able to prepare simple master budgets working from departmental information;
- prepare detailed cash budgets;
- understand the techniques for analysing performance against a budget or a standard;
- calculate flexible budgets;
- calculate simple standard costing variances;
- apply the generic skills.

Contents

Overview

What is a Budget?

Why Budget?

- Planning
- Control
- Coordination
- Communication
- Motivation
- Performance evaluation

The Planning and Control Cycle

- Define objectives
- Evaluate the external environment
- Select strategies
- Implement and organize
- Monitor and evaluate

Planning Levels

Budgeting for Planning

- The budget committee
- The budget manual
- The master budget

Budgetary Preparation

Cash Budgeting

Budgeting for Control

Performance Reporting

Variance Analysis and Reporting

- ▶ Variance reporting
- ▶ Determining the standard cost of a product
- ▶ Calculation of variances
- ▶ Direct material variances
- ▶ Direct labour variances
- ▶ Variable overhead variances
- ▶ Fixed overhead variances
- ▶ Sales margin variances
- ▶ Which variance to investigate

Behavioural Aspects of Budgeting

Conclusion

Unit Four

> " I think it's part of a corporation discipline programme for Disney executives ('Johnson, your department is over-budget again. You know what that means.' 'No! Please!' 'Yes! into the Goofy suit!')."
>
> Dave Barry, American columnist and comedian[1]

Overview

To a great extent we are all familiar with the process of budgeting as we manage our own finances. Some of us might be better at it than others, but basically all people do it. When going on holiday we do not spend endlessly, we keep within our budget of what we can afford to spend. When we apply for a mortgage or other form of loan we may be asked to plan our monthly income and expenditure, taking into account loan repayments. If we become overdrawn at the bank most of us look back and identify why it has occurred. We may discover that it was because of a one-off event that we did not anticipate, with no future consequences. Alternatively, we may find that it is the result of a particular regular expense that is likely to continue, and we must adjust our future expectations to accommodate this extra expense.

Although our budgeting may be simple it is not dissimilar to that practised by organizations, except that in organizations the budget may be used for additional purposes as part of the management process. Budgeting information can be used for disseminating information among people within the organization and for controlling and influencing the actions of people.

What is a Budget?

An organization's budget may be described as:
- a formal plan of business objectives;
- a yardstick against which performance can be monitored;
- a quantitative statement, which is usually expressed in financial terms;
- a 'map' of the organization's structure, with budgets existing for each sub-unit and for the organization as a whole.

Different budgets may cover different time scales. When one looks at the long-term future of the organization a five or ten year plan may be prepared, with this being translated into monetary terms to give a long-term budget. Long-term budgets tend to be in a very summarized form. They indicate the things that have to be done over several years to achieve the organization's long-term objectives. In the shorter term steps have to be taken so that the long-term plans can be achieved. A shorter-term budget will detail what needs to be done to maintain current activity and to implement the changes that result in the achievement of the long-term goal. These shorter-term budgets are usually prepared in detail and for a period of one financial year.

Why Budget?

In the smallest organization there is a role for budgeting in planning, particularly with regard to the cash resources of the business. As organizations become larger and more complex the budget takes on other roles. The roles of budgeting can be described as follows.

Planning

A major purpose of the budget is to help a business to plan ahead, to identify the resources required to achieve the organizational objectives. The simplest form of planning is *cash budgeting*, where income and outgoings are estimated in advance to identify any cash shortfalls. Once this information is available steps can be taken to ensure that an overdraft facility is organized to cover the shortfall (or that the best interest-earning opportunity is organized if a cash surplus is identified). If finance is to be raised from a high street bank, it is likely to want to see the cash budget before granting credit.

In larger organizations, budgets are also used to identify the way in which objectives are to be met. They detail the resources which are required so that action can be taken to obtain them. The budget plans activities within each sub-unit of the organization. It will detail the costs to be incurred and the revenues expected to be earned from ongoing activities. It will also detail the changes resulting from the introduction of new facilities or products, or from old products being deleted.

One of the advantages of having a formal budgeting process is that it gives line managers an opportunity to think about the future. Most managers are busy people dealing with urgent day-to-day matters. Priority may not be given to thinking about finding a better way of doing an activity or what would happen if an event was to happen, such as a large increase in the cost of an input. Preparing a detailed plan for their department allows them the opportunity to think about these things and thus to become more effective managers.

Control

For an organization to be in control, it must be achieving its objectives. To see how the organization is progressing, actual events must be monitored and then compared to what should have happened. When a deviation is identified steps can be taken to correct it. The budget is a statement of the objectives and plans for the organization, giving a yardstick against which actual results can be compared. Deviations from the plan are called *variances* in accounting terminology. When variances are reported to managers they can take steps to investigate their causes.

Coordination

This means making sure that all parts of the organization are working together. When planning how many units of a particular product are to be sold it is necessary to ensure that the production department is aware of the forecast and that it is able to manufacture sufficient numbers. Without coordination, changes in one department may not trigger changes in another. If sales of a product are lower than expected, fewer units will need to be manufactured or stocks will build up. A variance in one department should trigger a response in other departments or they too will incur variances.

Budgeting may also ensure that individual departments do not pursue their own objectives at the expense of the organization as a whole. For example, a sales department may wish to sell as many units as possible because this satisfies its own objectives to maximize sales. The sales team may not consider that this puts pressure on and causes inefficiencies in other departments, resulting in the organization earning less profit than it would have done with lower sales.

Communication

This is one of the means by which top management is able to express its plans and objectives to lower levels of managers. The budgeting process itself requires that managers communicate and the potential difficulties are identified ahead of their occurrence.

Motivation

The budget may provide a target towards which a manager can aim. A manager may be motivated to perform well and use the budget as a target because it satisfies his or her need for recognition from superiors or peers or for self-actualization. A budget can only be used as a target when the manager feels that it is reasonable. Participation in the budgeting process will increase a manager's commitment to the budget and its reasonableness.

Performance evaluation

One of the ways in which a manager's performance can be evaluated is by the performance of his or her department against its budget. It is quite common for managers to have an element of their total remuneration linked to performance against budget.

Sometimes the purposes of budgets and the way in which they are used are in conflict. If the target is too hard demotivation can occur; managers might be motivated by targets that are difficult, but not by those that are impossible to meet. Such targets are often missed and thought must be given, in budgeting, to whether to set a difficult target for motivation, or to set a realistic budget that can be used for accurate planning.

The Planning and Control Cycle

Planning and control go together: neither can be done effectively without the other. A plan is merely a dream unless steps are taken to ensure that it is achieved. Control merely restricts behaviour and activities unless it is done with a goal in mind. See Box AM4.1 and figure 4.1 for an example of a planning/control cycle. Box AM4.2 gives further details of the concept outlined in figure 4.1.

BOX AM4.1

Definitions of planning and control

Planning
The establishment of objectives and the formulation, evaluation and selection of policies, strategies, tactics and actions required to achieve these objectives.

Control
The continuous comparison of actual results with those planned, both in total and for separate subdivisions, and taking management action to correct adverse variances and to exploit favourable variances.

Source: Adapted from CIMA

BUDGETING FOR PLANNING AND CONTROL

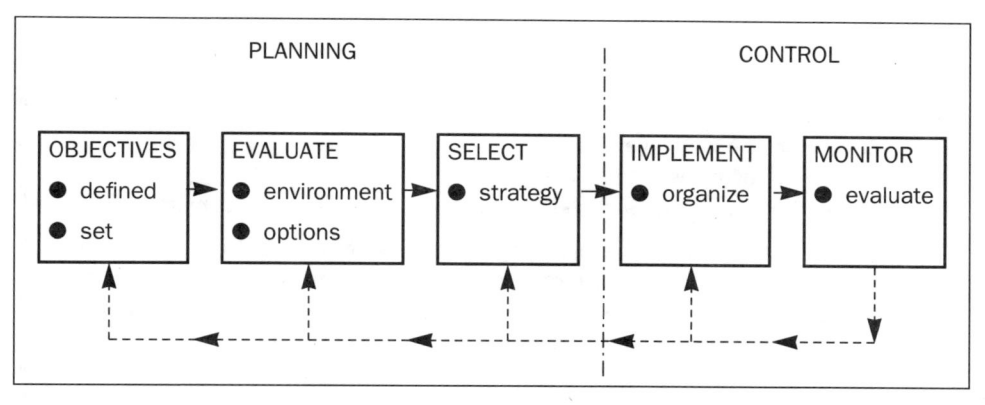

Figure 4.1 The planning and control cycle.

BOX AM4.2

The planning cycle

Without planning we are left to the vagaries of the marketplace. At the same time, the former Eastern European and Soviet bloc illustrates the limits of too much planning and not enough action.

At the organizational level a cycle of planning can be developed for every type of institution or enterprise.[1] In essence the cycle tends to be as shown in figure 4.2.

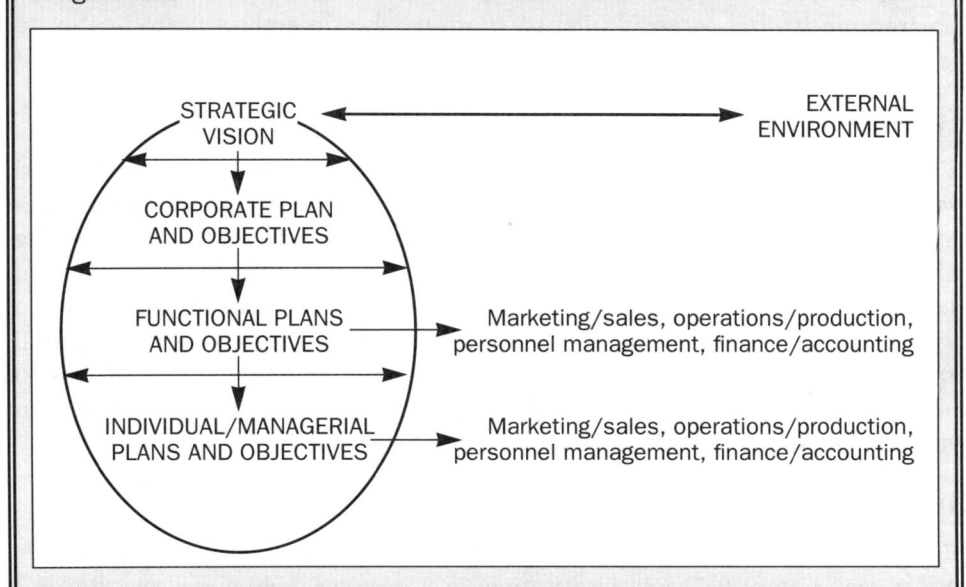

Figure 4.2 The planning cycle.

The cycle allows the following:
- adaptive objectives;
- feedback loops from various levels;
- comparison of results with the initial plans;
- revision of the overall plan and specific objectives according to circumstances.

One important variation of the planning cycle has been target or objective setting schemes. An outline of a more democratic scheme, which in theory incorporates the views of a bottom-up approach and a top-down view as above, is seen in some variations of MbO, or Management by Objectives.

Source:
1   Targets, key result areas and objectives are dealt with thoroughly in the sister volumes of this series, particularly *Effective Personnel Management*, *Effective Business Policy* and *Effective General Management*

Define objectives[2]

What is the purpose of the organization? What are managers trying to achieve? For a business organization, making a profit will be one of the major objectives. Even in a non-profit making organization there may be a financial objective, to provide value for money to the people it is serving. The definition of objectives is a task that does not need to be carried out too frequently. It is a good idea to examine the objectives periodically, to be reminded of what you are trying to achieve.

Evaluate the external environment

What is the environment in which the organization currently operates and what changes are likely to affect the way in which the organization operates in the future? Factors that might be identified here are the products being offered, the markets, the strength of competition and the political and economic climate. The factors to be examined are specific to an organization. A small business might only be concerned about the regional environment. A large multinational organization, on the other hand, has to look at its home environment and at the environment of any countries in which it has significant operations.

Select strategies

Identify alternate courses of action that will achieve the organization's objectives. Quantify each alternative in terms of achieving the desired results, incorporating the risk of each strategy given the environmental forecast. Once all the data relating to strategies are collected a choice can be made on which to follow. Some examples of the many strategies that might be selected are: to emphasize quality and aim for the top end of the market; to price low and go for volume; to develop new products or to enter new markets. The activity of identifying, evaluating and selecting strategies should be frequent and ongoing. At any one time strategies will be at different stages of development, with some being formulated, some being implemented and others nearing completion.

Implement and organize

Take the necessary steps over a period of time to implement the strategies selected. Tasks need to be defined and organizational sub-units (e.g. departments or divisions) need to take responsibility for their completion. The resources required for implementation, although broadly identified during the selection stage, now need to be planned in detail. The expected results of the strategies should also be developed. If at any time it seems likely that they are not going to be achieved they need to be reviewed and, if necessary, replaced.

Monitor and evaluate

Once tasks are under way they need to be monitored to ensure that they are indeed meeting their objectives. Tasks can be monitored by observation but it is usual to collect data and compare them to a quantitative plan. Accounting data are often used at this stage as they measure the resources used in carrying out the task and the results obtained in terms of revenues collected. If differences are identified the information can be fed back to the relevant management, who may be able to take steps to bring the activity back in line with the original plan. Alternatively, if this cannot happen because of a change in the environment, then plans can be made to accommodate the changed circumstances or new plans can be formulated.

Planning Levels

Planning and control take place at different levels within an organization. There is the strategic level, which is concerned with long-term plans over a long period of time. There is the management level, which is concerned with taking steps in the medium term to achieve the strategic plans. There is also the operational level, which is concerned with the operations on an ongoing basis. Table 4.1 shows some of the distinctions between the three levels.

Table 4.1 Planning levels

Feature	Strategic	Management	Operational
Time span	Long term 5–10 years	Medium term 1–24 months	Short term daily/monthly
Management level	Senior executives	Senior/middle managers	Middle/operational managers
Planning activities	Defining objectives, selecting strategies	Identifying actions and resources required to implement strategies	Identifying resources required for the performance of tasks
Control activities	Monitoring the environment, ensuring long-term goals are achieved	Identifying and responding to major divergencies from plan	Ensuring day-to-day activities are being carried out
Information and budget requirements	Strategic plan, broad based estimates, mostly in financial terms	Annual budgets, with shorter control periods, usually months, mostly financial data	Real time data, mostly non-financial

Accounting information is largely concerned with management planning and control and therefore the remainder of this unit concentrates on this level. We will first look at the planning process and the preparation of the annual budget. Then we will go on to look at the control process in more detail.

For both planning and control, *responsibility centres* are important concepts. Senior managers in an organization cannot carry out all the tasks themselves; they must delegate authority and responsibility to other managers. An organization structure defines the sub-units making up the whole and the managers given authority and held responsible for carrying out a task. These are called responsibility centres and each fulfils a prescribed and necessary role in attaining enterprise objectives. The planning of activities begins in these centres with the preparation of the centre's budget, as the manager should be in a position of having the most knowledge about the process and the likely outcomes. The individual managers of the centres have their own personal objectives and individual perceptions of what is required of them. In order for senior managers to be sure that responsibility centre managers are acting in a fashion congruent with organizational objectives, control mechanisms are required.

From an accounting perspective responsibility centres come in three forms, and the detail of budgeting and information required for control purposes differs for each. These are as follows.

- Cost centres, where a manager has responsibility for carrying out a task and also for the costs incurred in performing the task. The centre does not earn revenues and therefore managers will be concerned with keeping costs under control. Most departments in a functional organization structure are cost centres.
- Profit centres, where the manager is responsible for both costs incurred and revenues collected. The profitability of the centre can be determined and the manager will be concerned with controlling the profit earned. Each store in a retailing chain can be described as a profit centre.
- Investment centres, where the manager is responsible for costs, revenues and the amount invested in the centre. Not only can profit be measured, but the size of the investment can be analysed. The concern of the manager here will be to control profit earned in relation to the capital employed. In a divisionalized company each division is an example of an investment centre.

Budgeting for Planning

Before we look at the steps involved in the preparation of a budget it is useful to look at some organizational aspects of preparing the budget.

The budget committee

This is a group of people given responsibility for ensuring that the budget is prepared and that it achieves the desired results. On this committee will be top management and representatives of all areas of the organization, usually the most senior managers. Included on the committee will be a management accountant, who will be responsible for the preparation of the budgeted statements. He or she will also provide assistance to other members of the committee and to all managers preparing budgets.

The budget manual

The documentation for budgeting should contain the objectives of the organization and assumptions and guidelines of senior management in preparing for the period ahead. It also contains procedures to be followed in developing plans, details of the information to be prepared and dates for its completion.

The master budget

The master budget is that for the company as a whole. It is the result of bringing together all the departmental budgets. It comprises the major financial statements, that is:
- the budgeted profit and loss account;
- the budgeted balance sheet;
- the budgeted cash flow.

An additional statement may be also prepared, the *capital expenditure budget*. This is required for planning the acquisition of major items of capital expenditure and must be forecast to enable control of expenditure and to ensure that sufficient resources are available to pay for the items. Proposals for capital projects (e.g. the replacement of a broken down machine that cannot be repaired) sometimes have to be separate from the general budgeting process, but wherever possible they should be incorporated into the budget.

Budgetary Preparation

There are a number of stages to be followed in the budgeting process:

1. Define budget policy.
2. Identify restricting factors.
3. Prepare sales budget.
4. Prepare other budgets.
5. Negotiate budgets with more senior management.
6. Consolidate and review.
7. Resubmit and finalise budgets.
8. Communicate information.
9. Review.

Each of these stages will be looked at and demonstrated using the following worked example.

WORKED EXAMPLE: EXCELLENT MANUFACTURING CORPORATION

A company has a small factory in which it manufactures a single product, a widget. This involves just two stages: the assembly of bought-in components, and the finishing and packaging of the finished goods. All finished goods are transferred to another division of the company for sale and distribution. The other division estimates that demand for the product will be 20 000 units in the coming year. Revenue of £18 will be received for each unit transferred. Selling, distribution and administration costs were £60 000 in the past year and are expected to remain the same in the coming year.

Standard production requirements

	No.	Value
Materials		
Component X1	2	£1.5 each
Component Y2	4	£0.6 each
Labour		
Assembly	0.5 hour	£7 per hour
Finishing	0.2 hour	£6 per hour

	No.	Value
Machine hours		
Assembly	1 hour	
Finishing	0.10 hour	
Variable overhead costs		
Assembly	per machine hour	£2
Finishing	per machine hour	£5

Stockholdings at the beginning and end of the year are estimated as being:

	Opening stock	Closing stock
Finished goods	1000	1500
Component X1	10000	8000
Component Y2	15000	20000

(1) Define budget policy. The first stage in the budgeting procedure is the communication of information to all those involved in budget preparation. This will come from top management, and will include details of major changes expected to take place during the year, for example when a new product is to be introduced. This allows the department affected to plan for the change. Also communicated will be some assumptions about the external environment affecting the forecast, such as the predicted inflation rate or the level of salary increases.

(2) Identify restricting factors. In every company there will be crucial factors that restrict performance. It may be that production facilities are limited and that the company cannot make as many of a product as it could sell. Many companies might like to be in this situation but it is more likely that, being in a competitive situation, they would find that they are restricted by demand. Whatever the restricting factor, this is where budgeting should start. Until this is done plans made by other departments make no sense. The assumption in the worked example will be that sales are the restricting factor and subsequent comments will be on this basis.

(3) Prepare sales budget. This should be prepared for each product and for each department within the company. It should be prepared in terms of physical quantities and also in monetary terms. In the worked example the sales budget would be very simple.

Excellent Manufacturing Corporation – sales budget

Expected demand (units)	20000
Selling price	£18
Sales revenue	£360000

In a more complicated situation the sales budget might look as follows:

Region	Sales volume	Price (£)	Sales revenue (£)
North	4000	15	60000
South	7000	18	126000
East	5000	17	85000
West	4000	16	64000
Total	20000		335000

The sales budget would also have to be broken down into shorter time periods, normally months. This is particularly important when demand fluctuates during a year. Monthly budgets enable production and other activities to be planned accordingly. They also enable better control to be exercised over operations, as deviations can be identified against the monthly budget rather than at the end of the year.

In many ways, the sales budget is *the* budget where accuracy is most important. Unfortunately it is probably the most difficult budget to prepare. Approaches to sales budgeting might include the following.[3]

- Conducting or commissioning market research. An objective view is given but it is likely to be expensive and thus is often left to forecasting sales of new products.

- Building upon the previous year's sales. This can possibly incorporate a small increase or decrease. This approach is likely to be inaccurate but might be used for some minor products.

- Using the sales department to forecast sales according to regions. This is the most common approach used. It should result in a fairly reasonable estimate although it could present behavioural problems, with personnel being too optimistic or pessimistic.

(4) Prepare other budgets. Now the other departmental budgets can be prepared. Once the number of units to be sold has been forecast the number of units to be manufactured can be calculated. Once this is estimated the number of 'man hours' can be estimated. Following this, the number of people that have to be recruited (or laid off) can be estimated, and so on throughout the entire organization. The manager in charge of each organization sub-unit should be involved in the initial preparation of the budgets. This is the person who is likely to know most about the activities of the department and to be best able to prepare its budget. See figure 4.3.

The sales budget has been prepared and so the number of units that need to be manufactured can be determined. In this worked example 20 000 units are needed for sales. How many need to be produced? In addition, the company wants to hold some stocks at the end of the period so this increases the number to be produced to 22 000. However, there are already 1500 units at the beginning of the period, so this reduces the number to a total of 20 500 to be manufactured.

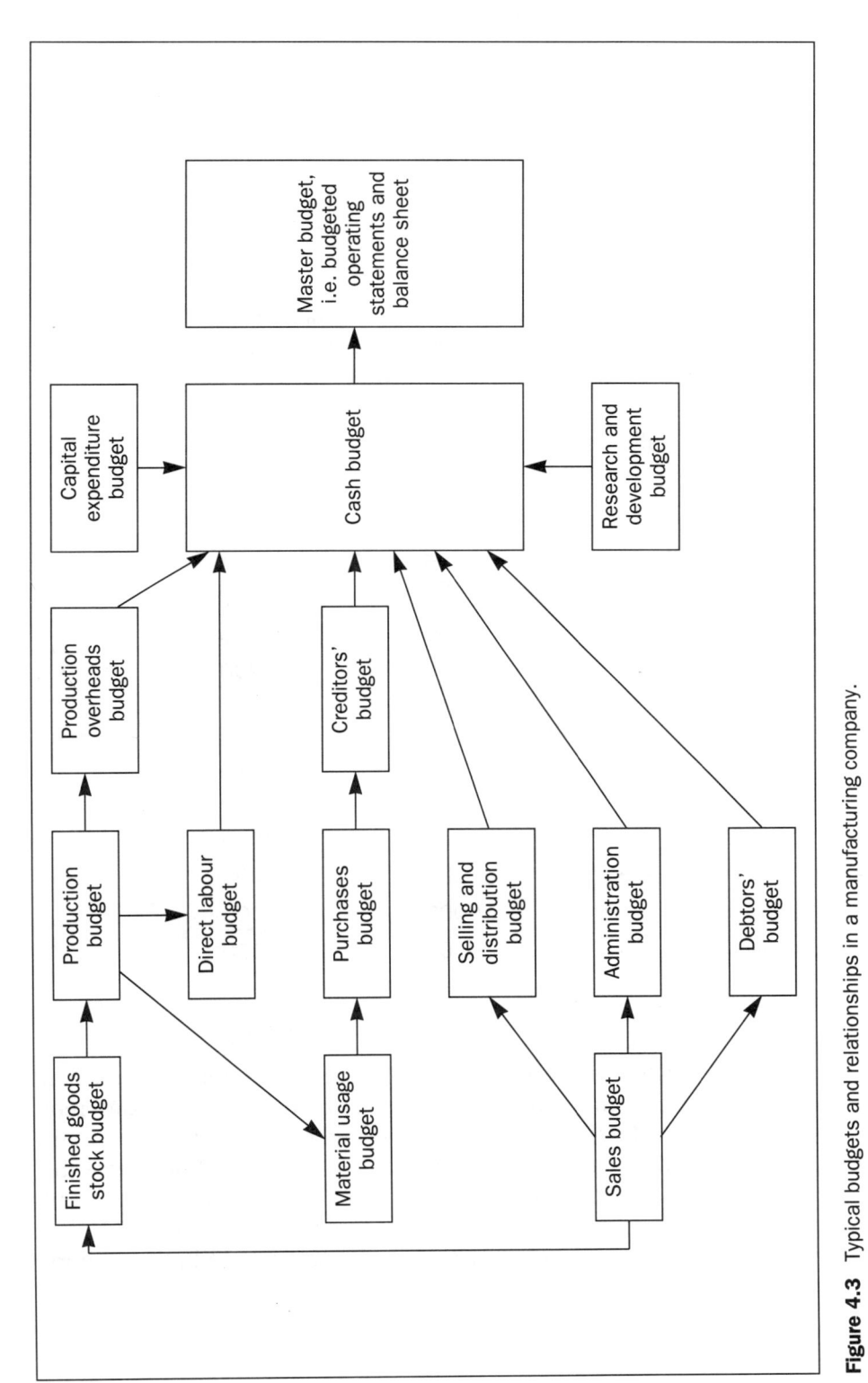

Figure 4.3 Typical budgets and relationships in a manufacturing company.

Production budget

Estimated sales	20000
Add: closing stock	2000
Total units required in year	22000
Less: opening stock	(1500)
Units to be manufactured	20500

When the number of units to be manufactured has been determined, the need for materials can be estimated. First the number of components to be used is estimated and then the number that have to be bought in is estimated.

Materials usage budget

Component	X1	Y2
Production (units)	20500	20500
Number of components per unit	2	4
Total components required	41000	82000
Price per component	1.50	0.60
Value	£61500	£49200

Material purchases budget

Component	X1	Y2
Production requirement	41000	82000
Closing stock	8000	20000
Total components required	49000	102000
Opening stock	10000	15000
To be purchased	39000	87000
Price per component	1.50	0.60
Value	£58500	£52200

A separate materials usage and purchases budget is required because in a large organization they may be the responsibility of different departments, the production department taking responsibility for usage and the purchasing department being expected to obtain and negotiate the best prices for materials. In times of changing prices there may be different component prices for items held in stock compared to those bought during the period. In such cases the production uses budget would have to adopt one of the stock valuation techniques discussed in Unit Two.

BUDGETING FOR PLANNING AND CONTROL

Direct labour budget

Department	Assembly	Finishing
Production (units)	20500	20500
Hours per unit	0.5	0.2
Total direct labour hours	10250	4100
Rate per hour	£7	£6
Direct labour costs	£71750	£24600

Once the number of direct labour hours has been estimated the number of employees required can be calculated. Employees are unlikely to spend all their time in productive activity and the most one person might reasonably spend on production would be 1500 hours a year. If this was so, in this case seven people would be required in the assembly department and 2.73 in the finishing department. If only six people were currently employed in assembly the personnel department would now know that one extra person had to be recruited and trained, and this would be incorporated into the departmental budget.

Machine utilization budget

Department	Assembly	Finishing
Production (units)	20500	20500
Machine hours per unit	1	0.1
Total machine hours	20500	2050

From this information we can determine how many machines are required. The maximum number of hours a single machine could operate in a year is 8760 (24 hours per day for 365 days). In reality the number of productive hours is likely to be much lower than this because very few factories operate continuously and even when they do there is likely to be downtime for maintenance and breakages. In this example assume that machines in both departments have a capacity of 4000 hours per year. If 20 500 units are to be manufactured six machines will be required in assembly and one in finishing. If the assembly department currently only has five machines plans will have to be made to provide extra capacity. This could be by extending the capacity of existing machines (by working an extra shift) or it could be by purchasing another machine. Either way, provision needs to be made in the budget or the department will not be able to produce all the items required.

In this worked example overheads have been assumed to vary with the number of machine hours worked. The worked example is very simplistic in that the aim is to demonstrate the budgeting process and not to get lost in a sea of calculations. In the real world, overheads would have to be budgeted for in detail and broken down into separate headings. The budgeted cost would then have to be estimated depending on whether the cost was considered to be fixed, variable or a combination of the two.

Production overhead budget

Department	Assembly	Finishing
Machine hours	20500	2050
Variable overhead per hour	£2	£5
Variable overheads	£41000	£10250

When the budgets for all the individual elements in the production area have been completed, departmental budgets can be produced. This will show how much expenditure is estimated to be incurred in each department over the year.

Assembly department budget

	£	£
Materials		
Component X1	61500	
Component Y2	49200	110700
Labour		71750
Variable overheads		41000
Total departmental budget		223450

Finishing department budget

	£
Labour	24600
Variable overheads	10250
Total departmental budget	34850

(5) Negotiate budgets with more senior management. Once the budgets have been prepared for the smallest sub-unit they can be agreed between the manager and his or her superior. The assembly and finishing departmental managers may have produced their individual budgets. Overall responsibility for the total production function lies with the production manager or director. He or she will want to be happy with the submitted budgets before passing them for consolidation. He or she might want to suggest changes to the departmental budgets and explore options. If the lower level manager has attempted to pad the budget this will need to be eliminated as far as possible at this stage.

(6) Consolidation and review. Once all departments have prepared budgets an overall company picture can be prepared. Preparation of the master budget is the responsibility of the management accountant on the budget committee. This may involve preparing a series of intermediate budgets to

move from the departmental budgets to the final statements. For example, a cost of goods sold budget will have to be prepared to take account of the value of closing stock.

Cost of goods sold budget

	Units	Value(£)
Opening stock	1500	18900
Production	20500	258300
	22000	277200
Closing stock	2000	25200
Sales	20000	252000

This budget is prepared using marginal costing principles for stock valuation, and assumes that stock from the previous year was manufactured at the same total cost per unit (£12.60) as in the current year.

Budgeted profit and loss account

	£
Sales revenue	360000
Less: cost of goods sold	252000
Gross profit	108000
Selling, distribution and administration	60000
Net profit before tax	48000

In addition to the budgeted profit and loss accounts, a balance sheet, a cash flow forecast and a capital expenditure budget would also be produced. These are not produced in this example because of the desire to keep the example simple. Cash budgeting is discussed in more detail below.

Once the budget committee have all the relevant departmental and master budgets they can examine the results. One of the first things they will look for is to see if activities are being coordinated. Can the production department produce sufficient to meet sales forecasts without excessive costs being incurred? Once they are satisfied that this is so the overall result will be examined. Are sufficient profits being generated in line with their expectations?

(7) Resubmit and finalize budgets. It is rare for a budget to be accepted at the first attempt. Following the review, departments will be asked to resubmit with changes that will result in the desired result being achieved. It is very much a case of organizational style as to how this is achieved. Some organizations will impose specific changes on departments. Others will ask for a saving and allow the manager to determine the best way of

achieving it. The process of submission and review will continue until the desired result is achieved.

(8) Communicate information. Once the budgets are finalized, the departments should be informed of their final budgets for the year. This is so that they can be identified as the target and yardstick against which actual performance can be monitored.

(9) Review. The budgeting process should not stop at this stage. If the budget is to be achieved progress must be monitored and action taken when necessary. Techniques of comparing the budget and actual results are looked at later. Meanwhile, tackle Activity AM4.1.

ACTIVITY AM4.1

BUDGETS

Activity code
- ✓ Self-development
- ✓ Teamwork
- ✓ Communications
- ☐ Numeracy/IT
- ✓ Decisions

Task

The principles of a major budgeting exercise are given. Your task (by group or individual) is to determine the detailed format of the practice for each of the headings. We are dealing with principles/practice – no figures are required. (Assume three products: x, y and z.) That is, you fill in the gaps and elaborate or question any of the stated principles.

The sales budget is the starting point. This assumes that a marketing plan has been developed and that the sales forecasts are readily available. This is the keystone of the whole operation. The budget must be divided into:

Operations budget. The firm must be able to meet the demand, so this is the supply side of the equation. Depending on the type of operation (service or manufacturing) the operation/production will include details of raw materials and stock levels going into the 'input'.

BUDGETING FOR PLANNING AND CONTROL

Materials used and any additional purchases of materials may be the next port of call. This may involve several departments, as various materials could be employed.

Next we need to replenish our stocks and plan in advance for the purchase of new materials.

- *Usage*

- *Labour* (direct)

- *Overhead budget.* This may involve such controllable items such as labour and material.

- *Budgets for administration, selling, distribution.* For example,

- *Capital expenditure budgets* for that period.

- *The master budget* is then prepared

Budgeted profit/loss for period.

Subtotal =

Less closing stock, raw materials and the cost of used raw materials

Total operating cost =

Cash budgets. Sufficient cash must be available to meet the ebbs and flows of the operation and the budgets that we have considered to date. The format is as follows:

Cash Budgeting

One of the most important planning activities for an organization is to budget for cash. If a company does not make a profit in a particular year it will probably survive. If it does not have cash to pay creditors it is unlikely to survive in its existing form. Ensuring that there are sufficient cash resources when required is an important task, and not one to be carried out once a year; it must be a continuous process throughout the year. It is important to take a realistic view of the timing of receipts and payments. We might like to think that customers will all pay within the due date but it would be foolhardy to make plans on this expectation. A simple example is demonstrated below.

A company manufactures and sells a single product. The selling price is £10 per unit, 20 per cent of sales are for cash and 80 per cent are on credit terms of one month. On average, 70 per cent of customers taking credit pay within the required time, with the remaining 30 per cent paying in the month after payment is due. Sales in January and February were 3000 and 2800 units respectively. Budgeted sales for March, April and May are 3200, 2900 and 3100 units respectively.

Production in each month is equivalent to sales in the previous month. The direct cost of production is £3 for raw materials and variable overheads and £2 for direct labour. In addition, fixed overheads are incurred at £15 000 per month, including £3000 depreciation on machinery. Wages are paid in the month incurred but one month's credit is taken for all other purchases.

As at 1 March there is a cash balance of £5000. On 1 May the company will have to pay to the Inland Revenue £20 000 in respect of tax due. A cash budget for the months of March, April and May is shown below, with workings and explanations following.

Cash budget

	March	April	May
Receipts			
Cash sales	6400	5800	6200
Debtors paid	22880	24640	23920
Other sources	0	0	0
Total receipts	29280	30440	30120
Payments			
Wages	5600	6400	5800
Materials and variable costs	9000	8400	9600
Fixed overheads	12000	12000	12000
Taxation	0	0	20000
Other payments	0	0	0

BUDGETING FOR PLANNING AND CONTROL

	March	April	May
Total payments	26600	26800	47400
Net surplus	2680	3640	−17280
Opening balance	5000	7680	11320
Closing balance	7680	11320	−5960

Workings (for March)

Cash sales	March sales = 3200 units Revenue earned: 3200 × 10 = £32 000 Cash sales: £32 000 × 20 per cent = £3200
Debtors payments	February sales = 2800 units Revenue earned: 2800 × 10 = £28 000 Credit sales: £28 000 × 80 per cent = £22 400 Collected in March: £22 400 × 70 per cent = £15 680 January sales = 3000 units Revenue earned: 3000 × 10 = £30 000 Credit sales: £30 000 × 80 per cent = £24 000 Collected in March: £24 000 × 30 per cent = £7200
Total collected in March	£15 680 + £7200 = £22 880
Wages	Production in March = 2800 units (= February sales) Wages: £2 × 2800 = £5600
Materials	February production = 3000 units Materials: £3 × 3000 = £9000
Fixed overheads	£15 000 less £3000 depreciation, which is an accounting adjustment that does not involve paying cash on a monthly basis.

As can be seen from this example, the company does not have enough cash resources to finance current operations and to pay the Inland Revenue. Managers will have to take action to avoid this situation. Having prepared the forecast in advance, they have over two months to negotiate the least costly source of finance.

Budgeting for Control

Before looking at the mechanism used by companies in controlling responsibility centres we shall take a closer look at the control process. At this stage it is also worth making the distinction between financial control and management control. Financial control means being in control of the company's resources, ensuring that sufficient funds are available to finance

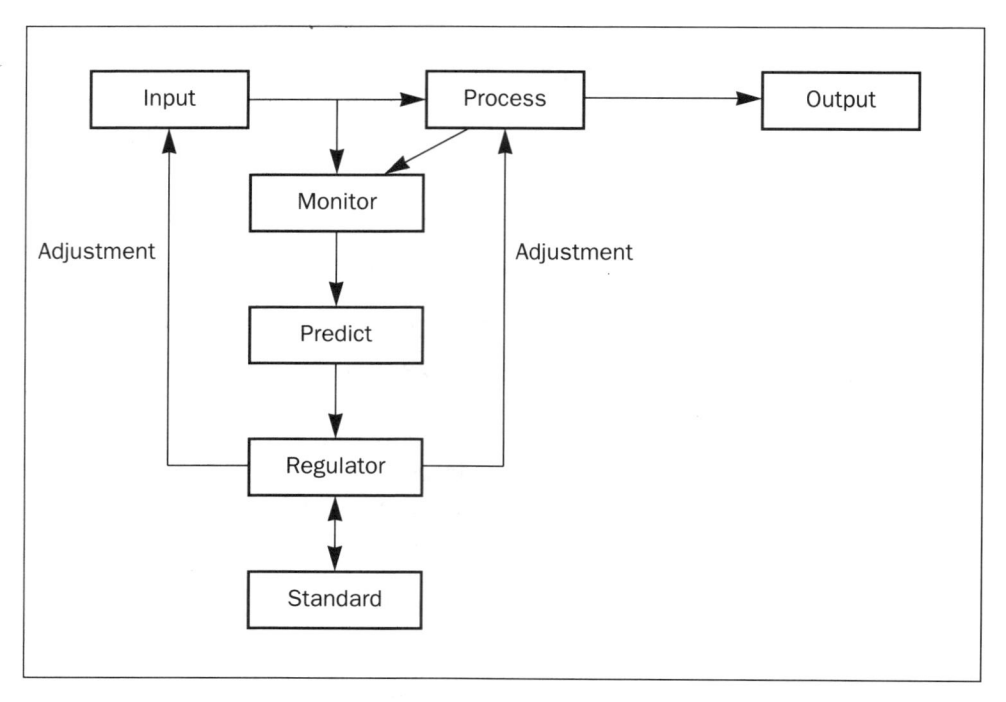

Figure 4.4 Feed-forward control.

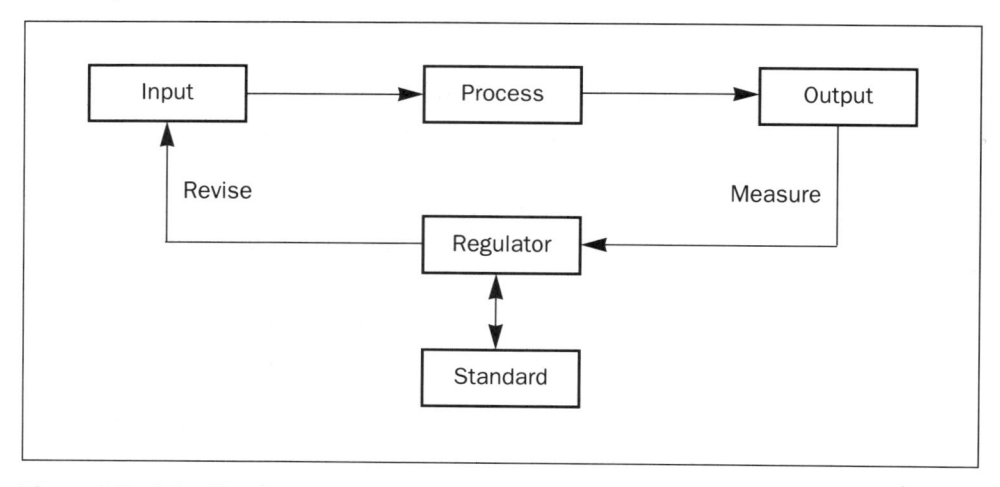

Figure 4.5 A feed-back control system.

the business. Management control, on the other hand, is about ensuring that all members of an organization act in a way that will achieve the organization's objectives. It is this aspect of control with which this section is concerned.

A general definition of control is: a process by which an enterprise adapts itself to its environment in order to achieve its goals.

BUDGETING FOR PLANNING AND CONTROL

A process that takes inputs (resources) and transforms them into an end product (results) can be controlled in two ways: feed-forward control, which happens before the process takes place (this is demonstrated in figure 4.4); and feed-back control, which takes place after the process (this is demonstrated in figure 4.5).

With feed-forward control the process is monitored, with the likely outcome being predicted. A regulator then compares the prediction to a planned target. If differences are identified then steps are taken before the process takes place to alter either the process itself or the planned target. We may practise feed-forward control in our everyday lives. If, when writing a cheque, we know that we will become overdrawn at the bank we can take steps before it is presented to our bank. We either arrange an overdraft facility or seek funds to pay into our account, we do not wait for the cheque to bounce (i.e. the process failing or being out of control). Organizations practise feed-forward control in many ways. Examples include the following.

- Stock control: placing orders for materials before the existing stocks run out.
- Cash planning: in the same way that we plan our finances so do organizations.
- The annual budgeting process, where results are forecast for the year: if this does not match the desired result managers resubmit their budgets until the budget reflects the desired result.

Feed-back control measures the output at the end of the process. This is then compared to the planned target. If differences are identified then action can be taken to eliminate them in the future, by adapting either the plan or the process itself. A commonly used example of a feed-back control is a central heating system. A desired temperature level is set as the target. The heating process then starts. The temperature in the room being heated is monitored. While there is a difference between the target and the measured temperature the boiler continues to operate. Once the desired target is reached the thermostat cuts off the boiler so that the temperature does not continue to rise. The temperature continues to be monitored until it falls below the desired level and the thermostat causes the boiler to start again.

An important component in any control system is the regulator. In the central heating system the thermostat is the regulator. The regulator can be described as the device that compares and recognizes variances, then reacts to take corrective action. In mechanical control systems the regulator can be relied upon to act in the proper way (unless there is a mechanical breakdown). The problem with control in an organization is that it is people who are the regulators. They cannot necessarily be relied upon to act in the same way as senior management to the signal that a variance exists. This might be the result of a different perception of the problem, but it could also be because individuals have their own personal objectives, which take precedence over those of the organization. A business is a pluralistic organization, where members may have conflicting objectives.[4] Rewards may have to be offered to ensure that members participate in a manner that is beneficial to all members.

Performance reporting is an important part of the control process. It makes the results of the sub-unit visible to the manager of the sub-unit, but also to senior managers who are able to make judgements about the manager's performance. In most organizations an important source of information is the accounting reports. Accounting reports are used because financial information can express the performance of all parts of the organization, and achieving a profit is one of the major objectives of the organization. Financial data give information about the use of resources and the success in earning revenues. There is the implication that good financial performance means effective management. However, as we noted in Unit One, other variables are also involved in this concept of effectiveness. Box AM4.3 emphasizes the importance of some types of financial control and prudent management.

BOX AM4.3

Budgetary control

A budget is a 'quantitative interpretation' prepared and approved beforehand, for a given period, to meet specific objectives. The continuous comparison of *actual results* with *budgeted forecasts* allows policy to be implemented and revisions made (if applicable). The budget is essentially a control mechanism to ensure that plans conform to policy. Certain advantages arise from using budgetary control.

- Cost awareness is stimulated. It may result in a thrifty approach.
- Senior managers can delegate more freely as subordinates have more job scope – assuming leeway in the budgets.
- Key tasks of managers can be undertaken using a quantified approach.
- Universal standards of performance across the organization can be made via budgets.
- The overall planning system is supported, allowing changes for the following period to be made and integrating the activities of the various functions of the organization.

Various types of budgetary controls exist:

- *Roll over.* Senior managers use this as a forecast of events for at least a year ahead.
- *Flexible.* There is an acceptance that fluctuations in turnover or output may occur, so the budget becomes more fluid.
- *Fixed.* Unchanged once agreed – irrespective of the turnover, output or other external or internal variables.

Various methods exist:

- *Top-down.* Decreed from above and often based on the budgeted profit, and 'given' to departments or managers.
- *'Inside out'.* Based on the corporate plan; using modelling techniques a computerized budget is made.
- *Bottom-up.* The normal method in many organizations, whereby the cost centre is responsible for the building blocks of the overall budget. The actual construction is monitored/reviewed/agreed by corporate managers at a senior level, who should have a wider vision of the organization and its profitability. 'Featherbedding' can be isolated in part at this stage.
- *Zero-based budgeting.* A useful device against too much featherbedding and building say 5 per cent on last year's budget. The budget starts at zero and each aspect has to be justified.
- *Probability budgeting.* A variation on the more fluid flexible budgets, which takes account of probability theory in that variations of risk can be built into each budget head to give a more dynamic picture, with parameters for each heading.
- *Change budgeting.* Justification with a given rationale for change (upwards or downwards) is required. Again this can counter featherbedding to some extent but the previous year's budget would have to be 'pure'.

Performance Reporting

The use of accounting information as the means of reporting is fraught with many problems, which means it does not always achieve the desired effect. Performance reports, communicating planned outcomes, actual results and resulting variances, can give managers information about efficiencies, but also inefficiencies. This second aspect may result in behavioural problems.

Performance reports need to be tailored to the specific needs of an organization. There is not one management reporting system that can be applied to all organizations. Some points to be considered in designing a management reporting system are as follows.

- *Managers' authority and responsibility must be clear.* Only when responsibility is defined can data relating to the task be matched to the task.
- *Senior management commitment.* Senior management must be seen to take the system seriously. One of the motivating forces for managers seeking to achieve good performance is the thought that they will receive senior management recognition.
- *Information must be relevant to the needs of the manager.* Managers at different levels of an organization require different degrees of aggregation in their reports. At the lower levels financial information may not be appropriate at all compared

MONTHLY OPERATING EXPENSES REPORT

DEPARTMENT: MANAGEMENT TRAINING **MONTH:** FEBRUARY 1994

DESCRIPTION	MONTH BUDGET	ACTUAL	VARIANCE	YEAR-TO-DATE BUDGET	ACTUAL	VARIANCE	TOTAL YEAR BUDGET	FORECAST	VARIANCE
Salaries	3,000	3,200	(200)	18,000	18,750	(750)	36,000	38,250	(2,250)
Staff expenses	500	450	50	3,000	2,800	200	6,000	6,000	0
Teamwork course	10,000	675	9,325	10,000	10,250	(250)	20,000	20,500	(500)
Leadership course	0	2,500	(2,500)	3,000	2,500	500	6,000	5,500	500
Miscellaneous	250	225	25	1,500	1,400	100	3,000	2,800	200
	13,750	7,050	6,700	35,500	35,700	(200)	71,000	73,050	(2,050)

MONTHLY OPERATING EXPENSES REPORT

DEPARTMENT: PERSONNEL **MONTH:** FEBRUARY 1994

DESCRIPTION	MONTH BUDGET	ACTUAL	VARIANCE	YEAR-TO-DATE BUDGET	ACTUAL	VARIANCE	TOTAL YEAR BUDGET	FORECAST	VARIANCE
Man training	13,750	7,050	6,700	35,500	35,700	(200)	71,000	73,050	(2,050)
YTS	5,000	5,200	(200)	30,000	32,000	(2,000)	60,000	65,000	(5,000)
General training	2,400	2,200	200	12,000	11,000	1,000	24,000	21,200	2,800
Recruitment	5,000	2,500	2,500	40,000	35,000	5,000	60,000	50,000	10,000
Fringe benefits	1,000	1,200	(200)	6,000	6,500	(500)	12,000	13,200	(1,200)
PERSONNEL ADMIN									
Salaries	3,500	3,500	0	21,000	21,200	(200)	44,000	44,600	(600)
Staff expenses	200	240	(40)	1,200	1,150	50	2,400	2,350	50
Computer expenses	2,500	2,750	(250)	15,000	16,500	(1,500)	30,000	33,000	(3,000)
Miscellaneous	300	300	0	1,800	1,800	0	3,600	3,600	0
	33,650	24,940	8,710	162,500	160,850	1,650	307,000	306,000	1,000

MONTHLY OPERATING EXPENSES REPORT

TOTAL COMPANY **MONTH:** FEBRUARY 1994

DESCRIPTION	MONTH BUDGET	ACTUAL	VARIANCE	YEAR-TO-DATE BUDGET	ACTUAL	VARIANCE	TOTAL YEAR BUDGET	FORECAST	VARIANCE
Personnel	33,650	24,940	8,710	162,500	160,850	1,650	307,000	306,000	1,000
Property Services	25,000	24,500	500	150,000	147,500	2,500	300,000	294,000	6,000
Finance	45,000	46,000	(1,000)	275,000	274,000	1,000	550,000	552,000	(2,000)
Computer Services	50,000	52,000	(2,000)	300,000	312,000	(12,000)	600,000	625,000	(25,000)
Marketing	80,000	85,000	(5,000)	450,000	440,000	10,000	1,000,000	980,000	20,000
Sales Support	20,000	18,000	2,000	120,000	115,000	5,000	250,000	250,000	0

Figure 4.6 Monthly operating expenses report.

BUDGETING FOR PLANNING AND CONTROL 145

with physical data (hours worked, numbers produced etc.). Figure 4.6 shows the different information that might be provided to a training manager, a personnel manager and a chief executive.

- *Training of managers in using financial data.* A problem with using accounting reports is that operational managers do not always understand the terminology of accounting or the meaning of cost variances. Managers cannot be expected to use the information contained in a report in the right way if they do not understand it. If this is a common problem, the method itself will need to be investigated.
- *Acceptance of the budget.* Managers will only be motivated to perform against a target if they feel it is reasonable and attainable. Participation in preparing the budget can help to increase this commitment.[5]
- *Timely feed-back of information.* The reports need to be prepared and presented as quickly as possible after the end of the period to which they relate. If a variance is identified immediate action is required. Waiting for the variance to be reported may result in inefficiency lasting longer than necessary. In the need to achieve speed some accuracy may have to be sacrificed.
- *Selection of an appropriate time horizon.* Most accounting reports are provided on a monthly basis and this will be the appropriate time horizon for most managers. However, it may be that a manager feels that information for control is required more frequently. For example, a sales director may want weekly data on the level of sales achieved. Senior managers who are concerned with the strategic direction of the organization will want the information less frequently, as it takes longer at the strategic level to identify trends affecting the business.
- *Routine and systematic feed-back.* For continuous control, regular reports are needed. Managers should not have to demand *ad hoc* reports. The information needed should be routinely made available.
- *Consideration of behavioural factors.* Managers should be aware of the likely reactions of people to the use of budget and financial information for performance evaluation and how this might affect their input into the budget process. Adverse behaviour might be aggravated when rewards are linked to performance against budget. Some of the behavioural implications of budgeting are considered in the final section of this unit.
- *Allow management by exception to be practised.* Identify the variances that need investigation and action. The major variances should be clearly visible and not hidden in a mass of irrelevant information.

146 EFFECTIVE ACCOUNTING MANAGEMENT

Variance Analysis and Reporting

First, we shall consider flexible budgeting through Activities AM4.2 and AM4.3. The rest of this section examines variance reporting using standard costing.

ACTIVITY AM4.2

BUDGETS AND VARIANCE 1

Activity code
- ✓ Self-development
- ☐ Teamwork
- ☐ Communications
- ✓ Numeracy/IT
- ✓ Decisions

The housekeeping department for the New Hotel had the following budgeted and actual costs in the month of February 1994. Has the department performed well or poorly in the month? Which variances should be investigated and action taken on?

Description	Budget	Actual	Variance
Manager's salary	1500	1500	0
Wages – chambermaids	7500	8500	(1000)
Wages – maintenance	1000	1050	(50)
Laundry	3600	3850	(250)
Consumables	1800	2000	(200)
Maintenance materials	500	400	100
Shrinkage	500	600	(100)
	16400	17900	(1500)

ACTIVITY AM4.3

BUDGETS AND VARIANCE 2

Activity code
- ✓ Self-development
- ☐ Teamwork
- ☐ Communications
- ✓ Numeracy/IT
- ✓ Decisions

Commentary
It appears that the housekeeping department shown in Activity AM4.2 has not performed well during the month, as it has overspent against the budget. A particularly large variance is that for chambermaids' wages, and managers may spend time looking for the cause of this variance. Upon investigation it is revealed that the original budget was prepared on the assumption that the occupancy rate for the rooms would be 70 per cent. The actual occupancy rate was 84 per cent. All costs are considered variable except for the manager's salary and maintenance materials. If the activity was higher, surely we would have expected more to be spent?

There are two accounting techniques that are used in situations where activity is different from that assumed in preparing the original budget. The first is *flexible budgeting* and this technique can be used in any responsibility centre. The second technique is *standard costing* and this is used in a manufacturing setting.

Flexible budgeting
This technique requires an understanding of the variable and fixed elements of costs in a department. Those which are variable can be expected to increase in direct proportion to activity. Those which are fixed remain the same regardless of the level of activity. In the above example the assumption was that rooms would be occupied for 70 per cent of the time, when they were occupied for 84 per cent of the time.

Using these new occupancy figures, calculate the variances and comment on them.

Variance reporting

This is a detailed accounting technique used by manufacturing organizations. The purpose is to plan and control costs and revenues, although the technique can also be used for stock valuation purposes. It is used in industries where there is a repetitive manufacturing process. Its use is widespread and includes car, electrical, printing, textile, brewing and chemical industries, to name a few.

The technique requires that revenue and cost standards be set for each product. For a particular quantity of that product the total cost will be the quantity multiplied by the standard cost. The expected profit is the standard profit margin (standard sales revenue less the standard cost) multiplied by the quantity sold. After sales and production have taken place the standard is used as a yardstick against which to check actual performance.

Determining the standard cost of a product

The first stage in determining the cost standard is to estimate *technical standards* in terms of the materials required, labour input, required machine time and other inputs. The technical standard can be estimated by a number of methods and is the responsibility of production managers. They may use engineering studies, time and motion studies or their own past experience of the process. Technical standards tend to remain constant over time, only changing when changes are introduced into the manufacturing process.

Once the technical standards have been established, *cost standards* can be determined using current prices. These can be updated annually, or more frequently where necessary.

In addition to the direct costs of manufacture it is usual to include some overhead costs in the product cost (particularly where the standard cost is being used for stock valuation purposes). The overheads will be allocated to products in the same way as described in Unit Three. Standard costing can be practised using marginal costing techniques and a benefit of this might be that variances are easier to calculate and understand. However, if a company wishes to use standard costs for stock valuation it will have to include fixed overheads.

A standard cost sheet for a typical product might look as follows:

Product 57	Quantity	Rate	Total cost
Direct materials ZZ63	2 kg	£16.00	£32.00
Direct labour	3 hours	£7.30	£21.90
Variable overhead	2 machine hours	£5.00	£10.00
Fixed overhead	per unit	£40.00	£40.00
Total standard cost			£103.90

In this example fixed overheads have been budgeted as totalling £40 000 in any period. The absorption rate for overheads is determined by dividing the budgeted cost by the budgeted output for the period, which in this case is 1000 units.

Calculation of variances

These will be calculated for product 57 using the following data, which relate to the actual cost in a period in which the budget was exceeded and 1200 units were produced.

Product 57	Quantity	Total cost
Direct materials ZZ63	2420 kg	£38 478
Direct labour	3644 hours	£26 419
Variable overhead	2450 machine hours	£12 250
Fixed overhead		£41 000
Total actual cost		£118 147

Before looking at the individual elements of cost let us see how much the difference is between what we would have expected to spend in producing 1200 units and the actual costs. With standard costing the costs are always recalculated to reflect the actual volume because changes in volume are assumed to be beyond the control of production managers.

Expected costs	1200 × £103.90 = £124 680
Actual costs	= £118 392
Difference: underspend	£6 288

The accounting terminology for this is a positive or favourable variance. Basically, a favourable variance means that less has been spent than was expected. Overspends are described as negative, unfavourable or adverse variances. Initially it looks as if the department has been operating efficiently, as the total expected cost is greater than the actual costs, but this may be hiding disturbing variances. Some of the costs were described as being fixed. If they were really fixed they should not increase with volume. When more units than budgeted are produced a favourable variance should be expected. (Conversely, an adverse variance should be expected if production is less than budgeted.) To investigate further what has happened to cost we need to calculate variances for each of the individual elements of cost.

Formulas are often used to calculate variances and are demonstrated below, with the following abbreviations being used:

AQ = actual quantity
BQ = budgeted quantity
SQ = standard quantity
AP = actual price
SP = standard price
AR = actual rate
SR = standard rate
BC = budgeted cost
AC = actual cost

Quantity relates to number of units, amount of materials used or number of hours worked, depending on the variance being calculated. The actual price and rate can be determined by dividing the actual cost by the quantity.

Direct material variances

If we first examine the actual cost of direct materials compared to expected cost we obtain the total variance for materials.

Material ZZ63

Expected cost: 1200 units × 2 kg × £16.00 =	£38 400
Actual cost:	£38 478
Variance, adverse:	£78

The variance for raw materials could be caused by one (or both) of two reasons:

- using quantity different from that implied in the standard;
- paying a different price for the material bought.

There are two variances that can be calculated to discover the cause of the overall variance:

Direct material usage variance = (SQ – AQ) × SP
(2400 – 2420) × £16.00
£320 adverse

Direct material price variance = (SP – AP) × AQ
(£16.00 – £15.90) × 2420
£242 favourable

These variances show that more material was used than was expected, but the cost per kilogram was lower. A possible cause of this variance is that an inferior quality (cheaper) material was used. Management should investigate to see if this was a wise move. It would seem not in this case, as the money saved on a lower price has not compensated for the higher usage of material.

Who is held responsible for material variances may cause a conflict between departments of the company. Should the production department be held responsible for the material usage variance when the supplies were obtained by the purchasing department (who can point to a favourable price variance as evidence of their efficiency)?

Direct labour variances

The variance for direct labour is the difference between the amount expected to be paid and the actual amount paid.

Expected cost: 1200 units × 3 hours × £7.30 per hour = £26 280
Actual cost: £26 419
Variance, adverse: £139

The direct labour variance could also be caused by one (or both) of two different factors:

- working a different number of hours from those expected;
- paying a different wage rate per hour from that expected.

Labour efficiency variance = (SQ – AQ) × SR
(3600 – 3644) × £7.30
£321.20 adverse

Labour rate variance = (SR – AR) × AQ
(7.30 – 7.25) × 3644
£182.20 favourable

Here the lower wage rate does not compensate for the extra hours that have been worked. The two variances may be connected: a lower grade of labour receives a low rate but may take longer to execute a task. They may be completely unconnected. The wage rate may be lower because general wage settlements are not as high as originally envisaged. If this is so the standard should really be adjusted for the future. The departmental manager will have to conduct an investigation to find the cause of more hours being worked and take corrective action if necessary.

Variable overhead variances

The total variable overheads variance is the difference between the expected overheads and the actual costs incurred.

Expected cost: 1200 units × 2 machine hours × £5 = £12 000
Actual: £12 495
Variance, adverse: £495

This variance could be caused by one (or both) of two reasons:

- a different number of machine hours from that expected;
- a different level of expenditure per machine hour being incurred.

Variable overhead efficiency variance = (SQ – AQ) × SR
(2400 – 2450) × £5
£250 adverse

Variable overhead expenditure variance = (SR – AR) × AQ
(5.00 – 5.10) × 2450
£245 adverse

The adverse efficiency variance reflects the fact that extra machine hours have been worked, and costs (such as electricity) are incurred while machines are in use. To find the cause of this variance the manager of the department will first need to investigate why more machine hours are being worked. The expenditure variance reflects the fact that costs for variable items are higher than expected. The departmental manager will not find this summarized variance of any use in investigating rising costs; he or she will need information on each element of variable cost.

Fixed overhead variances

The total variance represents the difference between the standard overheads (the expected overhead if the per unit rate remains constant) and the costs actually incurred.

Standard overheads: 1200 units × £40 per unit	£48000
Actual overheads:	£41000
Variance, favourable:	£7000

Now we can see the source of the overall budget's favourable variance. Only fixed overheads have a favourable variance. This has arisen largely because fixed overheads have been treated as if they were variable, and by their nature they are not. This has resulted from absorbing fixed costs into the standard costs. It is essential where this happens that the variances are further analysed to understand the true picture. The total variance can be caused by one (or both) of two factors:

- a different number of units being produced from that originally budgeted;
- actual expenditure being at a different level from that budgeted.

Fixed overhead volume variance = (AQ − BQ) × SR
(1200 − 1000) × £40
£8000 favourable

Fixed overhead expenditure variance = (BC − AC)
(£40 000 − £41 000)
£1000 adverse

The fixed overhead volume variance is pretty meaningless to the manager responsible for controlling costs in this department. All it tells him or her is that more units have been produced than budgeted for and that they have absorbed overheads when they should not have done. This variance represents over- or under-absorption of overheads, which we have already encountered in Unit Three.

The fixed overhead expenditure variance is the variance that requires investigation, to see why costs are higher than budgeted. Usually this is the result of costs having to be estimated before they are known with any certainty.

Bringing together all the variances calculated, it now becomes more clear which areas need investigation.

Variance	Favourable	Adverse	Total
Direct materials			
usage		(320.00)	
price	242.00		(78.00)
Direct labour			
efficiency		(321.20)	
rate	182.20		(139.00)
Variable overhead			
efficiency		(250.00)	
expenditure		(245.00)	(295.00)
Fixed overhead			
volume	8000.00		
expenditure		(1000.00)	7000.00
	8424.20	(2136.20)	6288.00

Sales margin variances

The standard cost analysis can also be extended to sales revenue from the products when sold. This enables gross profit to be completely analysed in terms of variances.

Extra data relating to the Product 57 example:

Budgeted selling price	£200 per unit
Budgeted sales	1000 units
Actual selling price	£190 per unit
Actual sales	1200 units

The total sales margin variance represents the value over the standard cost of production that is gained or lost from changes in sales revenue. The standard cost of production is always used in the calculation of this variance because any change in the cost of production is assumed to be the responsibility of the production manager.

Expected gross margin: $1000 \times (£200 - £103.90) = £96100$

Actual gross margin: $1200 \times (£190 - £103.90) = £103320$

Variance, favourable: £7220

The sales margin variance can be further analysed according to its two possible causes:

- a different quantity being sold from that originally budgeted;
- units being sold at a different selling price.

154 EFFECTIVE ACCOUNTING MANAGEMENT

Sales margin volume variance = (AQ − BQ) × BGM
(1200 − 1000) × (£200 − £103.90)
£19 220 favourable

with BGM being budgeted gross margin

Sales margin price variance = (BP − AP) × AQ
(£200 − £190) × 1200
£12 000 adverse

In this case a price reduction increases the volume of sales. The gross margin lost as a result of the lower price is more than compensated for by the gain from selling more units.

We can now bring together all the variances into one statement to reconcile the budgeted profit to the actual profit earned.

Budgeted profit:
(Selling price − cost of sales) × budgeted quantity

(£200 − £103.90) × 1000 =   £96100

Actual profit:
Sales revenue − actual costs
(£190 × 1200) −£118 392 =   £109608

Difference   £13508 F

Sales margin variances:
Volume   19220 F
Price   (12000) A   7220 F

Direct materials variances:
Usage   (320)A
Price   242 F   (78) A

Direct labour variances:
Efficiency   (321.20) A
Rate   182.20 F   (139) A

Variable overhead variances:
Efficiency   (250) A
Expenditure   (245) A   (495) A

Fixed overhead variances:
Volume   8000 F
Expenditure   (1000) A   7000 F

                                                                       13508 F

BUDGETING FOR PLANNING AND CONTROL

Which variance to investigate

A busy manager may be faced with a dilemma, with several variances being reported but insufficient time to investigate them all. Some companies will require that all are investigated but many require just the major variances to be investigated. One technique used to identify the major variances is to

---

ACTIVITY AM4.4

BUDGET VARIANCE AT THE NEWSPAPER

Activity code
- ✓ Self-development
- ✓ Teamwork
- ✓ Communications
- ✓ Numeracy/IT
- ✓ Decisions

The *Free Press* Ltd is a provincial newspaper in the UK, publishing a daily (morning) newspaper and an evening newspaper.

Advertising revenue as well as a growing or at least a constant circulation are important for profitability. Cost controls are important as well, and manpower is probably one of the most costly areas. Consequently, a form of budgetary control was installed some four years ago, and all additional posts had to be sanctioned by the managing director. Computerization of the production facility is ongoing. The MD sat down to review the figures, noting particular issues through a simple analysis using actual people in post compared to budget/establishment levels. The budget is set and the actual figures relate to the annual totals averaged over the past year.

Task
Highlight the key areas that need some further investigation.

NUMBERS OF EMPLOYEES AT YEAR END

Department	Year 4 Actual	Year 4 Budget	Year 3 Actual	Year 3 Budget	Year 2 Actual	Year 2 Budget	Year 1 Actual	Year 1 Budget
Editorial (day)	21	20	22	21	23	22	24	22
News desk	60	61	60	59	60	58	60	57
Subs	26	27	26	27	23+4 (p/t)	24	26	24
Features	15	15	15	14	15	15	15	16
Sports	6	6	6	6	6	6	6	6
Photographers	7	7	7	7	7	7	7	7

156   EFFECTIVE ACCOUNTING MANAGEMENT

Department	Year 4 Actual	Year 4 Budget	Year 3 Actual	Year 3 Budget	Year 2 Actual	Year 2 Budget	Year 1 Actual	Year 1 Budget
Editorial (evening)								
News desk	30	29	30	28	30	28	30	29
Subs	21	21	24	21	24	21	24	21
Features	11	11	11	11	11	10	11	10
Sports	9	9	9	9	9	9	9	9
Photographers	8	8	8	8	9	8	9	8
Library	5	5	5	5	5	5	5	5
Competitions	8	6	8	6	8	7	9	7
Photo sales	5	5	5	5	5	5	5	6
Production								
Communications room	16	15	16	15	16	15	16	17
Process	18	12	18	13	16	16	15	16
Composition	110	111	112	111	114	111	116	111
Machine	60	60	59	59	61	59	62	60
Packing	48	46	48	46	48	46	46	46
Returns	2	2	2	2	2	2	2	2
Reel Squad	8	8	8	7	8	7	8	7
Advertising								
Display (day)	16	16	18	16	17	15	16	14
Display (evening)	20	20	21	20	19	20	21	20
Administration	12	12	12	11	12	10	12	9
Classified (day)	40	40	47	41	49	42	50	43
Classified (evening)	40	40	45	41	47	42	48	43
Circulation								
Day paper	19	17	19	17	19	18	21	18
Evening paper	19	17	19	17	19	18	19	18
Administration	10	9	9	9	9	9	9	9
Distribution	14	12	13	12	13	12	13	12
Sales								
Publicity	9	9	9	9	9	9	10	9
Administration	3	3	3	3	3	3	3	3
Creative services	14	12	14	14	12	14	11	15
Personnel/Admin./Management								
Management	12	13	14	13	14	14	16	16
General	18	18	18	18	20	18	21	18
Telephones	12	12	12	12	12	12	12	12
Computing	5	8	4	8	3	8	5	8
Senior mgt	8	8	8	8	8	9	8	9

BUDGETING FOR PLANNING AND CONTROL

Department	Year 4 Actual	Year 4 Budget	Year 3 Actual	Year 3 Budget	Year 2 Actual	Year 2 Budget	Year 1 Actual	Year 1 Budget
Maintenance								
Cleaning	10	11	11	11	12	11	12	11
Canteen	14+2 (p/t)	16	16+2 (p/t)	17	16+2 (p/t)	17	17+3 (p/t)	16
Engineers	14	14	14	13	14	13	14	13

calculate the variance as a percentage of the standard cost. Only variances that exceed a target percentage figure (e.g. 5 per cent) are actually investigated.

Please complete Activity AM4.4.

Behavioural Aspects of Budgeting

Budgeting is not a purely passive technique: people can be expected to react in a number of ways, especially when their own objectives are affected by budgets. There are a number of behavioural aspects of budgeting that managers should be aware of before using budgets for control, motivation or as a basis for reward. This section is by no means extensive in looking at behavioural problems in budgeting, but highlights some aspects of which managers should be aware. Please consult Box AM4.4.

BOX AM4.4

'Featherbedding' or 'the best laid plans of mice and men'

All the control mechanisms open to organizations may still not result in accurate budgets and forecasting, particularly if a bottom-up view is taken of the budgetary process. But without the users doing the spadework, budgets imposed from above may become meaningless.

'Featherbedding' is about inflating the figures under your budget heads so that the target forecasts become 'looser', with more room for the individual manager to manoeuvre and less organizational control as a result.

It could be cheating. It could be a mechanism for an easier life. It could be the creation of a margin of safety, particularly if the managerial style is leaning towards a punitive culture where deviant budget breakers are taken to full

> account by more senior managers. It could also be down to the nature of the 'informal organization'.
>
> The formal organization, with its established mission, plans and objectives, tends to be very task-orientated at the expense of people within the organization. Partly as a reaction against this task orientation and partly as a result of the socio-emotional needs of individuals and groups, an informal organization develops with its own norms, values and perhaps separate 'culture', which may be contrary to the established 'culture'. Experienced managers realize the limits of managerial control and control mechanisms, so they may well build some leeway into the over-rigid control mechanisms to take account of this behavioural aspect.
>
> There may be another explanation. Decision making in management traditionally assumed some form of 'maximization'. However, as Simon[1] tells us, many managers may be in the market of 'satisficing', whereby a mentality of getting by or 'oh, that will do' may dominate.
>
> It is difficult, if not impossible, to prevent this 'featherbedding', but sound principles of costing should help form the springs of the mattress. At the same time, control mechanisms of management, from organizational and job allocations to accounting and budgetary controls, must take a behavioural view of control and its limits into account in preparing and monitoring budgets.[2]
>
> *Sources:*
> 1 Simon, *Models of Man: social and rational*
> 2 Cyert and March, *A Behavioral Theory of the Firm*

Budgets are part of the political power game in an organization. One of the reasons for this is that they are concerned with the allocation of scarce resources. A manager may seek to gain resources because they reflect his or her power. Other individuals may have influence on the selection of information to be included in the budget and reports. This may help to shape the outcome of the budgeting process and affect the future of the organization. Here budgets are not only a reflection of power, but an instrument of power. Managers may also use the budget as a signal to senior managers of their determination and motivation, by inflating their expected level of performance.

Budgets bring visibility to particular events and thus attention is focused on these aspects. They define economic aspects as being important and in need of consideration. Hard to measure non-quantitative elements may be ignored because they are included in reports. There is an often used expression in management accounting: 'what gets measured gets attention'. Budgets may thus have the effect of narrowing a manager's mind to considering only economic considerations and stifle new and innovative interpretations of a situation. Performance against budget is used to evaluate performance, if not competence. So budgets can be used as a form of reward and a punishment. When the budget is not achieved, 'uncontrollable' events may be blamed.

One of the problems that faces managers when they set budgets and standards is how difficult the target should be. If a target is set too low and is easily achieved there is no incentive to improve performance. On the other hand, too difficult a target, which is impossible to meet, will be thought to be unreasonable by the manager and he or she will not be motivated even to try to meet it. From a motivational point of view a difficult yet achievable target is best.[6]

Another problem facing managers is whether subordinates should participate in the budgeting process. A subordinate is in a position where he or she knows most about the department and is able to give the best estimates of likely performance. When their own performance is evaluated against the budget they may allow personal objectives to take precedence over objective forecasting. They might seek to introduce 'slack' into the budget because it makes it more easy to meet the target, and gives a buffer for events beyond their control if they feel the evaluation system does not accurately reflect changed circumstances. While in most cases managers might be expected to introduce 'slack', there are circumstances where the opposite is experienced. Where poor performance has been shown in the past an over-optimistic budget might be produced because it shows a determination to do better in the future. There may be disadvantages in participation but these are likely to be less of a problem than when budgets are imposed. Budgets are imposed by a manager with less information about the task than the subordinate. These diktats are less likely to be accepted as reasonable by the subordinate and thus are not good motivators.

Taking account of the aims and content of this unit, tackle Activity AM4.5.

Conclusion

This unit has studied an application of accounting to the managerial tasks of planning and control. The next unit continues this applied theme, looking at decision making.

ACTIVITY AM4.5

THE VALUE OF ACCOUNTING MANAGEMENT IN BUSINESS PLANNING AT MALMÖ

Activity code
- ✓ Self-development
- ✓ Teamwork
- ✓ Communications
- ☐ Numeracy/IT
- ✓ Decisions

Malmö Communications, a Swedish-based organization with its core business in telecommunications, had recently taken over an established peripheral systems company (Peripheral (UK)) in the United Kingdom. The products run from powerful minicomputers for introductory levels to the massive System 95, ideally suited to signal conditioning, process control and mass data applications.

The accounting information system is well established at Peripheral and budgetary control policy has been successfully applied for the past five years. Sales turnovers with margins are established by specific product. The planning of Peripheral (UK) has been 'slack' to date and Malmö is set on change.

Malmö believes that there are three possible ways of coming up with decent forecasts using accounting information for the business plan. They are:

1 *Basic forecast*
   - use sales turnover and trading profit figures for the past five years;
   - remove inflation;
   - add margin on sales ratio.
2 *Budget forecast*
   - use existing budget in the main functional areas;
   - take account of environmental change;
   - extrapolate figures for the forecast.
3 *Company forecast*
   - use all available management and cost accounting data;
   - take account of environmental change;
   - extrapolate figures for the forecast.

Task
Comment critically (report) on the three options from the perspective of an effective manager of accounting, recently employed by Malmö. In the third option, note which data you would seek. Assume that environmental scans[1] have been conducted and concentrate on the 'internal/company' environment.

Note
1 For details see Anderson and Barker, *Effective Business Policy*

Notes

1 D. Barry, American columnist and comedian, quoted in *The Observer*, 2 May 1993.
2 See Anderson and Barker, *Effective Business Policy*.
3 See Anderson and Dobson, *Effective Marketing*.
4 This pluralism is covered in Anderson, *Effective Labour Relations*.
5 Employee involvement in decision making is covered in Anderson and Kyprianou, *Effective Organizational Behaviour*.
6 Motivation is taken up in the context of Anderson and Kyprianou's text, *Effective Organizational Behaviour*.

Unit Five

Accounting Information for Decision Making

Learning Objectives

After completing this unit you should be able to:

- understand and apply the principles of financial decision making;
- understand why absorption costing does not provide good information for decision making;
- derive variable cost information and contribution, and apply them to decisions;
- conduct simple break even analyses;
- understand different approaches to pricing;
- understand and apply the techniques used to analyse long-term decisions;
- apply the generic skills.

Contents

Overview

Relevant Costing

- Differential/incremental
- Future
- Cash flow
- Contribution

Costing Techniques and Decision Making

- Effect on profit measurement
- Effect on decision making
  - Deleting a segment
  - Make or buy
  - Accepting a special order
  - Scarce resources

Break Even Analysis

- The break even chart
- Calculation of the break even point
- The relevant range
- Sensitivity (what if?) analysis

Pricing

- Cost-based pricing
- Full cost plus
- Variable cost plus

Long-term Decision Making

- Time value of money

Methods of Appraising Investments

▶ Net present value (NPV)
▶ Internal rate of return (IRR)
▶ Payback period
▶ Accounting rate of return (ARR)

Capital Rationing

Conclusion

Unit Five

> " The firm makes two types of decisions: input decisions and output decisions. The input decisions answer questions such as 'Which factors of production should the firm buy?' and 'In what quantities?'... The output decisions are ... 'Which products should the firm produce' and 'In what quantities?' "
>
> *Naylor, Vernon and Wertz, Managerial Economics*[1]

Overview

Managers are faced with many decisions that affect the future of their companies. Making a decision means choosing between at least two courses of action. It may be a 'do something' or a 'do nothing' decision. It may be choosing between a series of alternatives. Some examples of decisions using accounting information are:

- to make a product or subcontract;
- to discontinue a product or a branch of the company;
- what price to charge;
- to accept a special order;
- to introduce a new product or start a new venture.

What criteria do managers use when making these decisions? One criterion should be the financial outcome; certainly it will be evident for profit-making organizations. Non-financial criteria can be just as important in arriving at a decision. Qualitative factors can, and should, override the financial criteria in some situations. Examples include:

- maintaining employee morale;
- maintaining the company's image;
- quality;
- reliability;
- future prospects;
- complementary business.

Financial data used in a decision will come from cost–benefit analysis. All the costs resulting from the decision are compared against the benefits, which are either revenues gained or costs saved. For example, by investing in a new machine labour costs might be saved. If the benefits are greater than the costs the investment decision should go ahead.

Some decisions are long term and may involve large sums of money being expended. Some are short term and may have no long-term implications. There is a slight difference in the approach taken with long- and short-term decisions. In the short term many costs will be unaffected by the decision, as they are fixed. As the time horizon expands fixed costs can become variable: rent on buildings is usually fixed for a period of a year, for example a short-term decision about what to do with the building will not affect the amount of rent payable. A longer-term decision may result in the building being vacated or sublet, so the cost is no longer fixed.

This unit is about identifying the financial data necessary for decision making and evaluating these data.

Relevant Costing

Relevant costing is the name that is generally given to the activity of identifying the costs affected by a decision. Although the term 'costing' appears in the name the same principles apply to identification of the revenues affected by a decision. The principles are fairly simple; to a great extent they are merely the application of common sense. Costs and revenues that are relevant to a decision can be summed up in four words: differential, future, cash flows.

Differential/incremental

These are costs and revenues that change as a result of the decision. If they remain the same, they are not relevant. Consider a business that will incur a certain level of fixed overheads for the year, but has some spare capacity. In any decision about using the spare capacity fixed overheads are irrelevant, as they will be incurred regardless of the decision. Only the extra revenue and costs actually incurred are relevant.

Another point to remember is that the change must affect the organization as a whole. If one department makes a saving, only for the cost to be passed on to another department, there is no saving for the organization as a whole. This 'saving' should therefore be irrelevant to the decision.

Sometimes making a decision to do one thing may preclude you from doing another. There is an *opportunity cost* associated with the decision. To identify differential costs fully you must therefore evaluate all alternatives. For example, you have been approached to produce one order, which will use up all your spare capacity. If it is taken other orders might have to be rejected. So in making the decision you need to identify the potential profit from the alternative forgone.

Future

These are costs and revenues that will be incurred after the decision has been taken. The past might be a good indicator of the future, but it should not be assumed that because something has cost a particular amount in the past it will cost the same in the future.

When looking into the future we should forget about what has been spent in the past. The fact that we spent £2 million on a machine just two years ago should not be considered when we are deciding what to do with the machine now. If we want to keep the machine we have to look at future earnings; if we want to get rid of it we have to consider its resale price. Costs which have been expended in the past and are irrecoverable are called *sunk costs*, and are always irrelevant for decision making.

Cash flow

This is the actual cash that will be expended and collected as a result of the decision. For long-term decision making it is important to identify the timing of the cash flows, as we will see in the section at the end of this unit. Cash flow information is needed to provide fair financial reports. When considering the purchase of a new machine, we need to know how much it will cost and when it has to be paid for, not what the annual depreciation charge will be.

These principles applied together are demonstrated in the following worked example.

WORKED EXAMPLE

Angus makes special order engineering products and has received an enquiry from a customer for supply of a product. He has discovered the following information about the order.

Materials. Material A, 10 kg. This is already held in stock, having been purchased at a cost of £13/kg. Buying it was a mistake. It cannot now be used except on this order. It could, however, be sold as scrap for £40 the lot. Material B, 5 kg. This material is regularly in use. There is 20 kg in stock which cost £25/kg. The current price is £35/kg.

Labour. John is required for 12 hours, and the cost of employment for John is £9 per hour. John is fully employed at present and if used on this order would have to be taken off the manufacture of another job. A temporary worker could be employed for £150 to finish this work.

Overheads. Plans are needed for the product. There are some that had been drawn up for another order, which had subsequently been cancelled. These had cost £50. Variable overheads: assumed to vary at £2.00 per hour with direct labour hours. Fixed overheads: charged to jobs at £5.00 per direct labour hour.

What is the minimum price that Angus could quote for this job and be no worse off than he is at present?

The minimum price that could be charged is the relevant cost of completing the order. Any price higher than that would make Angus better off than he is without the order. The relevant costs are:

	£
Materials	
Material A	40
Material B	175
Labour	
John	150
Overheads	
Variable	24
	389

Why is this the relevant cost? Let's look at it item by item.

Material A. No cash has to be expended as materials are held in stock. The original cost of purchasing the material was £130, but this cost is irrelevant as it is a past cost and is irrecoverable. The only alternative would be to sell the material for its scrap value. By using the material in the order we are losing this opportunity, so this is the relevant cost.

Material B. Again there is some of this material in stock. If it is used on this order, more will have to be purchased for use on existing work. This will mean the company having to pay £175 (5 × £35) for the replacement materials. The cost of £25/kg is not relevant because it is a past cost and not affected by the decision.

Labour. John is needed to work on the order. If the order is not taken on he will be employed for 12 hours elsewhere in the factory. The cost of employing John will be incurred whether or not the order is taken on. The only extra costs that will be incurred are those associated with the temporary worker.

Overheads. The only overhead cost that will be incurred as a result of taking on the extra work is the variable overhead. The cost of plans are a sunk cost. The fixed overhead allocation is merely an accounting adjustment; taking on the extra work does not mean that any extra expenses will be incurred.

Contribution

A point to note in the above example is the exclusion of allocated fixed overheads. In the short term, fixed costs are unlikely to change. If they do change, the predicted amount should be separately identified. An important principle in short-term decision making is *contribution*. This is calculated by deducting variable costs from the revenue earned from the sale of a product or service. The excess of revenue over variable cost provides a 'contribution' to the fixed overheads of the company and then it 'contributes' to the profit. It can be calculated for an individual product or service, or for a product line, a branch of a company or the company in total. In the short term a decision that results in a positive contribution higher than an increase in fixed costs is good for the company. Please tackle Activity AM5.1.

ACTIVITY AM5.1

THE ALBION

Activity code
- ✓ Self-development
- ✓ Teamwork
- ☐ Communications
- ✓ Numeracy/IT
- ✓ Decisions

Tomson and Smythe had started working in the hotel sector some twenty years ago. Tomson's family wealth and Smythe's industry had allowed the two friends to buy a medium-sized three-star hotel near Duxford in Cambridgeshire. Their initial motive had been to provide a stopover facility on the A505 for passing trade and to act as an overspill hotel for the tourist-infested city of Cambridge, a pleasant fifteen to twenty minutes' drive from the hotel. The Albion, as it was called (George Tomson and Phil Smythe being quite patriotic), had prospered over the past few years. It had a further shot in the arm with the opening of the north-bound London motorway, the M11. More passing trade came off at the Duxford exit for a comfortable night's rest, a reasonably priced meal and a soothing drink. Duxford is fairly close to the expanding 'third' London airport at Stansted.

The coffee bar had been opened in a section of the lounge bar. It took up a quarter of the seating space as the non-alcohol drinkers were kept separated by a row of plants in huge pots from the alcohol-serving part of the bar. It meant that passing trade could be served without the full bar being open or the people in the restaurant being troubled.

The sales for the year, including pre-packaged sandwiches, amounted to some £125 000. The cost of the goods sold came to £60 000, labour (a proportion of the total) based on hours came to £18 000. The fixed overheads

> came to £30 000. There were problems in manning and extra bodies would have to be taken on in the next accounting period to push labour costs up to £25 000. Raw materials were creeping up too and a 10 per cent rise was expected to give costs of £66 000. The pricing was tight (and some felt expensive), so only a 5 per cent rise could occur. The fixed overheads were expected to rise by 10 per cent as well, to £33 000. The bar takings had remained static in the past year while other non-bar turnover had increased by some 8–10 per cent. The existing turnover of the bar was £350 000.
>
> **Task**
> Determine whether this unit is a viable proposition. Note the contribution forgone and take a view on opportunity cost as well.

For financial reporting purposes companies use *absorption costing*, which includes an allocation of overheads for product costs. Sometimes this can lead to incorrect short-term decisions being taken. The next section looks at the use of costing techniques and their effect on profit measurement and decision making.

Costing Techniques and Decision Making

In Unit Three we were introduced to two methods of costing: absorption and variable costing. Absorption costing sought to trace all costs to products. Variable costing only traced variable costs to products, with any fixed costs being deducted in the profit and loss account as a period cost. The accounting profession has decided that for financial reporting purposes, stock valuation and profit measurement, companies should use the absorption costing method. This does not mean that it must be used internally, when making decisions. Whether or not a company decides to prepare variable costing data as well as absorption costing data depends in part on the perceived benefits from making better decisions compared to the cost of collection. The decision is usually left to the finance staff as most other managers are unaware of the use of the alternative technique. There has been a long running debate among accountants over which technique is superior, with some strong views being held. This section looks at the differences between the two techniques, concentrating particularly on their use in *decision making*, but starting with a look at their effect on *profit measurement*.

Effect on profit measurement

When stocks are being built up or run down, the reported profit earned will vary depending upon whether absorption costing or variable costing is used. This is demonstrated in the following worked example.

WORKED EXAMPLE: GARDEN GNOMES (PERIOD 1)

A company manufactures a single product, garden gnomes, which sell at £20 per unit. It manufactured 5000 gnomes in period 1 but was only able to sell 4500 gnomes. It had no stocks at the start of the year. Fixed costs of £20 000 were incurred and were absorbed to products on the basis of units manufactured. The variable costs of manufacture were £12 per unit.

1 *Absorption costing.* See Unit Three for a reminder of how costs are absorbed to products and how profit is calculated using this technique. In this simple example the £20 000 is divided equally between the 5000 units manufactured, that is £4 per unit. The total cost for each product made is therefore £16 (£12 variable plus £4 fixed). The profit earned in the past year is:

	£	£
Sales revenue (4500 × £20)		90000
Less: cost of goods sold		
Opening stock	0	
Manufacturing costs (5000 × £16)	80000	
	80000	
Less: closing stock (500 × £16)	8000	
(4500 × £16)		72000
Gross profit		18000

2 *Variable costing.* The difference here is that only variable costs, at £12 per unit, are included in the cost of goods calculation. All fixed costs are deducted from the contribution earned. Making the calculation in the same format as above, the profit is:

	£	£
Sales revenue (4500 × £20)		90000
Less: variable cost of goods sold		
Opening stock	0	
Variable costs (5000 × £12)	60000	
	60000	

174 EFFECTIVE ACCOUNTING MANAGEMENT

	£	£
Less: closing stock (500 × £12)	6000	
(4500 × £12)		54000
Contribution		36000
Fixed overheads		20000
Gross profit		16000

There is an alternative format for the calculation of profit using variable costing.

Profit = (contribution per unit × volume) − fixed costs
= (£8 × 4500) − £20 000
= £16 000

where contribution is £8 per unit (sales revenue £20 − variable costs £12).

As can be seen from the simple example used here, the profit earned varies according to which method is used. Absorption costing gives the higher profit and stock valuation when production exceeds sales (that is, when stocks are being built up). The difference in profit is exactly matched by the difference in stock values.

Period 1	Gross profit	Closing stock
Absorption	£18 000	£8000
Variable	£16 000	£6000

It is hardly surprising that in such a situation companies will want to use the absorption costing figures in their financial accounts. They give a higher reported profit and higher stock values in the balance sheet. The problem comes when stocks are reduced. With absorption costing the fixed costs are written off in the profit and loss account when stocks are sold. So when stocks are run down/sold profits are reduced, as demonstrated below.

WORKED EXAMPLE: GARDEN GNOMES (PERIOD 2)

In the following period costs incurred remained identical. Five thousand gnomes were again manufactured but 5500 were sold, using up all the stock of gnomes.

1 *Absorption costing*

	£	£
Sales revenue (5500 × £20)		110000
Less: cost of goods sold		
Opening stock (500 × £16)	8000	
Production costs (5000 × 16)	80000	
	88000	
Less: closing stock	0	
		88000
Gross profit		22000

2 Variable costing

	£	£
Sales revenue (5500 × £20)		110000
Less: variable cost of goods sold		
Opening stock (500 × £12)	6000	
Variable production costs (5000 × £12)	60000	
	66000	
Closing stock	0	
		66000
Contribution		44000
Fixed costs		20000
		24000

A summary of the situation this time is:

Period 2	Gross profit	Closing stock
Absorption	£22 000	0
Variable	£24 000	0

When stocks are run down variable costing gives a higher profit than absorption costing. In the long run, if sales equal production, then both techniques will give the same reported profit. The difference between the techniques for profit measurement is merely in the timing of reporting the profits. However, use of the absorption costing technique could encourage managers not to reduce stock levels, contrary to the belief that stock sitting in a warehouse is a wasted resource.

Effect on decision making

Deleting a segment
Decisions that businesses often have to make relate to the content of their product ranges. Some lines that were profitable in the past may become unprofitable. Should the company continue to manufacture or should it delete the product?

WORKED EXAMPLE

Newfash Ltd produces its accounts using absorption costing principles. The results obtained in the past financial year for three of its products are:

	Small	Smaller	Smallest	Total
Sales revenue	240	180	70	490
Variable costs	−120	−100	−35	−255
Fixed costs	− 85	− 60	−45	−190
Gross profit	35	20	−10	45

The company is considering deleting the Smallest product, which it sees as loss making. Before arriving at a decision it asks the management accountant to look into the matter further. She discovers that if Smallest was discontinued, in the short term fixed costs would remain the same. Assuming that all other things remain the same, are there financial reasons why Smallest should be discontinued?

It would seem that Smallest is indeed making a loss and should be discontinued. From the information provided, we might be forgiven for thinking that deletion would mean the total profit rising to £55 (£35 Small + £20 Smaller). This is not the case and, to demonstrate this, the table is reproduced using variable costing principles:

	Smaller	Smaller	Smallest	Total
Sales revenue	240	180	70	490
Variable costs	120	100	35	255
Contribution	120	80	35	235
Fixed costs				190
Profit				45

It should be clear from this table that Smallest makes a contribution towards the fixed costs and profits of the company. If it was discontinued the contribution would be reduced to £200 (£120 Small + £80 Smaller). With fixed costs remaining at the same level the profit would be reduced to £10. This is worse than the existing situation, where £45 is being made. Only if the fixed costs can be reduced should Smallest be deleted.

The use of absorption costing information at face value without further investigation may lead to incorrect decisions being taken. Before any such decision is taken the effects on fixed costs must be examined. It may be that there are no cost reductions initially, but in the longer term there will be savings. In such a case it may be worth reducing profit now if there will be increased profits in the future.

In the same way that fixed overheads are allocated to products, head office charges in service industries are often allocated to branches. The rationale for this is that the branches would have to incur extra costs if the head office did not carry out certain tasks, such as advertising, recruitment and accounting. This may be true but in consideration of whether a branch should be closed they should be excluded, unless head office costs will be reduced by the closure.

Make or buy

In an age when assembly industries are increasing, one of the major decisions to be made by companies is whether to make a component themselves or to buy it in from a supplier.

WORKED EXAMPLE

A company makes a finished product using a number of components that the company currently makes itself. It has identified potential suppliers who can deliver as required and can guarantee quality at least equal to that in existing components. Overheads are absorbed to products on a direct labour hour basis, at a rate of £10 per hour. In the short term there would be no reduction in overheads. Which, if any, of the three components should be bought in?

	Z100	Z102	Z103
Direct labour hours	1	0.6	1.2
Cost per unit (£)	25.00	17.50	33.00
Outside price (£)	16.50	18.00	20.00

From the absorption cost information, components Z100 and Z103 would be bought in as the quoted price is less than the cost of producing them internally. However, if fixed costs do not actually reduce as a result of the decision they should not have been taken into account in making the decision. The variable costs per unit need to be found by taking out the fixed cost allocation.

	Z100	Z102	Z103
Direct labour hours	1	0.6	1.2
Overhead allocated (£)	10.00	6.00	12.00
Cost per unit (£)	25.00	17.50	33.00
Variable cost (£)	15.00	11.50	21.00
Outside price (£)	16.50	18.00	20.00

The variable cost shows the actual cost that will be incurred by the company if the components are manufactured internally. This can be compared to the outside price (which if bought in would become the variable cost). Only component Z103 can be bought in at a price lower than the variable cost, so only this component should be bought in.

Accepting a special order

Sometimes companies are asked by customers to produce a special order at a lower than usual price. Assuming there is spare capacity available, will it be financially viable for the company to accept the order?

WORKED EXAMPLE

Thyme Ltd manufactures a range of products for export. It normally produces and sells 5000 spice racks and expects to make £0.60 profit from each unit. Details of the cost (based on absorption costing) and revenue per unit are given below. The factory has some spare capacity and has been approached by a local customer to supply 500 units at £3.60 each. For this order there will be no selling and distribution costs incurred and fixed overheads will remain the same. Should Thyme Ltd accept the order?

178 EFFECTIVE ACCOUNTING MANAGEMENT

	£	£
Selling price		5.00
Variable manufacturing cost	2.60	
Fixed manufacturing cost	0.80	
Variable selling and distribution costs	0.40	
Fixed selling cost	0.60	4.40
Profit		0.60

If we take the product cost information at face value the company will make a loss of £0.80 per unit (£3.60 − £4.40) by accepting the order. Before the order is rejected we need to look in greater detail at the costs that will be incurred by taking on the order. The variable selling and distribution costs of £0.40 per unit will be saved. There will be no additional fixed costs at all and the amount allocated to the product can be ignored for the purposes of considering this contract. The only cost that will be incurred is the variable manufacturing cost of £2.60. This leaves a contribution of £1.00 per unit and, as there are no extra fixed costs, £500 extra profit.

Scarce resources
When resources are in short supply you may be unable to manufacture all the products you would like. You are then faced with the question of which product mix will maximize profit.

WORKED EXAMPLE
Newtech Industries manufactures printed circuit boards. Owing to a shortage of microchips it is unable to produce enough to meet the demand for its three product lines. The following information relates to the three products:

	Quick	Quicker	Quickest
Maximum demand (units)	10 000	8000	5000
Microchips per unit	3	4	5
Selling price per unit (£)	100	120	150
Cost per unit (£)			
Microchips	30	40	50
Other materials	13	17	20
Direct labour	10	10	15
Variable overheads	5	5	10
Fixed overhead	20	20	30
	78	92	125
Profit per unit (£)	22	28	25

ACCOUNTING INFORMATION FOR DECISION MAKING

Fixed overheads have been absorbed to products at 200 per cent of direct labour costs, in accordance with the company's absorption costing system. However, all three products share the same facilities and overheads for the year are estimated as being £400 000.

The total number of microchips that the company can purchase is restricted to 60 000. What combination of products will maximize the company's profit?

The first thing to do is to calculate how many components in total are required and to check that this is more than is available.

Quick	10000 units × 3 microchips	30000
Quicker	8000 units × 4 microchips	32000
Quickest	5000 units × 5 microchips	25000
Total microchips required		87000
Microchips available		60000

Looking at the absorption costing data we might think that the best combination would be to manufacture in the following order: Quicker, Quickest then Quick. This is the order of each product's profitability. The profit earned under this plan would be:

Product	Chips used	Units produced	Profit per unit	Profit
Quicker	32000	8000	£28	£224000
Quickest	25000	5000	£25	£125000
Quick	3000	1000	£22	£22000
	60000			£371000
Less under-absorbed overheads[a]				£70000
Total profit				£301000

[a] There is an under-absorption of overheads because the number of units produced will be insufficient to absorb all the costs incurred. The amount absorbed, £330 000 ((8000 × £20) + (5000 × £30) + (1000 × £20)), is £70 000 short of the £400 000 estimated overheads.

Ranking products by their profitability does not maximize overall profit. To find the optimal combination the products need to be ranked in order of the contribution earned for each unit of the limited resource used. First the contribution per unit must be calculated; then the result is divided by the number of microchips used.

Product	Profit per unit	Fixed overhead	Contribution per unit	Chips used	Contribution per chip
Quick	£22	£20	£42	3	£14
Quicker	£28	£20	£48	4	£12
Quickest	£25	£30	£55	5	£11

The order of ranking has changed. Now the preferred order of production will be: Quick, then Quicker, with no units of Quickest. The profit earned will be:

Product	Chips used	Units produced	Contribution per unit	Contribution
Quick	30000	10000	£42	£420000
Quicker	30000	7500	£48	£360000
	60000			£780000
Less fixed overheads				£400000
Total profit				£380000

The profit earned with this product mix is £54 000 higher than when the products are ranked in order of absorption costing profitability. In this example the problem with using the absorption costing information is exaggerated by the under-absorption of overheads. The optimal product mix can always be found by using the contribution per unit of scarce resource.

A few examples have been given above of how absorption costing figures can be misleading in decision making. Before we move on it is worth emphasizing, by repetition, that before any decision is made all the costs need to be investigated. In the short term fixed costs may not change and therefore the variable costs should be looked at. Decisions have long-term implications and it may be that fixed costs can be avoided over a longer time horizon (see figure 5.1). Changes to fixed costs should be identified and not estimated inaccurately by using the overhead allocated for absorption costing purposes.

Break Even Analysis

A business will break even when it makes neither a profit nor a loss; that is, when the costs incurred are exactly equal to the revenues received. A useful thing to know about your company is how many units of a product or what amount of services have to be sold before a profit is made. This type of analysis is known as break even analysis. It makes use of the marginal costing technique introduced in Unit Three. This means that costs and revenues are analysed according to their cost behaviour patterns. It is a technique that applies to the short term, within a period of about a year, in which time costs are unlikely to change dramatically. The technique will be demonstrated using the following example.

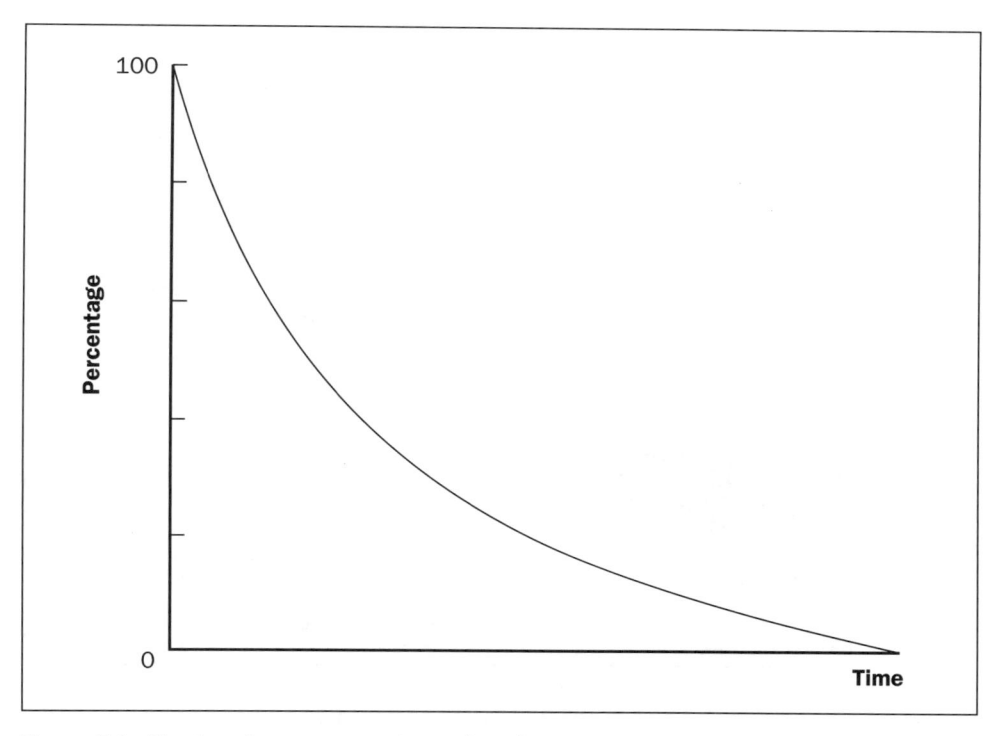

Figure 5.1 Fixed costs as a percentage of total costs.

WORKED EXAMPLE

The Greenton Guest House opens for 30 weeks during the 'season'. It has 20 double rooms, which are let for bed and breakfast at £25 per night. Fixed costs of £40 000 are incurred per annum. Variable costs are incurred at £5 per room per night occupied. An occupancy rate of 75 per cent is expected. How many nights do rooms need to be let during the season for the guest house to break even?

The break even chart

To be able to analyse this situation we need to construct a graph showing costs and revenue against the volume of activity. The first thing to do is to calculate the maximum number of rooms that are available for letting. This is 20 rooms, for seven nights a week, for 30 weeks, a total of 4200 nights. If all these were let £105 000 (4200 × £25) would be received. This gives us the maximum values that will be needed on the graph. All costs and revenue should now be plotted on the graph, as shown in figure 5.2.

Sales revenue is simply calculated as the number of nights rooms are let multiplied by the rate per night. If no rooms are let there will be no revenue. If rooms are occupied for 1000 nights the revenue will be £25 000. Where the revenue is earned at a constant rate per unit, total sales revenue will form a straight line. There is no need to work out the

182 EFFECTIVE ACCOUNTING MANAGEMENT

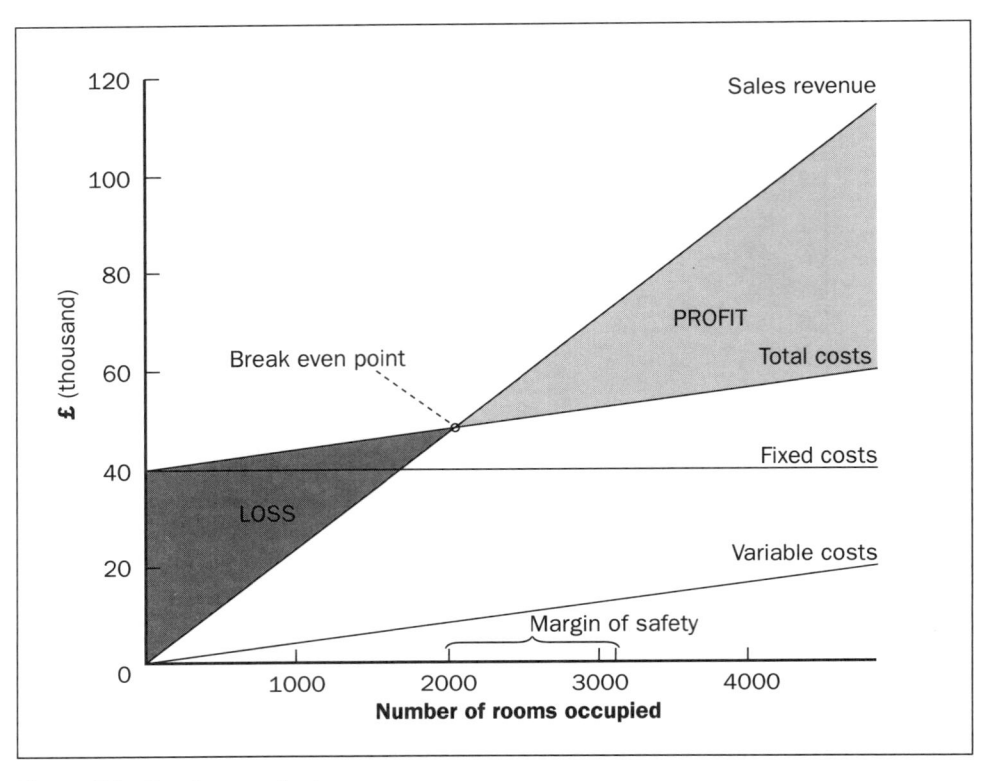

Figure 5.2 Break even chart.

revenue for each level of occupancy. Two values can be calculated and then a straight line is drawn passing through the two points.

Costs should first be calculated as separate elements, according to cost behaviour patterns, and then added together to give total costs. Fixed costs are constant regardless of occupancy, so are drawn as a straight horizontal line. Variable costs increase with occupancy and should be calculated in the same manner as sales revenue. At any given level of occupancy total costs are fixed costs plus variable costs, forming a line parallel to the variable cost line.

The break even point is the point where the sales revenue line meets the total cost line, and can be read easily off the graph. It can be expressed either in physical terms, that is rooms let for 2000 nights, or in monetary terms, that is sales revenue and total costs of £50 000. A profit is made at any volume to the right of the break even point and a loss is made at any point to the left. The size of the profit or loss at any level can be measured as the distance between the cost and revenue lines. For example, with rooms occupied for 4000 nights the costs are £60 000, the revenue £100 000 and the profit £40 000.

The margin of safety is an expression used to describe the difference between the expected volume and the break even volume. In this example

ACCOUNTING INFORMATION FOR DECISION MAKING

the expected occupancy rate is 75 per cent; that is, 75 per cent of the maximum 4200 lettings, 3150 lettings. The margin of safety is therefore 3150 − 2000 = 1150. This is the number of lettings by which volume can fall below that expected before a loss-making situation is experienced. It is sometimes expressed as a percentage of the expected level; in this example the number of lettings can drop by 36.5 per cent before a loss is made.

Calculation of the break even point

The break even point can be found by calculating some simple formulae, as well as from the construction of a graph. The graphical method has the advantages of good presentation and of being easily understood by those without a financial background. The formulae give results very quickly and should be used when conducting initial analysis or considering alternative scenarios, using the graphs for presentation.

The formulae make extensive use of *contribution*, as introduced earlier in this unit. A quick reminder of how it is calculated may be helpful: sales revenue earned less variable costs. Once sufficient revenue has been earned to cover the variable costs the remainder contributes towards the fixed costs and profits of the company. The break even point occurs where the contribution earned exactly meets the fixed costs.

In the example, the contribution per room per night is £25 − £5 = £20.

$$\text{Break even point (in volume)} = \frac{\text{Fixed overheads}}{\text{Contribution per unit}}$$

$$= \frac{40\,000}{20} = 2000 \text{ lettings}$$

Break even point in (£) = break even volume × sales revenue per unit
= 2000 × £25 = £50 000

Profit at any volume level = (volume × contribution per unit) − fixed overheads

For example, at the 75 per cent occupancy rate (3150 room lettings):
(3150 × £20) − £40 000 = £23 000

$$\text{Volume to meet required profit} = \frac{\text{Required profit + fixed costs}}{\text{Contribution per unit}}$$

If £30 000 is the required profit:

$$= \frac{£30\,000 + £40\,000}{£20} = 3500 \text{ lettings}$$

Now tackle Activity AM5.2.

184 EFFECTIVE ACCOUNTING MANAGEMENT

ACTIVITY AM5.2

TEFL

Activity code
- ✓ Self-development
- ✓ Teamwork
- ✓ Communications
- ✓ Numeracy/IT
- ✓ Decisions

A report by independent government assessors on the local college had emphasized the competence, if not the excellence, of the language department and of the business section. These points confirmed what the staff already knew. Tom, the unit leader for languages, and Bill, who ran the business courses, discussed matters as follows.

Tom: 'Frankly, Bill, your business courses have come out top and so have my language team. With a joint academic staff of ten people, we should start a Business English College.'

Bill: 'A buy-out.'

Tom: 'No, don't be daft, Bill, we can't buy them out. But, at the end of the day, this place pays a salary which is none too impressive, and the number of students increases daily, with more and more tutorials, marking and demands being placed on us. Add to that the 1950s scientific management view of the directorate who wish to treat us like proletarians while they award themselves bonuses for additional student numbers, and where does it leave us?'

Bill: 'Nowhere, and things are going downhill fast. What can we do, though? Most of the lecturers in the business area may get work outside the college, but the language people are trapped – unless some nice translation job comes up in the EC. I'm tired of the whole thing: we used to be a college, now we're a factory for degrees and technical business qualifications at the lower end of the educational spectrum. The lecturers are demotivated, they are sick of all these new bureaucratic controls, the management style stinks and the labour relations around here are not worth a candle!'

Bill: 'I agree Tom. I would add that this place has some limited government funding – which is decreasing year by year – along with its staff. It is the expertise of its lecturers which makes a college a place of excellence. We have the expertise that the market wants.'

Both 'partners' sat down later on. Both agreed that although their salaries were not brilliant they had, unlike most, tenure. The pension was poor compared to other peers and the motivation to remain in this profession for the next twenty-odd years was certainly not there.

'We'll need to work through a business plan and we need to work out the pennies. In essence, we'll need a cash flow projection for ensuring the business runs and a break even analysis.' Both agreed that this break even analysis would make or break the embryonic venture.

They agreed that there were several 'products' in the new venture and a break even analysis would focus the decision making of the parties on the 'product' that would run faster than the others.

'Principles first: practice follows' was the time-honoured motto of these academics. They picked up a handout from the business department on costs.

Principles
Costs can be broken down into fixed costs, which remain constant over a period, and variable costs, which are seen to relate to the level of activity.
- Fixed costs tend to include property rate and government taxes on property etc., leasing of vehicles and some fixed salaries (at least for a given period).
- Variable costs will include direct labour (e.g. lecturers paid by the hour), electricity, heating and materials from books to manuals of instruction.
- Some costs are 'step fixed' which behave as fixed costs but may jump if the college has to expand dramatically in floor space, to accommodate more students, for example. Other costs do not fit neatly into the fixed/variable categories as they include elements of both fixed and variable costs. The phone rental will be fixed but the phone call costs, particularly if there is telephone selling, will be variable.
- Fixed costs tend to remain the same irrespective of the output but fixed costs per unit (student) will vary with output.
- Variable costs tend to vary with the level of activity, but they remain reasonably constant at all levels of output.
- The 'contribution' made by a product or service is the sales price less its variable costs.
- A break even analysis can be constructed via charts (vertical axis, money; horizontal axis, output in units or students) to show the potential point of profit/loss.
- A margin of safety can be built into these groups to ensure that losses are not sustained.

Practices
Various options (A to D) are open to the new partners.

Option A
- Rent a college and recruit permanent staff.
- Fixed costs would be considerable, amounting to about £200 000 p.a.
- The short public course selling price per student is based on a monthly figure of £120 per student.
- The variable costs per student are some £40 per month.
- The expected monthly 'turnover' is some 100 students.

Option B
- Rent a college and recruit only temps to do the inputs. Fixed costs reduced to £120 000 p.a.
- The short public course selling price per student on a monthly basis is £120 per student.
- The variable costs per student increase to £70 per student per month owing to the labour dimension.
- Some 100 students are expected in a month.

Option C
- Rent a smaller college, recruit a core full-time staff and do 'in-house' work for companies in language training. Fixed costs are £100 000 p.a.
- The 'in-house' selling price per student on a monthly basis is £160. The variable costs increase through advertising and some non-core labour to £80 per student per month.
- Some 100 students are expected in a month.

Option D
- Rent a smaller college, operate with only temporary staff and do 'in-house' work for companies in language training. Fixed costs are reduced to £65 000.
- The selling price is £160 per student per month. The variable costs, including advertising and non-core labour, amount to £100 per student per month.
- Some 100 students are expected in a month.

Tasks
1. Construct break even charts for each scenario.
2. Allow, in addition, for a margin of safety of some 10 per cent.
3. Make a decision on which of these scenarios is the best option. Note why (in about 100 words).

The relevant range

One of the flaws of the break even analysis conducted above is the assumption of linearity. That is, it is assumed that fixed costs stay the same regardless of volume and that variable costs rise in a constant proportion. An economist would say that the preceding analysis was too simple. Cost patterns are not linear but curved, reflecting bulk discounts received, efficient working and economies of scale. Revenue patterns are also not linear. To achieve increased sales volume prices must be reduced. A break even chart as might be drawn by an economist recognizes the non-linearity and shows the true pattern of costs at different volume levels. Such a chart is compared to the accountant's version (see figure 5.3).

As can be seen, there is a range of volumes over which the two charts look very similar. This is known as the *relevant range*. The accountant's model provides a close approximation to the true underlying pattern of costs within this range. As long as we are aware that the accountant's

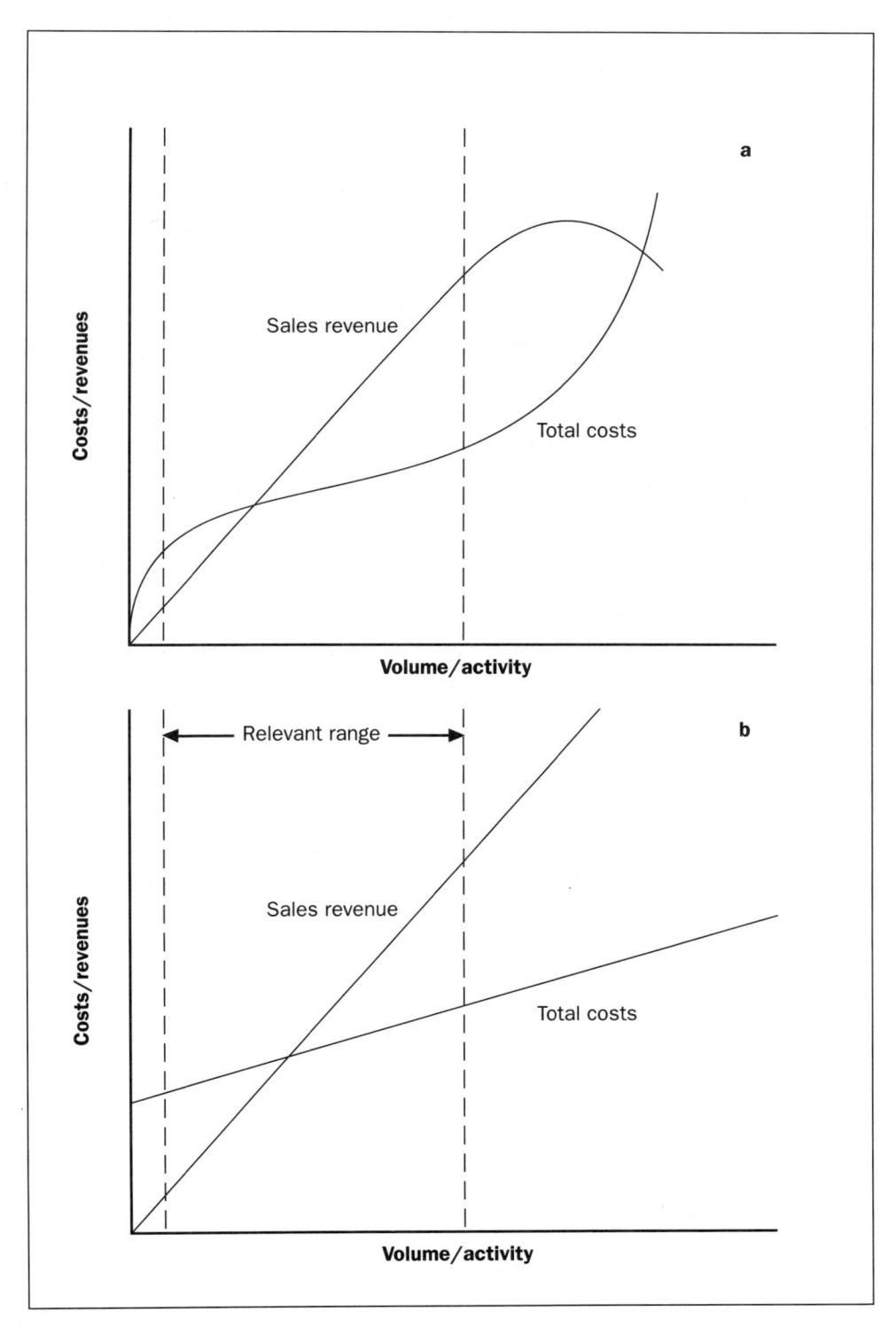

Figure 5.3 The economist's chart (a) and the accountant's chart (b): a comparison.

188 EFFECTIVE ACCOUNTING MANAGEMENT

model is only accurate within the relevant range we may use it. The data on which the accountant's model is based relate to the most likely level of activity. The relevant range is therefore around the most likely level of operation and extends to perhaps plus and minus 50 per cent (that is, with a likely volume of 5000 units the relevant range would be 2500–7500 units). Outside this range special studies need to be conducted to investigate behaviour, as there is a significant change to the activity level.

Sensitivity (what if?) analysis

Once the initial data have been analysed, changes can then be introduced to see what effect they have on profits earned or the break even point. If one of the raw materials used in your manufacturing process is susceptible to major price fluctuations you can anticipate the effect on your operations ahead of time. You may want to analyse the effect of a change in interest rates if a large proportion of fixed costs are interest related. Consider the effect on Greeton's profit if fixed costs were to rise from £40 000 per annum to £45 000. Break even volume = £45 000 ÷ £20 = 2250, an increase of 250 nights, or 12.5 per cent, on the previous break even volume of 2000 nights. Expected profit (at 75 per cent) = (3150 × £20) − £45 000 = £18 000, a fall of 21.7 per cent from the previous profit of £23 000.

Rather than just analysing minor changes to the existing situation, you can also analyse the effect of major changes. Before going ahead with changes you will probably want to know the effect on profit. This can be done quite easily on the break even chart, as shown in the following example.

WORKED EXAMPLE

A company manufactures a single product. It expects to sell between 800 and 1200 units in the coming year, with the most likely level being 1000 units at a selling price of £100 per unit. It is considering the purchase of a machine that would reduce the amount of labour required. The costs for the two methods are:

	Existing	New machine
Cost per unit (£)		
Direct materials	25.00	25.00
Direct labour	30.00	10.00
Variable overhead	15.00	5.00
Annual costs (£)		
Fixed overheads	15 000	40 000

Sales revenue will be the same for the two methods, the only difference on a chart being the costs. Both are plotted on figure 5.4.

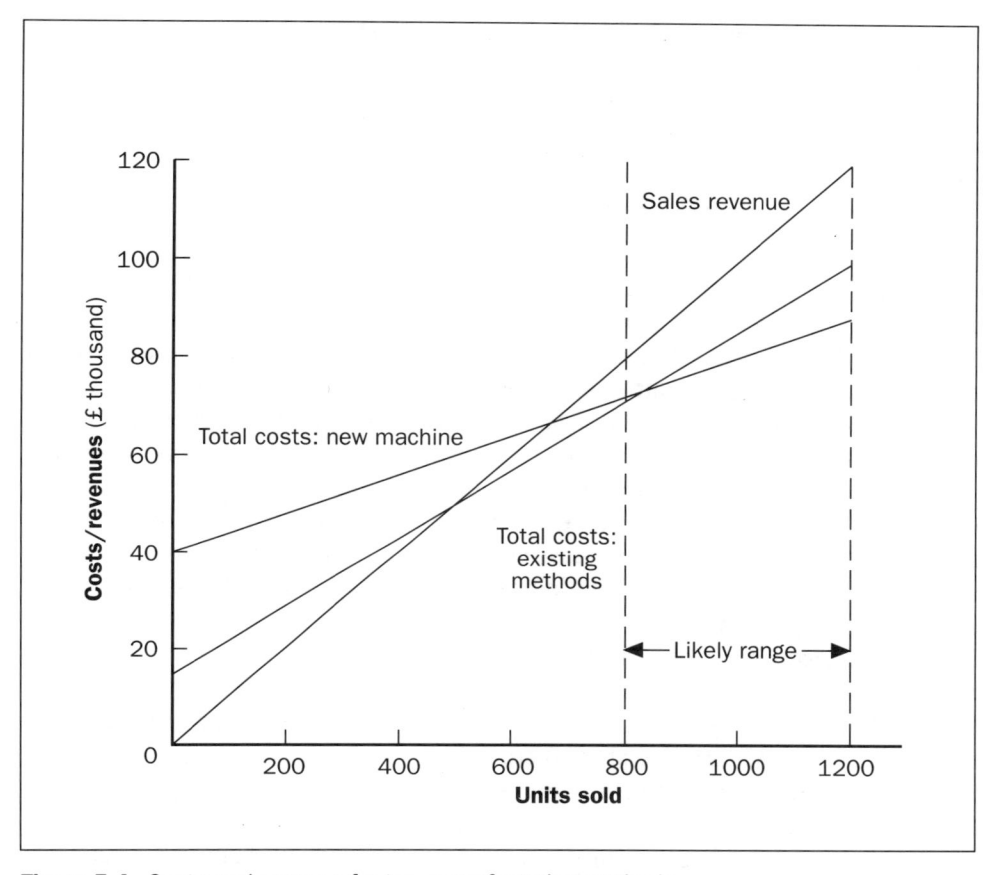

Figure 5.4 Costs and revenue for two manufacturing methods.

The second cost line starts much higher than the original line, but rises less quickly. The break even point is much higher for the method using the new machine (667 units) than for the existing method (500). Conversely, the margin of safety is much lower for the second method (333 units) than for the first method (500). You may conclude from this that the existing method is preferred to the new, but is this in the relevant range? We have been told that sales are expected to be between 800 and 1200 units, so this is where we should be looking. First look at the most likely level, 1000 units. The expected profit under the old method is £15 000, but under the new method it is £20 000. At the 1200 unit level the increase in profit is even greater (£32 000 compared to £21 000). It is only at the lower level of 800 units that there is cause for concern. The profit from the new method (£8000) is less than for the old (£9000). At all levels above 833 units (where the two cost lines meet) the new method is preferred.

Pricing

One of the most important decisions facing a business is how much to charge for its goods and services. The level the price is set at will help to determine the level of demand for the product. If the price is high few will be demanded, if the price is low a high quantity will be demanded. In economists' terms the relationship between price and demand is known as the *price elasticity of demand*. For some goods, typically non-essential goods, elasticity is high. This means that the volume of sales will drop very quickly as prices go up. For other goods, typically essential goods, demand is inelastic. That is, as price goes up volume does not fall very much. There are many factors affecting the elasticity of demand for a particular product, and it is management's responsibility to understand these before it attempts to set a price.[2]

In some circumstances there is no decision to be made, as the company is a price taker. If the price is not set at the market level no sales will be achieved. In such cases, a company whose average costs are higher than the selling price will not be able to survive.

Most companies operate in what is called an *imperfect* market. They will have some degree of freedom in choosing the price level. It is generally assumed that in such cases prices will be set at a level that will maximize profits. In order to determine the maximum profit, analysis has to be conducted, looking at both the sales revenue generated and the costs incurred. Maximizing sales revenue does not always maximize profits, as demonstrated in the following example.

WORKED EXAMPLE

Drummond Ltd has been formed to manufacture a single product. Estimated production, selling, distribution and administration costs include a fixed element of £20 000 per year and variable costs of £2 per unit. They wish to set a selling price that will maximize profit. They have received the results (below) of some market research, which identifies the most likely demand for the product at a range of different price levels.

Price (£)	3.00	3.50	4.00	4.50	5.00
Sales volume	20 000	17 500	15 000	12 500	10 000

As we are seeking to maximize profit, we need to calculate profit at each of these price/demand levels. First the sales revenue is calculated and then total costs are deducted to give the expected profit.

Demand	20000	17500	15000	12500	10000
Price (£)	3.00	3.50	4.00	4.50	5.00
Sales revenue (£)	60000	61250	60000	56250	50000
Variable costs (£)	40000	35000	30000	25000	20000
Fixed costs (£)	20000	20000	20000	20000	20000
Total costs (£)	60000	55000	50000	45000	40000
Profit (£)	0	6250	10000	11250	10000

As can be seen from the table, the best price level is £4.50, where 12 500 units are demanded and a profit of £11 250 will be earned. Note this is not where sales revenue is maximized; that is when a price of £3.50 is charged and 17 500 units are demanded. The optimal price gives £5000 less sales revenue but the variable costs are £10 000 less, making a £5000 difference in profit earned. Note that the largest sale quantity gives no profit at all. Although many units are sold there is very little contribution coming from each unit, and in this example the total contribution only just covers the fixed costs.

It is important when setting price levels to consider costs as much as the revenue in the short term. However, in order to achieve longer-term strategic objectives the price may be set at a level different from that which would be optimal in the short term. The sales or revenue maximizing price may be chosen to eliminate competitors or to develop customer preferences. Once the volume of sale is achieved, a company can then look at its cost structure to see where reductions can be made and efficiencies of scale achieved.

Cost-based pricing

There are some circumstances where there are no generally available market prices; for example, products that are highly specialized and perhaps made to the customer's own specifications. Orders will go to the business that can deliver adequate quality at the lowest price. If there is no market guidance, how do these businesses determine a price? Often the approach taken will be to start by estimating costs and then to add on an allowance for profit.

Before we address the question of what costs to use let's deal with the issue of mark-ups. A simple example is where an item is sold for £1.00, the cost is 75p and the profit earned is therefore 25p. The profit element could be described in relation to the cost element: this is known as the *mark-up*. In this case the profit of 25p is divided by the cost of 75p, giving a mark-up ratio of one-third or 33 per cent. Alternatively, the profit element could be described as a percentage of the total selling price: this is known as the *profit margin*. In this case the profit of 25p is divided by the selling price of

100p, giving a profit margin of 25 per cent. Different companies and different industries use the two different conventions in expressing the profit element, so it is as well to establish which method is being used by a particular company.

We now move on to the question of what definition of cost to use. We again come back to the old argument about how to treat overheads. Problems encountered earlier mostly dealt with product costing for stock valuation and profit measurement. There the cost of a product included only manufacturing costs, other overheads being treated separately in the profit and loss account. When making pricing decisions you need to make sure sufficient revenue is being generated to cover *all costs*, including selling, distribution and administration. There are two basic approaches to costing for pricing, each of which is looked at below.

Full cost plus

This is similar to absorption costing except that all costs are included. Appropriate bases need to be found to absorb sales, distribution and administrative costs to individual products and services. Prices will need to be quoted and agreed before an order is placed. As the actual costs that will be incurred are not yet known they must be estimated and predetermined overhead absorption rates used. Absorption rates will be calculated using estimates of costs and also estimates of the level of activity. Once costs have been estimated a profit element can be added on to find the final price. This method of pricing is frequently used in practice. One advantage is that a well tried formula allows pricing to be delegated to fairly low levels of management.

The disadvantage of this approach is that orders might be lost by pricing too high. If this occurs, it is possible that the volume of work received is less than that assumed when absorption calculations were made. This may lead to under-absorption of overheads and could lead to a loss being made, despite only orders with a good profit margin being accepted.

WORKED EXAMPLE

Peter's Posters has the capacity to print 50 000 posters a year. It has operated at full capacity for a number of years and was expecting to again at the start of this year. Estimated costs are 20p variable costs per poster and fixed costs of £50 000 per annum. Prices are set by adding a 20 per cent mark-up to the predetermined absorbed cost per poster, and no discounts are given on this price. A downturn in the market meant that because of the pricing policy orders for only 40 000 posters were actually received during the year. Assuming costs were as estimated, what profit was earned?

Calculation of selling price:

Variable cost	20p
Fixed costs (£50 000 ÷ 50 000 posters)	100p
	120p
Mark-up (20 per cent of 120p)	24p
Selling price	144p

Profit and loss account:

	£	£
Sales revenue (40 000 × 144p)		57600
Variable costs (40 000 × 20p)	8000	
Fixed costs	50000	58000
Loss		(400)

The loss is the result of failing to achieve full capacity. In making the price calculation it had been assumed that 50 000 posters would be sold. The 10 000 posters that were not sold had been allocated fixed overheads of £1 each. This cost has not been recovered. If the company had a more flexible pricing policy it might have been able to achieve full capacity. Although the profit earned would not have been as high as initially estimated, the company would stand a better chance of making a profit than with unused capacity.

Variable cost plus

The absolute minimum price that a company can charge is the variable cost. Anything above this produces some contribution towards fixed costs and eventually profit. However, if all orders were priced at or just above variable cost, insufficient contribution would be earned to meet fixed costs. In order to avoid this, guidelines are usually given to add on a percentage to the variable costs, sufficient that all costs are covered and a profit is earned. The profit percentage would of course be higher than when using full cost plus; for example, variable cost plus 100 per cent rather than full cost plus 10 per cent.

Now please tackle Activity AM5.3.

ACTIVITY AM5.3

THE LONDON BREWING COMPANY

Activity code
- ✓ Self-development
- ✓ Teamwork
- ☐ Communications
- ✓ Numeracy/IT
- ✓ Decisions

The London Brewing Company has some 7500 employees and sales of almost £800 million per annum. As the name suggests, it was founded in London, and the head office remains there. Times have moved on, though, and given its national and increasing international market, it should perhaps be renamed 'the UK Brewing Company'.

The company moved out of London into geographical 'divisions' after the Second World War. With acquisitions and the removal of some of the fiercest local competition through a policy of attrition, the six geographical divisions became regional companies responsible for their own costs and profitability. Increasingly, each of the regional companies has been given fuller autonomy. Apart from the corporate plan, capital/investment projects and the overall marketing plan, each company is virtually independent.

The focal point of each regional company is a brewery, so there are six breweries altogether making over forty-five different beers and lagers. On the retail side there are 4221 tenanted public houses, thirty-two shops specializing in selling wines, beers and spirits, and eight 'inherited' inns-cum-restaurants, all in East Anglia. The pubs and inns are controlled by the regional companies while the shop side is controlled by a specialist company based in Stevenage, Hertfordshire. Each of the companies has a regional board of directors, whose chairperson is on the main board in London.

The management meeting on pricing strategy for the new product was dragging on. Even the accounting advice was divided. The marketing team, as ever, gave several options but did not come down on one side or the other. The views can be summarized as follows.

The *sales* unit within the auspices of the overall marketing department wanted lower prices. Their argument was that this not only would give market entry but would sustain a longer-term policy of increasing market share.

The mainstream *marketing* view was to have a steady rate of return, avoiding the quick buck vision of some of the competition but pricing higher than the sales people suggested. The company was too well established for such 'loss leaders'. Even then, a minority view was that the overall portfolio was the issue and that this new product was neither here nor there, so it could be sold as a 'loss leader'. The sales people were not unhappy with this perspective.

The *mainstream marketeers* felt that the marketplace dictates the price. Within that market, the aim of the steady rate of return over the projected life span (five years, with perhaps another three or four with revamping) would give the best return.

The *accountants* believed that the marketplace did not have to be 'right'. Others were pursuing their policies from loss leading to milking the market in the short term. The costs of manufacturing plus some 'add on' was the main pricing advice of the accountants. One view was that the total cost method should be used. All production costs need to be absorbed: the raw materials, the labour, the ongoing overheads from maintenance to cleaning and the costs of advertising and selling would all have to be taken into account. *A minority view among the accountants* believed in another formula. 'Look, a lot of these costs are fixed, so we need to go for the variable cost per unit. Ally this to demand or expected demand and we can pitch in at the best selling price according to its contribution. This route takes account of the market rate (via demand expectation) and our real costs, which are variable, not fixed.'

Tasks
1 Examine the figures below.
2 Determine a pricing policy from each of these perspectives and calculate a contribution table for the fourth perspective.
3 Which final pricing policy should be adopted and why? Justify your response in a mini-report.

Sales: 'take home' beer
This is not a premium beer. The main competition in our region sells a four pack low/medium standard of beer as follows (main supermarket chains):

	Four pack selling price	
'Crusader'	£2.00 to £2.20	average £2.15
'Swordsman'	£1.80 to £1.95	average £1.90
'Gallant'	£1.50 to £1.90	average £1.80
'Warrior'	£2.60 to £2.90	average £2.65
'Gladiator'	£2.95 to £3.10	average £2.95
'Victor'	£2.50 to £2.59	average £2.53
'Merrymate'	£2.20 to £2.25	average £2.24
'The King'	£1.80 to £1.90	average £1.85
'The Queen'	£2.35 to £2.60	average £2.52
'Prince'	£2.00 to £2.50	average £2.40

196 EFFECTIVE ACCOUNTING MANAGEMENT

Marketing

The life span of this beer is some eight years in all. It is not particularly unusual and it is not the cheapest, but it fills a hole in our overall product portfolio.

Product portfolio			Retail price (£)	Approx. demand (daily × four packs)
Lager	premium	XX	3.30	10 000
	↓	X	3.00	12 000
	↓	yy	2.70	18 000
	Lower level	y	2.50	17 500
Beer	Super	AA	3.30	9000
	↓	A	3.00	11 000
	↓	ZZ	2.30	17 000
	Lower level	Z	2.00	16 300

Product Z has been going too long, and advertising, which is costly, is keeping it up. We need to replace Z or ZZ ultimately with this lower/medium beer.

Accounting

All overheads must be met. We have carefully worked out the overhead cost of each four pack of the new brand. Indirect materials, labour, expenses, all according to the total costs incurred by each centre with an allowance for service departments, means that the true cost in overheads of our new four pack is some £1.50. Assuming our normal mark-up (25 per cent) and the allowance for the retail outlets of about $12\frac{1}{2}$ per cent on top of that, the price of our new beer speaks for itself.

The other group within the accountants favoured a different approach. The fixed costs should be asided and really written off against the 'contribution'. (The difference between sales and the variable costs.)

The demand is seen as between 16 300 and 18 500.

The variable cost per unit (4 can pack): amounts to 20p/unit on sales of 16 300, rising to 22p/unit on 17 000, and falling to 19p/unit on 17 500 and to 16p on 18 500.

Fixed costs: they amount to £16 300 on the 16 300 total; to £17 000 on the 17 000 total; £17 000 on 17 500; and slightly up at £17 800 on the 18 500 throughput.

The Company likes a profit of some 25 per cent (total contribution less fixed costs).

The price cannot really alter with volume given the nature of the product.

If we pitch in with a price of £1.80 per four pack how will this impact on our 'contribution' table? Is there a more realistic price structure than £1.80 (plus retailer's mark-up of $12\frac{1}{2}$ per cent)?

Long-term Decision Making

Long-term decisions (sometimes called capital investment or investment appraisal decisions) typically involve the outlay of cash now, in the expectation of receiving cash flows in the future. Exactly the same principles are used as with any decision. It is much more important to identify the timing of the cash flows because differences in timing need to be taken into consideration. In any analysis care needs to be taken to identify exactly when cash flows occur, taking into account such things as when taxes will be paid.

Time value of money

People attach different values to money depending on when they will receive the cash. If you were given a choice between £1000 now or £1000 to be received in one year's time, which would you choose? Probably the £1000 today. Generally we expect to get more in the future because of the delay in receipt.

Worked example: adjusting for the time value of money

Fred is due some money and has been given a choice between receiving £1000 now or £1200 in two years' time. If the money is taken now it could be invested in a building society and earn a nominal rate of interest of 10 per cent per annum. Which should Fred choose?

One way of looking at this choice is to work out the value of the £1000 after it has been invested for two years in the building society.

In year 1: £1000 × 1.1 = £1100
In year 2: £1100 × 1.1 = £1210

Taking the money now and putting it in the building society would give Fred £1210 after two years. He should select this option as it gives him £10 more after two years than he is currently being offered.

Another way of working out the value of an amount invested for a period of time is to use the compound interest rate formula. This is useful when an amount is to be invested for a long period of time.

Future value = Present value × $(1 + r)^n$

where r is the interest rate (expressed as a decimal) and n is the number of time periods. In the above example:

Future value = £1000 × $(1.1)^2$ = £1210

Another way of looking at the value of receipts is to look at the future values of cash flow and express them all in today's terms. This is the approach usually taken in textbooks when they look at investment decisions. It is known as the *present value approach*, and it is calculated by rearranging the formula used above.

$$\text{Present value} = \frac{\text{Future value}}{(1+r)^n}$$

The part of the formula below the line is called the discount factor, and this can be looked up in discount tables. An extract from such a table is shown below. What is being shown is the present value of £1, depending on the interest rate and when it is to be received.

Year	5%	6%	7%	8%	9%	10%
0	1.000	1.000	1.000	1.000	1.000	1.000
1	0.952	0.943	0.935	0.926	0.917	0.909
2	0.907	0.890	0.873	0.857	0.842	0.826
3	0.864	0.840	0.816	0.794	0.772	0.751
4	0.823	0.792	0.763	0.735	0.708	0.683
5	0.784	0.747	0.713	0.681	0.650	0.621
6	0.746	0.705	0.666	0.630	0.596	0.564

To use the tables you simply look down the rows for the number of years required and along the columns for the interest rate. For example, the present value of £2000 to be received in three years' time with an interest rate of 8 per cent is

£2000 × 0.794 = £1588

Using the formula for Fred, the present value of the £1200 to be received in two years' time is

$$\text{Present value} = \frac{£1200}{(1.1)^2} = £991.68$$

Or, using the discount table,

Present value = £1200 × 0.826 = £991.20

Note that there is a slight difference in the results obtained from the formula and the discount table. The formula gives the accurate result, while the discount table results in a small rounding error. Either method can be used but in the following examples we will use the formula.

The meaning of the calculation is that £1200 to be received in two years is equivalent to £991.68 today. This present value can be compared to the other choice, which is already expressed in today's terms. The conclusion is the same as that made when looking at future values: take the first option of £1000 now.

When making comparisons it does not really matter which method you use. Whether future values or present values are used, the conclusion will be the same. It is more usual for the present value to be used because it is today that decisions have to be taken and therefore values are expressed in today's terms. Please refer to Box AM5.1.

> **BOX AM5.1**
>
> ### Factors affecting the time value of money
>
> The value people attach to money to be received in the future is influenced by three factors:
>
> - *Interest rates*: how much the money would earn in the intervening period, by being deposited in a bank, building society or other investment.
> - *Inflation rates*: the quantity of goods and services that can be bought today compared to how much could be bought next year. In making a comparison you may have to predict prices a year ahead and see what quantity can be bought. You may not have to do this if the price of goods is expected to rise in line with general inflation (in the UK called the retail price index, which measures the increase in the price of a basket of goods). Nominal interest rates predict the general inflation rate. The nominal interest rate is that rate which is quoted by a bank or building society. The nominal rate includes both the real rate of interest and the expected inflation rate. If you use the nominal rate of interest to make comparisons there is no need to adjust for inflation too. However, if you are affected by specific inflation (the increase in price of the particular items you want to buy), you will have to make an adjustment.
> - *Urgency for consumption*: if we need to buy goods and services now, it is of no interest to us how much we can buy in the future.

Methods of Appraising Investments

A number of methods are used by companies to analyse investments. Some are simple rules of thumb and others are more complex. Sometimes these different methods give conflicting advice, especially when more than one project is being compared. The more complex methods have been proved to be theoretically superior, yet the simple rules still find favour in practice. Four different methods of appraisal will be looked at, using a simple example to demonstrate each technique. Before looking at the techniques of appraisal it is worth noting that the quality of the appraisal is only as good as the data being analysed. The most important part of looking at an investment is correctly to identify all cash flows and when they occur.

WORKED EXAMPLE

Bluebell Ltd is thinking about launching a new product. It would involve making an initial investment of £100 000 for plant and machinery. The product would have an expected life of four years. After this time the machine will be sold for scrap, estimated as giving £10 000. Funds can be borrowed to finance the project at an interest rate of 10 per cent. The company expects to earn net cash flows (revenue received less costs incurred) of:

Year 1	(10 000)
Year 2	60 000
Year 3	95 000
Year 4	65 000

Net present value (NPV)

This uses the concept of present values, introduced above, to express all the cash flows in today's terms. For each period of the investment the net cash flow is identified and is discounted at the appropriate interest rate. The initial investment, which is already expressed as a present value, is then deducted from the other present values. If the result is positive, the investment should go ahead. If the result is negative, it should be rejected. The calculations could be conducted on a monthly basis to obtain a really accurate result. However, it is more usual for some accuracy to be sacrificed, with annual cash flows being used.

In Bluebell Ltd the net cash flows have been estimated for each year. There is one adjustment to be made to these figures. At the end of year 4, when the project is complete, the plant and machinery will be sold, bringing in another £10 000 cash in that year. The discounted cash flows for the project will be:

Year	Cash flow	Discount factor		Present value
1	(10000)	× 1/(1.1)	=	(9091)
2	60000	× $1/(1.1^2)$	=	49587
3	95000	× $1/(1.1^3)$	=	71375
4	75000	× $1/(1.1^4)$	=	51226
				163097
Initial investment				(100000)
Net present value				63097

From this analysis we can see that this investment is worthwhile, as it produces a positive net present value.

Although these calculations might look quite difficult, they can in fact be performed very easily on a computer spreadsheet, using the NPV function. To use this function you first have to enter the cash flows in a range of cells, with the initial investment in the first cell of the range. The NPV function runs by taking information about the interest rate and the location of the cash flows. The result appears in seconds.

Internal rate of return (IRR)

This second technique (sometimes known as the discounted cash flow yield) also makes use of the concept of present values. It is the interest rate that will give a net present value of zero for the investment. It is found by trial and error. The higher the interest rate the lower the net present value, which eventually becomes zero and then negative. Again it looks complicated to calculate, but it too can be performed on a computer spreadsheet, using the IRR function, which works in a similar fashion to the NPV function.

For the project being considered by Bluebell the net present values at various interest rates are shown below.

Year	Cash flow	PV (20%)	PV (25%)	PV (30%)
1	(10000)	(8333)	(8000)	(7692)
2	60000	41667	38400	35503
3	95000	54977	48640	43240
4	75000	36168	30720	26260
		124479	109760	97311
Initial investment		(100000)	(100000)	(100000)
Net present value		24479	9760	(2689)

As you can see, the net present value at 25 per cent is positive but at 30 per cent it is negative. The internal rate of return lies somewhere between 25 and 30 per cent. An approximate value can be found using a mathematical technique known as interpolation. It is not demonstrated here owning to its complexity and it does not give a completely accurate result. Making use of a computerized spreadsheet package will always give the correct result and is much faster. In the Bluebell example the internal rate of return is calculated as being 28.8 per cent. The net present values obtained at different interest rates can be plotted on a graph to form a curve, as shown for Bluebell in figure 5.5. You can see from this that the internal rate of return is the point where the curve cuts the horizontal axis.

Payback period

This is a simple rule of thumb that is often used for the initial assessment of projects. It is the amount of time that elapses before the initial investment is repaid. The calculation is very simple, the total cash flows

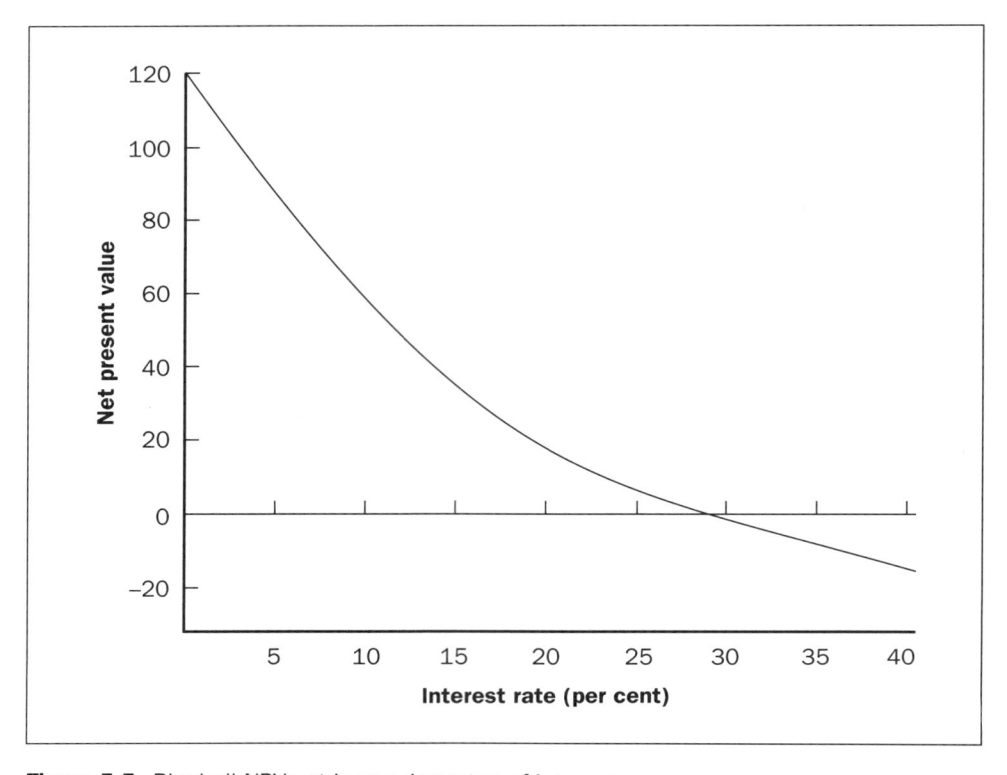

Figure 5.5 Bluebell NPVs at increasing rates of interest.

(both outgoing and incoming) are added together to give a running total, as shown for Bluebell below.

Year	Cash flow	Cumulative cash flow
0	(100 000)	(100 000)
1	(10 000)	(110 000)
2	(60 000)	(50 000)
3	95 000	45 000
4	75 000	120 000

Here we can see that the project has a negative cash flow at the end of the second year but by the end of the third year it is positive. The payback period is between the second and third year. We can find the exact period by finding the proportion of the year that has passed when the cumulative cash flow reaches zero. At the start of the year another £50 000 needed to be received, and during the year a total of £95 000 was received. Assuming that the cash comes in equally during the year a direct proportion can be taken: £50 000 ÷ £90 000 = 0.53. Just after half way through the year payback is achieved, so the payback period for this project is 2.53 years.

Companies set minimum payback targets, for example five years. If a project's payback period is less than the target it will be accepted. Any

ACCOUNTING INFORMATION FOR DECISION MAKING

project taking longer than the target will be rejected. It is likely that the project being considered by Bluebell will be accepted because of its very short payback period.

The popularity of this method lies in its simplicity, in terms of both calculation and understanding. It does, however, have a major disadvantage in that it ignores anything that happens after the payback period. It merely measures the time taken to repay and does not look at the relative profitability of projects.

Accounting rate of return (ARR)

This method differs from the others in that it looks at *accounting profits* rather than cash flows. In this respect it fails to meet one of the three principles of decision making. It assesses the effect that investment will have on accounting profit. It is very similar to the ratio that is sometimes used to assess managers' performance, return on capital employed (see Unit Six). It is hardly surprising that managers will want to know the effect of a project on this ratio before deciding whether to go ahead. One of the problems with using this method is that there are so many different definitions of profit and investment that could be used. When making comparisons between projects it becomes important to ensure that like is being compared to like. Two versions of the accounting rate of return will be demonstrated with the Bluebell example. The first will show annual profit as a proportion of annual investment and the second average profit as a proportion of the average investment, using the following formulae.

(a) $\dfrac{\text{Annual profit}}{\text{Annual investment}} \times 100$

(b) $\dfrac{\text{Average profit}}{\text{Average investment}} \times 100$

Before starting any analysis we need to work out, for each year of the project, the accounting profit and the value of the investment in terms of accounting net book value. With this approach the investment is written off (depreciated) over its useful life. This affects both profit and the value of the investment. See Unit Two for a reminder of the accounting treatment of depreciation. For simplicity's sake we will assume that Bluebell depreciates its assets over a four-year period on a straight-line basis.

$$\text{Depreciation per annum} = \dfrac{\text{historic cost} - \text{residual value}}{\text{useful life}}$$

$$= \dfrac{£100\,000 - £10\,000}{4}$$

$$= £22\,500$$

Accounting profit: cash flow minus depreciation

Year	Cash flow		Depreciation		Profit
1	(10 000)	–	22 500	=	(32 500)
2	60 000	–	22 500	=	37 500
3	95 000	–	22 500	=	72 500
4	65 000	–	22 500	=	42 500
Total profit					120 000

$$\text{Average profit} = \frac{£120\,000}{4} = £30\,000 \text{ per year}$$

Net book value: historic cost minus depreciation

Year	Historic cost		Accumulated depreciation		Net book value
1	100 000	–	22 500	=	77 500
2	100 000	–	45 000	=	55 000
3	100 000	–	67 500	=	32 500
4	100 000	–	90 000	=	10 000

The average investment is the net book value half way through the project (at the end of year two), £55 000.

(a) *Accounting rate of return: annual*

Year	Profit (£)	Investment (£)	Ratio (%)
1	(32 500)	77 500	–41.9
2	37 500	55 000	68.2
3	72 500	32 500	223.1
4	42 500	10 000	425.0

(b) *Accounting rate of return: average*

$$\frac{\text{Average profit}}{\text{Average investment}} = \frac{£30\,000}{£55\,000} = 54.5 \text{ per cent}$$

Companies have target rates of return and will normally accept investments above this rate. The target rate depends on the industry and the historic average (see Unit Six on assessing performance using ratios). For the project that Bluebell is considering, if we look over the entire life of the project it gives a high return, whichever method is used. However, a problem could exist, which may cause the project to be rejected. In the first

ACCOUNTING INFORMATION FOR DECISION MAKING

year it makes a loss, and gives a negative ratio. The manager making the ultimate decision may be assessed by the ratio, and may even have an annual bonus linked to achieving a certain level. Although in the long term the project gives good returns, the manager could take a short-term view and reject the project, depending on his assessment of being around to profit in the long term.

Capital Rationing

Sometimes in investment decisions you may have to choose between various projects. For example, there might be two different methods of manufacturing a particular product, each of which results in different cash flows (perhaps because one requires an expensive machine to be purchased initially, but thereafter operating costs are low). Only one can be selected and the options have to be ranked and the best chosen. Sometimes a company may have more investment opportunities than it can raise funds to finance. Here again those available need to be ranked and the best selected. How is the selection made? Each of the investment appraisal techniques has a rule for ranking choices:

- net present value – select the project giving the highest value;
- internal rate of return – select the project with the highest rate;
- payback period – select the project with the shortest period;
- accounting rate of return – select the project with the highest rate.

Unfortunately these rules are sometimes contradictory, as demonstrated by the following example.

WORKED EXAMPLE

Bluebell has identified another method of manufacturing the product. The original method is referred to as method A, and the alternative as method B. The same initial investment is required and the same residual value is estimated. The operating cash flows in each year differ.

Year	Method A	Method B
1	(10 000)	50 000
2	60 000	50 000
3	95 000	50 000
4	65 000	40 000

The adjusted cash flows after sale of the machinery will be £75 000 and £50 000 respectively.

Net present value

Method B

Year	Cash flow	Discount factor		Present value
1	50 000	× 1/(1.1)	=	45 454
2	50 000	× 1/(1.1)^2	=	41 322
3	50 000	× 1/(1.1)^3	=	37 566
4	50 000	× 1/(1.1)^4	=	34 151
				158 493
Initial investment				(100 000)
Net present value				58 493
Method A: net present value				63 097

Decision rule: choose the alternative with the highest NPV; in this case, method A.

Internal rate of return

Method B

Year	Cash flow	PV (20%)	PV (30%)	PV (40%)
1	50 000	41 667	38 461	35 714
2	50 000	34 722	29 585	25 510
3	50 000	28 935	22 758	18 221
4	50 000	24 113	17 506	13 015
		129 437	108 310	92 460
Initial investment		(100 000)	(100 000)	(100 000)
Net present value		29 437	8 310	(7 540)

The internal rate of return lies between 30 and 40 per cent; the actual value is 34.9 per cent. The internal rate of return for method A was 28.8 per cent.

Decision rule: choose the alternative with the highest IRR; in this case, method B.

Payback period

Method B

Year	Cash flow	Cumulative
0	(100 000)	(100 000)
1	50 000	(50 000)
2	50 000	0
3	50 000	50 000
4	50 000	100 000

ACCOUNTING INFORMATION FOR DECISION MAKING

The payback period is two years. With method A the payback period was 2.53 years.

Decision rule: choose the alternative with the shorter payback period; in this case, method B.

Accounting rate of return

Intermediate calculations are not shown, but made in the same way as for method A.

(a) Accounting rate of return: annual

Year	Profit (£)	Investment (£)	Ratio (%)	Method A ratio (%)
1	27 500	77 500	35.5	−41.9
2	27 500	55 000	50.0	68.2
3	27 500	32 500	84.6	223.1
4	17 500	10 000	175.0	425.0

(b) Accounting rate of return: average

$$\frac{\text{Average profit}}{\text{Average investment}} = \frac{£25\,000}{£55\,000} = 45.5 \text{ per cent}$$

Average for method A: 54.5 per cent

Decision rule: choose the alternative with the highest accounting rate of return. Because of the wide fluctuations when using the annual method, the average will probably be used. This recommends that method A be selected.

Summary of results

The results from each technique, with the recommended alternative highlighted, are shown below.

	Method A	Method B
Net present value	**63 097**	58 493
Internal rate of return	28.8%	**34.9%**
Payback period	2.53 years	**2 years**
Accounting rate of return	**54.5%**	45.5%

As can be seen, the advice being given is contradictory: two recommend one alternative, two the other. Which alternative should be selected? The answer is the alternative chosen by the *net present value technique*. This technique always selects the best alternative. To see why the deficiencies of the other techniques need to be considered.

(1) Internal rate of return. The two techniques (net present value and internal rate of return) that discount cash flows in their analysis will often

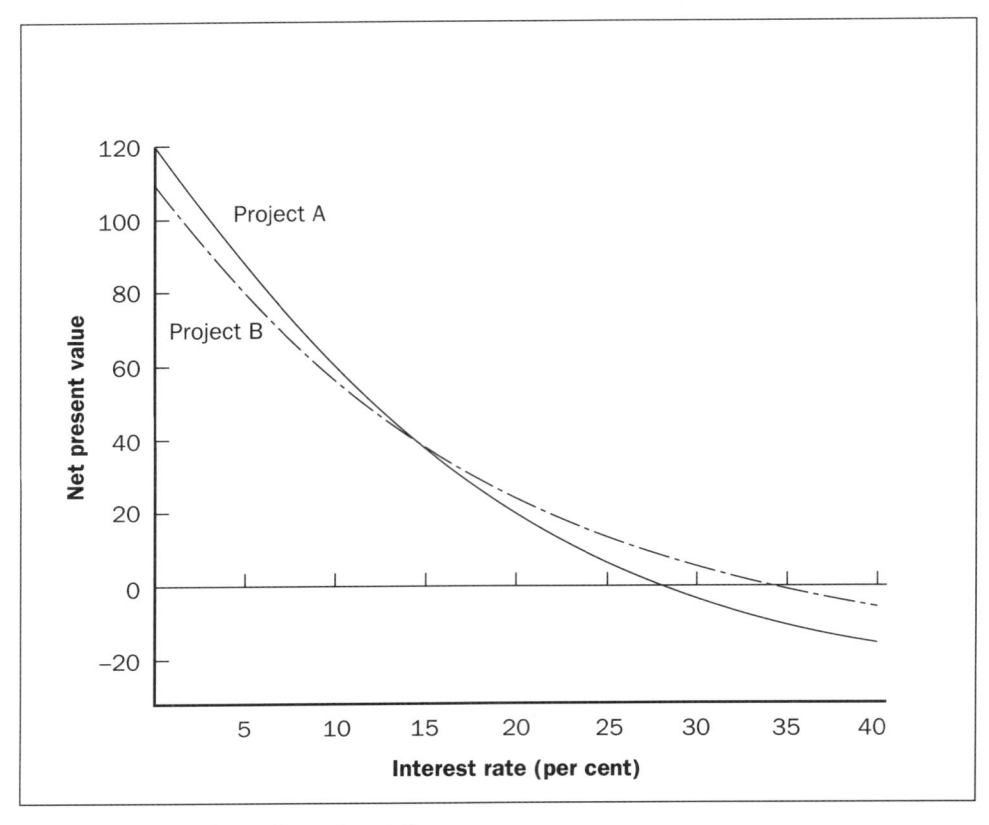

Figure 5.6 NPVs for projects A and B.

give the same conclusion. Occasionally they will give conflicting advice, as seen in this case. Figure 5.6 shows the net present value curves from projects A and B.

All things being equal, projects should be taken on if they give an internal rate of return that is higher than the cost of capital. The project being considered by Bluebell has an internal rate of return of 28.8 per cent compared to a borrowing rate of 10 per cent. They should go ahead with the investment. The actual interest rate that is paid could rise as high as the internal rate of return before the project should be rejected.

As you can see, at low interest rates method A gives the higher net present value. When the interest rate is about 14 per cent both methods give the same net present value. At higher rates of interest method B gives the higher net present value. Method A reaches the internal rate of return more quickly than method B. Method B remains profitable at a higher interest rate than for method A. However, the internal rates of return are very high when compared to the likely interest rate (28.8 and 34.9 per cent compared to 10 per cent). Is looking to see what happens at very high interest rates relevant? Are interest rates ever going to be this high? They might rise by a few percentage points, but are they going to double or treble? The internal rate of return gives the highest interest rate that can be charged before a project becomes unprofitable. When making a decision we should be looking at the results obtained at the likely interest rate.

(2) Payback period. As already has been mentioned, this technique does not look at what happens beyond the payback period. It merely looks at which project is paid back most quickly. It does not attempt to see which alternative would increase wealth most. It also has the disadvantage of not making any adjustment for the timing of receipts. It treats £1 received in two years' time as having the same value as £1 now.

(3) Accounting rate of return. This technique also suffers from a failure to adjust for the timing of cash flows. The timing issue is made worse by the fact that actual cash flows are not identified because of the use of accounting conventions such as depreciation.

Activity AM5.4 concludes this unit, drawing upon concepts previously covered in the book, not just in this unit.

ACTIVITY AM5.4

GIFT IDEAS LTD AND PROFITABILITY

Activity code
- ✓ Self-development
- ✓ Teamwork
- ✓ Communications
- ✓ Numeracy/IT
- ✓ Decisions

Gift Ideas Ltd is a company which manufactures a range of products. It is considering making a number of changes to its operations, which it hopes will lead to improved profitability. You are to answer questions and comment on each of these proposals.

Proposal A

One of the products is a souvenir clock. The company is considering subcontracting manufacture of this item at a cost of £8 per unit. At present 5000 units are produced each year. The standard cost of manufacture is:

	£
Direct materials	4.00
Direct labour	1.50
Variable overheads	0.50
Fixed overheads	4.00
	10.00

If the work is subcontracted the company expects to save £5000 per annum

Required
1. Calculate the effect of subcontracting on the company's profits. Do you recommend acceptance?
2. What is the maximum price the company should pay for the work to make the proposal financially viable?
3. What qualitative factors might influence a company's decision to subcontract work?

Proposal B

The company produces jigsaw puzzles of pictures of English towns, which it sells for £0.60 each. 100 000 jigsaws are produced each year but the equipment used in their manufacture is not fully utilized. The company has been approached to produce for a total price of £4000 a trial batch of 10 000 jigsaws of Moscow. The standard cost of manufacture is:

	£
Direct materials	0.20
Direct labour	0.07
Variable overheads	0.03
Fixed overheads	0.10
	0.40

If the order is accepted the company expects to receive a 5 per cent discount on all its material purchases. Fixed overheads are not expected to rise as a result of accepting the order.

Required
4. Calculate the effect on the company's profits if it accepts the order. Do you recommend acceptance?
5. If fixed overheads were to rise by £50 as a result of taking on the order, would you recommend acceptance?
6. What qualitative factors might a company consider before accepting a special order?

Proposal C
The company makes computerized toys and wishes to expand its range from two to three models. The new product is called Zap. Data relevant to the production of the three products are given below:

	Zap	Kill	Shoot
Estimated demand (units)	500	600	400
Microchips per unit	3	2	2
Selling price	£30	£20	£25
Direct materials	12	8	8
Direct labour	4	2	4
Variable overheads	2	1	1
Fixed overhead	6	3	6

Fixed overheads are allocated to products on the assumption that production will be at the maximum level for all three products.

There is a temporary shortage of microchips, which will restrict production. In the coming year only 2500 microchips are expected to be obtained.

Required
7 Calculate the profit earned if sufficient microchips could be obtained to meet estimated demand for all products.
8 Calculate the maximum profit the company could earn given the shortage of microchips. What quantity of each product would be produced to maximize profit?
9 Calculate the profit that would be earned if at least 25 per cent of the demand for each product was met.
10 Why might the company choose to supply at least 25 per cent of demand rather than the solution which maximizes profit?

Conclusion

In this unit, we spent considerable time examining costing techniques and their impact on decision making. Salient 'decision types' were noted: break even analysis, pricing and long-term decision making. We touched upon investment appraisal although this is covered in greater detail in *Effective Financial Management*. However, some 'feel' for the subject is necessary, for we are about to put all of the work of Units One to Five together when we start examining the performance of organizations in Unit Six.

Notes
1 Naylor, Vernon and Wertz, *Managerial Economics and Strategy*.
2 See, for example, Lipsey, *An Introduction to Positive Economics*.

Unit Six

Measuring Performance with Accounting Information

Learning Objectives

After completing this unit you should be able to:

- calculate financial ratios;
- interpret the meanings of financial ratios;
- evaluate the performance of a company over time or compared with other companies;
- apply the generic skills.

Contents

Overview

Ratio Analysis: Concept

Profitability

- ▶ Return on capital employed (ROCE)
- ▶ Gross profit percentage
- ▶ Mark-up percentage
- ▶ Net profit percentage
- ▶ Turnover ratio
- ▶ Percentage increases
- ▶ Costs as a percentage of sales value

Liquidity

- ▶ Working capital
- ▶ Current ratio (working capital ratio)
- ▶ Acid test (liquid ratio)

Activity

- ▶ Fixed asset usage ratio
- ▶ Working capital turnover ratio
- ▶ Debtors' ratio
- ▶ Creditors' ratio
- ▶ Rate of stock turnover

Financing

- ▶ Borrowing and gearing ratios
- ▶ Interest cover
- ▶ Dividend cover

Investment Ratios

- Earnings per share (EPS)
- Dividend yield
- Earnings yield
- Price–earnings (PE) ratio

Conclusion

Unit Six

> " It is crucial that new performance measures are established to capture the most salient aspects of the new manufacturing technology. There will be a need to supplement financial measures with non-financial measures."
>
> Drury, Management and Cost Accounting[1]

Overview

Drury is correct. The introductory unit examined the research of Campbell,[2] and his non-financial measures are indeed quite relevant, as is the effectiveness concept and the application of his whole series across the range of disciplines. To be effective we must adopt this multi-disciplinary stance. At the same time, each discipline has its own 'inner value' concerning effectiveness. As far as accounting is concerned, there is still considerable value in using performance indicators, from budgetary control to ratio analysis. These techniques do need supplementing by non-accounting indicators and this needs to be recognized. While accepting this premise, which underpins the series, in this final unit we will focus on performance measurement through accounting information. The non-accounting indicators can be seen in the remaining books of the series.[3]

In Unit Four we analysed one of the ways in which accounting information is used in performance measurement through responsibility accounting and comparison to budget. This is just one aspect of performance and the final unit in this book expands upon this theme of performance. Budgetary analysis is the concern of internal managers but managers are not the only people interested in the performance of the business (please refer back to Unit One and the list of users or potential users of accounting information). While we are still thinking of the needs of managers as our central theme, more attention is given to the needs of other users. One of the problems facing other users is the lack of information. The only accessible source available to most will be the annual report and accounts. We will use this format in this unit.

Ratio Analysis: Concept

Accounting ratios are used in the interpretation of financial statements. By themselves they are meaningless but when compared to ratios for different

218 EFFECTIVE ACCOUNTING MANAGEMENT

time periods for the same entity, or when compared to those for different entities in the same time period, they can assist in identifying trends and highlighting strengths and weaknesses. These ratios can be calculated by people outside an organization using the published financial accounts of the company. The assumption would then be that the balance sheet position is representative of the true position during the period, although this may not always be the case. For example, stocks in the balance sheet may be higher than usual if the year end is just prior to a peak in anticipated demand, or they may be lower than usual if it follows a sale. Managers within the business may use the same ratios in trying to manage the business. They are less affected by occasional fluctuations in particular figures.

Ratios are useful in examining five areas of performance:

1 Profitability; that is, measuring management's overall effectiveness in generating profits from the resources available.
2 Liquidity ratios; that is, measuring the ability of a business to meet its short-term obligations.
3 Activity ratios; that is, measuring how effectively a business is employing its resources.
4 Financing ratios; that is, measuring the contribution of shareholders compared to providers of loan capital.
5 Investment ratios; that is, measuring the performance of shares in the stock market.

Each of these ratios will be demonstrated in this unit using the following example. This shows the accounts for two years of a company which has been undergoing rapid expansion. Comparisons are made between the two years.

WORKED EXAMPLE

SUMMARIZED BALANCE SHEET FOR GREEN RETAIL PLC AS AT 31 DECEMBER 1994

	1994		1993	
	£000	£000	£000	£000
Fixed assets				
At cost		1450		900
Depreciation		600		300
		850		600
Current assets				
Debtors	220		100	
Stock	190		125	
Cash at bank and in hand	15		25	
	425		250	

**Creditors: amounts falling due
within one year**

Trade creditors	140		40	
Dividends	60		60	
	200		100	
Net current assets		225		150
Total assets less current liabilities		1075		750

**Creditors: amounts falling due
after one year**

Debenture loan (15 per cent)		300		0
		775		750

Capital and reserves

Called-up share capital (600 000 shares at £1)		600		600
Profit and loss account		175		150
		775		750

Memo:

Share price at year end	£2.50	£2.00

GREEN RETAIL PLC SUMMARIZED PROFIT AND LOSS ACCOUNT
FOR THE YEAR ENDED 31 DECEMBER 1994

	1994		1993	
	£000	£000	£000	£000
Turnover		1200		700
Less: cost of sales		600		300
Gross profit		600		400
Distribution costs	240		140	
Administration expenses	195	435	145	285
		165		115
Interest payable		45		0
		120		115
Taxation on profit on ordinary activities		35		35
Profit for the financial year		85		80
Retained profit brought forward from last year		150		130
		235		210
Proposed dividend on ordinary shares		60		60
Retained profits carried forward		175		150

Profitability

One way to assess a business is to look at the profit generated in a period. The profit for the financial year for Green Retail has gone up, which seems to be a good trend. However, it is useful to put the profit in some sort of context, as a business with huge resources would be expected to generate more profit than one with few resources.

Return on capital employed (ROCE)

Probably the most frequently used ratio in assessing management's efficiency in utilizing resources is the return on capital employed. It has the greatest meaning when the true values of assets are known. When they are not known the balance sheet values of assets must be taken.

$$\text{ROCE} = \frac{\text{Profit}}{\text{Capital employed}} \times 100$$

When you look at a profit and loss account you will see that there is more than one measure of profit. There is profit on ordinary activities, both before and after interest and taxation, and there is profit before and after extraordinary items. Which one should be used? It does not really matter which is used, as long as the same definition is always used.

Profit before interest and taxation (sometimes abbreviated to PBIT) is often used. The reason is that it shows profit earned from the normal operations of the business, before the influences of factors beyond management's control. It might be argued that profit after interest and taxation should be used, as management should seek to ensure that they are minimized. Profits for one year might be distorted by extraordinary items, so generally a measure of profit that excludes them is used. It will be interesting to see what happens after the widespread adoption of Financial Reporting Standard 3, which defines very few transactions as being extraordinary.

Capital employed is the money invested in the business and used to provide assets. As with profit, there is more than one definition of capital employed that can be used. Again, the important thing to remember is to be consistent and always to compare like with like. The three most likely measures are:

- Total assets, which equal all funding, whether short- or long-term creditors or shareholders. In the example the value can be found by adding together fixed assets and current assets: £1275 and £850 respectively.
- Net assets, which are all assets less short-term creditors. These are equal to funding from long-term creditors plus shareholders' funds. In the example the value can be found by adding together fixed assets and net current assets: £1075 and £750 respectively.
- Equity, which is the shareholders' funds that have been used to finance total assets, less all creditors. In the example it is found by taking the value at the

MEASURING PERFORMANCE WITH ACCOUNTING INFORMATION

bottom of the balance sheet: £775 and £750 respectively. When we are calculating the ratio here, the definition of profit that should be used is the profit for the financial year after all other deductions. This is the profit left for the shareholders and can be compared to the funds that are provided by the shareholders.

Return on capital employed will be calculated for Green Retail using the net asset definition. This definition is chosen as it is the most widely used, to examine a company from the outside but also internally to assess the performance of divisions. If you were a shareholder of the company, you would probably want to calculate the return on equity as well, as this is of more direct relevance to your interests.

The year end value of net assets will be used. It is possible that an average for the year could be used but it is more useful to look at the latest situation if we want to look at where a trend is leading. Within a company managers are able to calculate the ratio on a monthly basis, to give them a more accurate picture of trends.

$$\text{Return on capital employed} = \frac{\text{Profit before interest and taxation}}{\text{Net assets employed}} \times 100$$

$$1994: \frac{165}{1075} \times 100 = 15.4 \text{ per cent}$$

$$1993: \frac{115}{750} \times 100 = 15.3 \text{ per cent}$$

Green Retail's profit has improved between the two years, but it has been matched by an increase in capital employed. When profit is expressed as a percentage of the capital employed there has only been a marginal improvement.

Theoretically a ROCE ratio as high as possible is desirable. However, you cannot judge performance without looking into the company and its circumstances more closely. Different industries will have different ratios as the norm, and comparisons should be drawn. Even within the same industry there can be wide differences in the ratios. A franchising business with few assets but large profits will have a very high return. Another retail business that has held retail property for a length of time will have high asset values. Increases in property values cannot be used to increase profits until the property is sold, and are held in a revaluation reserve. This means the ratio will be very low. How can a comparison be made between the two?

A change in ROCE can be the result of two things: change in profit or change in the capital employed. To some extent this ratio can be manipulated by reducing capital employed (by off balance sheet funding or failing to invest in new assets) rather than improving profitability.

When looking at the ROCE earned by a business you might compare it to what it could earn by investing all its money in a bank. If a bank would pay 10 per cent on deposits, then a business might be expected to earn a higher return, considering the risk involved of being in business.

Gross profit percentage

This measures the profit percentage included in the price of goods sold by a company. We encountered this ratio when we looked at pricing in Unit Five. It is calculated using information in the profit and loss account.

$$\text{Gross profit percentage} = \frac{\text{Gross profit}}{\text{Turnover}} \times 100$$

1994: $\frac{600}{1200} \times 100 = 50$ per cent

1993: $\frac{400}{700} \times 100 = 57.1$ per cent

In 1994, for every £1 worth of sales made, 50 pence was gross profit; in the previous year it had been 57.1 pence.

Mark-up percentage

An alternative measure, the mark-up percentage, gives basically the same information. This shows the profit earned as a percentage of the costs.

$$\text{Mark-up percentage} = \frac{\text{Gross profit}}{\text{Cost of sales}} \times 100$$

1994: $\frac{600}{600} \times 100 = 100$ per cent

1993: $\frac{400}{300} \times 100 = 133$ per cent

In 1994, for every £1 in cost of sales incurred an additional £1 of gross profit was earned; in the previous year it had been £1.33.

As we noted in Unit Five, an increase in volume of sales is normally only made by a decrease in the price charged. The cost of goods coming in for resale does not often fall, meaning a reduction in the profit earned. This appears to be what has happened with Green Retail. More sales are being made but with a lower margin. Another reason for a change in the percentage might be a change in the sales mix. Growth might be experienced for lower margin items, which bring down the overall company average.

Different industries are able to charge different profit or mark-up percentages. A newspaper wholesaler would expect to have a very small mark-up, but would have large volumes. A car manufacturer would have a large mark-up but smaller volumes. A useful comparison to make might be of the mark-up of a company against the industry average. Even within an industry some companies will be supplying the lower end of the market: they will have lower than average mark-ups. This is not necessarily a bad thing, and many companies have successfully made profits supplying the lower end.

Net profit percentage

Similar to the gross profit percentage is the net profit percentage. It is more meaningful in providing an overall feeling of profitability as it includes all costs and not just the cost of sales. Net profit here is the same profit before interest and taxation figure as used in the ROCE ratio.

$$\text{Net profit percentage} = \frac{\text{PBIT}}{\text{Turnover}} \times 100$$

1994: $\dfrac{165}{1200} \times 100 = 13.75$ per cent

1993: $\dfrac{115}{700} \times 100 = 16.4$ per cent

What this means is that for every £1 of turnover generated in 1994, 13.75 pence is left as operating profit; this compares to 16.4 pence in 1993. We should expect this to happen given the change in the gross margin percentage.

Turnover ratio

This measures the turnover generated by assets and shows how fully a company is utilizing its assets. The definition of capital employed used for the ROCE ratio should also be used here.

$$\text{Turnover ratio} = \frac{\text{Turnover}}{\text{Capital employed}} \times 100$$

1994: $\dfrac{1200}{1075} \times 100 = 112$ per cent

1993: $\dfrac{700}{750} \times 100 = 93$ per cent

This ratio is similar to the ROCE, except that this time it is the value of turnover generated from capital employed rather than profit. In 1994, for every £1 employed in the business £1.12 is raised in sales turnover, and after costs £0.15 is left as profit. In 1993, £0.93 was raised in sales value for every £1 employed, and after costs £0.15 was left as profit. So profits are virtually unchanged but turnover has increased, again showing the change in gross margin.

Percentage increases

A simple way of analysing performance is to look at individual costs from one year to the next, to see if they have increased disproportionately to revenues.

$$\frac{\text{Value this year} - \text{value last year}}{\text{Value last year}} \times 100$$

$$\text{Turnover} = \frac{1200 - 700}{700} \times 100 = 71.4 \text{ per cent}$$

$$\text{Cost of sales} = \frac{600 - 300}{300} \times 100 = 100 \text{ per cent}$$

$$\text{Distribution} = \frac{240 - 140}{140} \times 100 = 71.4 \text{ per cent}$$

$$\text{Administration} = \frac{195 - 145}{145} \times 100 = 34.5 \text{ per cent}$$

We already know from other ratios that costs of sales have risen more than turnover. This is confirmed here: while turnover has increased by 71.4 per cent the cost of sales has risen by 100 per cent, resulting in the fall in gross profit.

The increase in distribution costs exactly matches the increase in turnover. This is an item of cost that we might expect to move with turnover. If it rises by more than turnover there may be cause for concern. The increase in administration expense is much less than for anything else. This may be because increases in administration staff and expenses often tend to lag behind other areas. While a lower increase in costs might seem good, it could be problematical if it results in overloading areas, to the detriment of the company. For example, not increasing credit controllers might mean a rise in debtors.

Costs as a percentage of sales value

Another simple way to analyse the performance is by taking each cost category as a percentage of turnover. This is the same calculation as was made for cost of sales in the gross profit percentage.

$$\frac{\text{Costs}}{\text{Turnover}} \times 100$$

Distribution

1994: $\dfrac{240}{1200} \times 100 = 20$ per cent

1993: $\dfrac{140}{700} \times 100 = 20$ per cent

Administration

1994: $\dfrac{195}{1200} \times 100 = 16.25$ per cent

1993: $\dfrac{145}{700} \times 100 = 20.71$ per cent

This gives basically the same information as the previous percentages. Distribution costs remain constant as a percentage of turnover but administration costs are falling.

To analyse the profit performance of a company you must look at all the information available. You should not rely on one simple ratio, such as the ROCE. It is only by looking at the whole picture that you get a feel for what is happening.

Liquidity

Many failed businesses fail not because they are not profitable but because they are unable to pay creditors on time. *Liquidity is having cash or near cash items available to pay short-term obligations.* A lender or a supplier to a company will be particularly interested in looking at liquidity.

Working capital

Working capital is the term used to describe the short-term assets and obligations of the business. Every business needs working capital to survive. Credit needs to be extended to customers for sales to be made. Stocks need to be held ready for supply to customers or for using in production. Some cash (or short-term investments) is also needed to pay current liabilities when they fall due. The amount of working capital required can be reduced by taking advantage of short-term credit, given by suppliers of goods and services, or delays in paying taxation or dividends. If insufficient cash is available then short-term finance can be extended by banks in the form of overdrafts.

It is possible to have negative working capital, where the current liabilities are greater than the current assets. There are a few businesses that can survive in this situation; for example, a supermarket can raise new cash very quickly from buying goods on credit and selling them before it has to pay for them. Generally it is not a good sign when a business has negative working capital. Most businesses are not in the fortunate situation of large supermarkets and need positive working capital. Funds need to be raised from shareholders and lenders to finance working capital. The business will have to pay a return to the providers of finance, so it is desirable if working capital is kept to a minimum.

Working capital = Current assets − creditors: amounts falling due within one year

1994: 425 − 200 = 225

1993: 250 − 100 = 150

Green Retail's working capital has risen by £75 000 in 1994. This is not surprising given that it has been expanding. To be able to assess if the increase is higher or lower than expected we need to look in more detail at the working capital.

Current ratio (working capital ratio)

This ratio indicates the extent to which the claims of short-term creditors are covered by current assets. The assets used in this measure include cash, debtors and stocks. Debtors can be expected to be turned into cash in a fairly short time span. Stocks can be sold and cash collected reasonably quickly, if not as quickly as with debtors.

$$\text{Current ratio} = \frac{\text{Current assets}}{\text{Current liabilities}}$$

1994: $\frac{425}{200} = 2.125$

1993: $\frac{250}{100} = 2.5$

A ratio of between one and two is generally an indicator of good liquidity, although this is very much dependent on the type of industry and the speed at which the business can raise cash. The lucky supermarket might easily have a ratio closer to zero than one, while a company building aeroplanes that take a long time to complete might have a ratio much higher than two. Comparisons should be made to the industry average.

A very low ratio indicates poor liquidity and unless the business has access to funds it may fail to survive. Too high a ratio might indicate that too much stock is being held, that too much credit is being given or that too much cash is held. Green Retail's liquidity looks good, although it has worsened during 1994.

MEASURING PERFORMANCE WITH ACCOUNTING INFORMATION

Acid test (liquid ratio)

This is a measure of the ability to meet obligations in the very short term. It excludes stock because of the time taken to convert stock into cash (via sales and debtors).

$$\text{Acid test} = \frac{\text{Current assets} - \text{stock}}{\text{Current liabilities}}$$

1994: $\dfrac{425 - 190}{200} = 1.175$

1993: $\dfrac{250 - 125}{100} = 1.25$

Interpretation of the result is again dependent on the business activity, but a ratio of one is generally considered safe.

Please tackle Activities AM6.1 and AM6.2.

ACTIVITY AM6.1

RATIO ANALYSIS IN THE RETAIL ORGANIZATION

Activity code
- ✓ Self-development
- ✓ Teamwork
- ☐ Communications
- ✓ Numeracy/IT
- ✓ Decisions

Task

Please scan the consolidated balance sheet and profit and loss accounts attached. Derive the overall 'health' of this company using the appropriate performance/efficiency ratios.

	1991 £ million	1990 £ million
Turnover (excluding sales taxes)	1208.6	1310.3
Cost of sales	(1119.5)	(1201.4)

228 EFFECTIVE ACCOUNTING MANAGEMENT

	1991 £ million	1990 £ million
Gross profit	89.1	108.9
Administrative expenses	(69.9)	(69.7)
Profit	19.2	39.2
Share of results of associated undertakings	1.3	2.0
Interest and other items	0.5	(8.6)
Profit before exceptional items	21.0	32.6
Exceptional items	(14.8)	(19.8)
Profit on ordinary activities before taxation	6.2	12.8
Tax on profit on ordinary activities	(2.1)	(4.3)
Profit on ordinary activities after taxation	4.1	8.5
Extraordinary items	(11.2)	(7.4)
Profit/(loss) for the financial year	(7.1)	1.1
Retained profit at beginning of year	332.8	348.9
Dividends paid and proposed	(20.5)	(20.5)
Translation differences	(4.1)	3.3
Retained profit at end of year	301.1	332.8
Earnings per share		
Excluding exceptional items	3.7p	5.1p
Including exceptional items	1.0p	2.1p

Consolidated balance sheet

	1991 £ million	1990 £ million
Current assets		
Stocks	142.3	167.3
Trade debtors	12.9	26.2
Other debtors	48.8	93.2
Cash at bank and in hand	136.9	142.9
Total current assets	340.9	429.6
Fixed assets		
Tangible assets	429.6	470.6
Investments	28.0	27.7

Total fixed assets	457.6	498.3
Total balance	798.5	927.9
Current liabilities		
Creditors (within 1 year)		
Trade creditors	75.3	97.5
Other creditors	176.7	204.3
Total current liabilities	252.0	301.8
Long-term liabilities		
Debentures	77.6	122.3
Reserves	114.3	117.6
Ordinary shares at 10p per share	41.0	41.0
Share premium	12.5	12.4
Profit and loss account	301.1	332.8
Total long-term liabilities	546.5	626.1
Total balance	798.5	927.9

ACTIVITY AM6.2

RATIOS AND THEIR IMPLICATIONS

Activity code
- ✓ Self-development
- ✓ Teamwork
- ✓ Communications
- ✓ Numeracy/IT
- ✓ Decisions

Below you will find a whole range of ratios for a leading company. Your task is to write a commentary on the implications of the trends for the company of these ratios using a comparison with the year before. You may wish to do additional personal research on the theory behind these ratios.

1 Performance ratios

Gross profit margins

1990

$$\frac{362.2}{2694.5} \times 100 = 13.4 \text{ per cent}$$

1991

$$\frac{296}{2790.5} \times 100 = 10.6 \text{ per cent}$$

ROCE

1990

$$\frac{362.2}{535.5} = 0.68 \times 100 = 68 \text{ per cent}$$

1991

$$\frac{296}{496.1} = 0.60 \times 100 = 60 \text{ per cent}$$

Return on shareholders' funds or equity

1990

$$\frac{150}{184.8} \times 100 = 81.2 \text{ per cent}$$

1991

$$\frac{210.80}{186.1} \times 100 = 113.3 \text{ per cent}$$

Net profit margin

1990

$$\frac{322.3}{2694.5} \times 100 = 11.9 \text{ per cent}$$

1991

$$\frac{217.0}{2790.5} \times 100 = 7.8 \text{ per cent}$$

Credit period (using sales, not cost of sales)

1990

$$\frac{597.2}{694.5} \times 52 = 11.52 \text{ weeks}$$

1991

$$\frac{592.8}{2790.5} \times 52 = 11.04 \text{ weeks}$$

Debtor period (using sales, not cost of sales)

1990

$$\frac{1043.4}{2694.5} \times 52 = 20.14 \text{ weeks}$$

1991

$$\frac{789.4}{2790.5} \times 52 = 14.7 \text{ weeks}$$

2 Liquidity

Gearing: interest cover

1990

$$\frac{364.7}{42.4} = 8.7$$

1991

$$\frac{296.5}{79.5} = 3.7$$

Borrowed capital: shareholder funds

1990

$$\frac{394.4}{514.7} \times 100 = 76.6 \text{ per cent}$$

1991

$$\frac{423.8}{472.8} \times 100 = 89.6 \text{ per cent}$$

Income gearing

1990

$$\frac{42.4}{353.8} \times 100 = 12 \text{ per cent}$$

1991

$$\frac{79.5}{289.6} \times 100 = 27 \text{ per cent}$$

Quick ratio

1990

$$\frac{874.8 \ (1055.4 - 180.6)}{1943.4 \ (356 + 687.4)} = 0.84:1$$

1991

$$\frac{728.9 \ (878.3 - 149.4)}{789.4 \ (196.6 + 592.8)} = 0.92:1$$

Liquidity ratio

1990

$$\frac{597.2}{687.4} = 0.87:1$$

1991

$$\frac{553}{592.8} = 0.93:1$$

Current ratio

1990

$$\frac{1055.4}{1043.4} = 1.01:1$$

1991

$$\frac{878.3}{789.4} = 1.1:1$$

Activity

These look at how efficiently directors and managers are managing the business. Managers themselves will be interested in them. They will want to look at them on a monthly basis to ensure that they stay in control.

Fixed asset usage ratio

This ratio looks at how fixed assets are being used to generate sales. You can look at individual categories of assets or you can use the total value of assets. One of the problems with making comparisons using this ratio is the valuation of the assets. Ideally you should use the current values of assets and not out-of-date historic cost values.

$$\text{Fixed asset usage ratio} = \frac{\text{Turnover}}{\text{Fixed assets}}$$

$$1994: \frac{1200}{850} = 1.41$$

$$1993: \frac{700}{600} = 1.17$$

For every £1 of fixed assets held by Green Retail, sales of £1.41 are generated, an improvement on the previous year. The investment in fixed assets over the year has resulted in sales per asset not only being maintained but improving.

Working capital turnover ratio

First we will take an overall view of working capital, before we look at the individual elements. This first ratio looks at the value of sales generated in a year from working capital, and thus is similar to the fixed asset utilization ratio.

$$\text{Working capital turnover ratio} = \frac{\text{Sales}}{\text{Working capital}}$$

$$1994: \frac{1200}{225} = 5.33$$

$$1993: \frac{700}{150} = 4.67$$

The higher the value, the more quickly that working capital is working. Green Retail's ratio has increased over the year, showing that working capital has not increased as quickly as sales during the year.

Another way of interpreting this ratio is to see it as the number of times in a year that working capital is replaced. In 1994 it has been replaced 5.33 times. The more quickly it is replaced the less investment needs to be made in working capital.

To examine what is happening to working capital it is necessary to look at the individual elements.

Debtors' ratio

This measures the average credit period given to customers. Ideally, only sales made on credit terms and trade debtors would be included in the calculation. As an outsider looking into the company you may be unable to get this information and have to use total sales and total debtors from the published accounts instead.

$$\text{Debtors' ratio} = \frac{\text{Trade debtors}}{\text{Sales}} \times 365 \text{ days}$$

$$1994: \quad \frac{220}{1200} \times 365 \text{ days} = 66.9 \text{ days}$$

$$1993: \quad \frac{100}{700} \times 365 \text{ days} = 52.1 \text{ days}$$

What is a 'good' or a 'bad' ratio will depend on the industry. Some industries give very little credit to customers in comparison to the sales made; for example, most retailers (although store credit cards have changed this over recent years). In manufacturing industry it is the norm for 30 days' credit to be given to customers. Companies who do not give credit do not get the business.

A period in excess of the credit terms given indicates poor credit control. If a company gives 30 days' credit and the credit period taken is 60 days then it is waiting twice as long as necessary to receive money, and the funds required to finance the debtors are twice as high as they need be.

The credit period given by Green Retail has worsened and should set off some alarm bells. Perhaps the higher volume of sales has been achieved through the granting of credit to people who are not creditworthy.

Creditors' ratio

In the same way that credit is extended to customers, businesses expect to receive credit from their suppliers. This ratio measures the average credit given by suppliers.

$$\text{Creditors' ratio} = \frac{\text{Trade creditors}}{\text{Purchases}} \times 365 \text{ days}$$

To be able to calculate this ratio we must first calculate how much has been spent on goods and services during the year. Unfortunately we cannot always deduce this from the profit and loss account. The expenses shown there include wages and salaries, for which there is not usually a credit period. Also included is depreciation, which involves no payments at all. If we use costs including wages and salaries the credit period will be understated. Ideally we would want to find the value of goods purchased on credit and compare it to the amount owing to trade creditors.

Without ideal information we must do our best with the information available. We can easily see the distribution and administration expenses in the profit and loss account, but what about production costs? All we have in the Green Retail example, as found with many published accounts, is the cost of goods sold. A stock adjustment has been made to arrive at this figure, so the adjustment needs to be undone. (Assume that at the end of 1992 stocks were £125, the same as in 1993.)

Cost of goods sold	1994	1993
Opening stock	125	125
Production costs	?	?
	?	?
Less: closing stock	190	125
Cost of goods sold	600	300

Working backwards, the missing numbers are £665 and £300 respectively. Adding production to distribution and administration costs, total costs are £1100 and £585. We can now calculate the creditors' ratio.

$$1994: \frac{140}{1100} \times 365 \text{ days} = 7.85 \text{ days}$$

$$1993: \frac{40}{585} \times 365 \text{ days} = 6.84 \text{ days}$$

On average Green Retail is taking less than eight days to pay amounts owed. As already mentioned, the creditors' ratio is distorted by using all costs rather than just credit purchases. It may be so distorted that for someone outside the company it is a useless ratio. Internally, managers should find the required information and monitor how long is being taken to pay creditors.

In theory, the longer taken to pay creditors the better. However, if too long a period is taken it may lead to problems, such as having supplies cut off or being taken to court for the recovery of amounts owed. It is quite interesting to compare this to the debtors' ratio.

Rate of stock turnover

Stocks provide a buffer between various stages of production, allowing the company to supply customers on demand, or against future price rises. While it might be nice to hold stock it is a costly thing to do. Not only does stock require financing, it needs to be stored, insured and looked after. The trend over the past 15 years has been to reduce stocks as far as possible by better planning and the introduction of just-in-time techniques.

This ratio measures the number of times stock is replaced at cost during a given period.

$$\text{Stock turnover} = \frac{\text{Cost of goods sold}}{\text{Stock}}$$

1994: $\dfrac{600}{190}$ = 3.15 times

1993: $\dfrac{300}{125}$ = 2.4 times

The ratio tells us how often in a year stock is replaced. You could buy all the required stock for the year and run it down over the year: this gives a stock turnover of 1, as demonstrated in figure 6.1. No sensible person would do this (unless they were being given a very hefty bulk discount). The stock would be replaced at several points during the year, as is also shown in figure 6.1. The higher the stock turnover ratio the less finance is required.

Interpretation of this ratio depends on the nature of the business. An aircraft manufacturer will probably have a ratio of 1, whereas a baker will have a ratio of 365 (depending on the number of days he or she is open for business). Green Retail's ratio is probably below that for an average retailer. However, there has been a considerable improvement from the previous year.

Stock turnover can also be expressed as a period rather than as the number of times it is replaced. To do this one simply divides 365 days (or 52 weeks or 12 months) by the turnover ratio. For example, in 1994 the stock turnover period is 365/3.15 = 115.9 days.

Financing

These ratios look at how the company is financed and how the providers stand in relation to getting returns in dividends or interest payments.

Borrowing and gearing ratios

These ratios find the proportion of net assets that have been financed from fixed interest securities. The borrowing ratio includes only loans (debentures). The gearing ratio includes both loans and preference shares (which pay a fixed dividend similar to interest).

$$\text{Borrowing ratio} = \dfrac{\text{Fixed interest loans}}{\text{Net assets}} \times 100$$

$$\text{Gearing ratio} = \dfrac{\text{Fixed interest loans} + \text{preference capital}}{\text{Net assets}} \times 100$$

As Green Retail has no preference shareholders the two ratios are identical

1994: $\dfrac{300}{1075}$ × 100 = 27.9 per cent

1993: nil

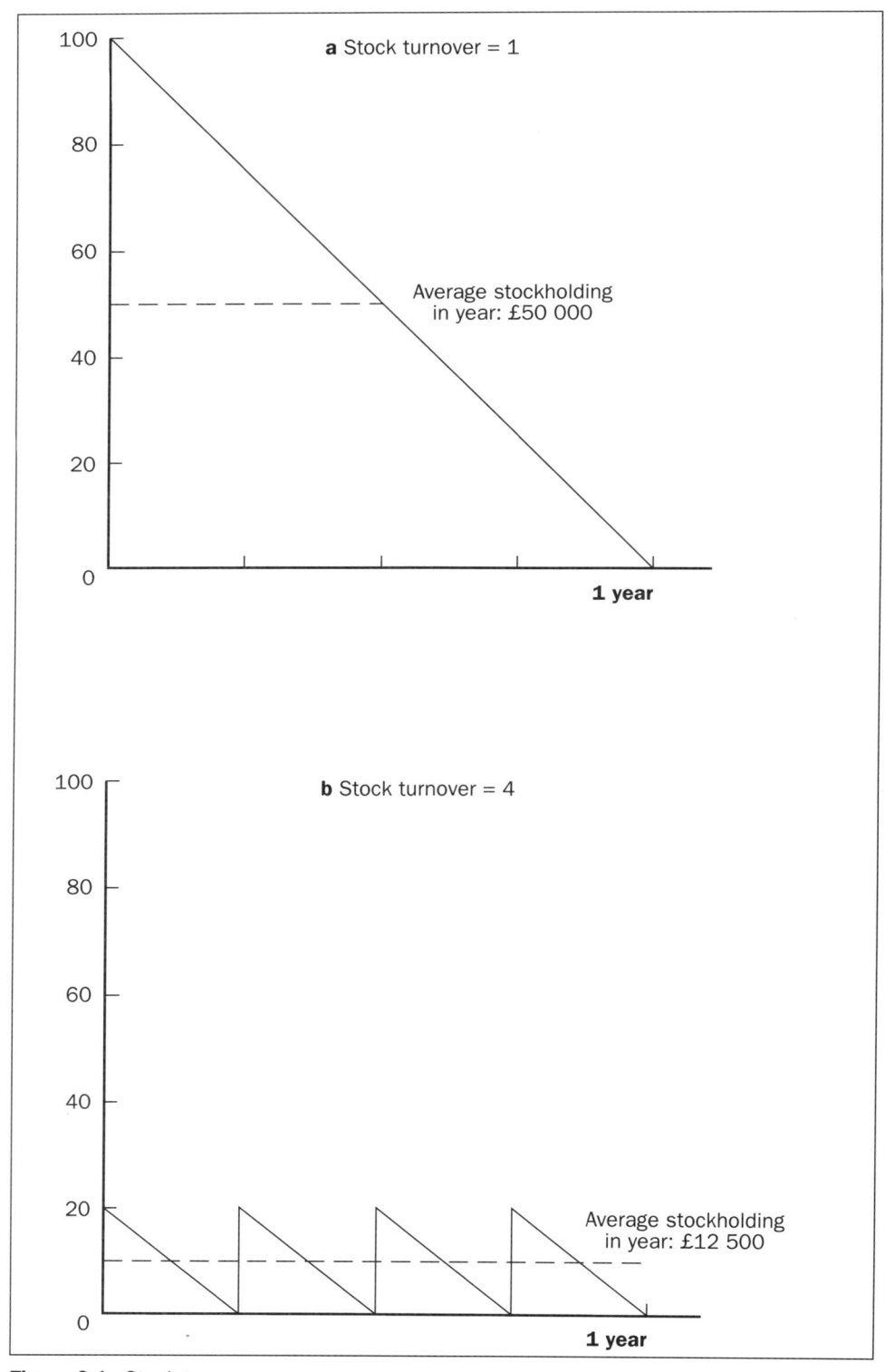

Figure 6.1 Stock turnover.

Green Retail had no fixed interest loans until 1994. A high borrowing ratio can be a good thing or a bad thing, depending upon circumstances. If a company is generating high profits, interest is paid at a fixed rate, leaving high profits for the shareholders. If a company is not generating high profits it must still meet the interest payments on debt and there may be no profits left over for shareholders.

Interest cover

This measures the ability to make interest payments from current earnings.

$$\text{Interest cover} = \frac{\text{PBIT}}{\text{Interest payment}}$$

$$1994: \frac{165}{45} = 3.67$$

A high ratio indicates that interest payments are easily met from profits. A ratio of less than 1 indicates that a company is having to dip into its reserves to meet the payments. Green Retail is easily able to pay interest from current earnings, which are 3.67 times the amount to be paid.

Dividend cover

This is a similar measure but looks at the company's ability to make dividend payments from current earnings.

$$\text{Dividend cover} = \frac{\text{Profit attributable to shareholders}}{\text{Dividend payments}}$$

$$1994: \frac{85}{60} = 1.42$$

$$1993: \frac{80}{60} = 1.33$$

The higher the ratio the more easily dividends payments are met. There has been a slight increase in the ratio for Green Retail over the two years.

Investment Ratios

These ratios are of interest to shareholders, who invest their money in a company in the hope of receiving dividends each year and of making a capital gain (as the share price increases) over the period shares are held.

Earnings per share (EPS)

This is the profit earned by the company that belongs to each of the shareholders. The number of shares in issue can vary from year to year, so this allows comparisons to be made year on year.

$$\text{Earnings per share} = \frac{\text{Profit attributable to shareholders}}{\text{Number of shares in issue}}$$

$$1994: \quad \frac{85}{600} = £0.1417$$

$$1993: \quad \frac{80}{600} = £0.1333$$

For each shareholder in Green Retail a profit of 14 pence is earned in 1994, an improvement on 1993. Many company directors think that EPS growth is one of the most important things that investors look for. So the directors of Green Retail can report a growth of EPS over the period as evidence of their good management.

Dividend yield

This is one of the ratios you can find when looking at the share price in a quality newspaper. A low ratio means that a company is paying out small dividends, thus keeping profits to invest in the future.

$$\text{Dividend yield} = \frac{\text{Dividend per share}}{\text{Share price}} \times 100$$

$$1994: \quad \frac{0.10}{2.50} \times 100 = 4 \text{ per cent}$$

$$1993: \quad \frac{0.10}{2.00} \times 100 = 5 \text{ per cent}$$

Some investors look for high dividend payouts while others look for capital growth, depending on their personal income and tax position. Those wanting dividends will favour shares with a high dividend yield.

Green Retail has a low dividend yield and is typical of a company that is expanding. Few dividends are being paid as money is being reinvested, but the stock market still values the share highly because it is likely to make high profits (and pay out high dividends) in the future.

Earnings yield

This expresses current earnings as a percentage of the current share price.

$$\text{Earnings yield} = \frac{\text{EPS}}{\text{Share price}} \times 100$$

MEASURING PERFORMANCE WITH ACCOUNTING INFORMATION

1994: $\dfrac{0.1417}{2.50} \times 100 = 5.67$ per cent

1993: $\dfrac{0.1333}{2.00} \times 100 = 6.67$ per cent

A low yield indicates that the market expects earnings to grow in the future. This ratio is hardly ever seen, as it is the inverse of the next ratio.

Price–earnings (PE) ratio

This is the inverse of the earnings yield and is the more commonly used ratio. It will be found quoted with the current price of a share in quality newspapers.

$$\text{Price–earnings ratio} = \dfrac{\text{Share price}}{\text{EPS}}$$

1994: $\dfrac{2.50}{0.1417} = 17.6$

1993: $\dfrac{2.00}{0.1333} = 15.0$

A high PE ratio indicates that the market expects the earnings of the company to grow in the future.

Now, please tackle Activities AM6.3 and AM6.4.

ACTIVITY AM6.3

RATIOS AND ORGANIZATIONAL HEALTH

Activity code
- ✓ Self-development
- ✓ Teamwork
- ✓ Communications
- ✓ Numeracy/IT
- ✓ Decisions

Company B is being affected by the recession. Debt and a hangover from the integration of previous acquisitions are causing general problems. By using key ratios, determine the state of this organization for internal managerial consumption.

Consolidated profit and loss account

For the year ended	X 30 March (Current) £ million	Y 31 March (Last year) £ million
Revenue		
Subsidiaries	2635.9	2585.9
Share of associated undertakings	154.6	108.6
	2790.5	2694.5
Operating profit	289.6	353.8
Income from interest in associated undertakings	6.4	8.4
Total operating profit	296.0	362.2
Investment income	0.5	2.5
	296.5	364.7
Interest	(79.5)	(42.4)
Profit on ordinary activities before taxation	217.0	322.3
Tax	(56.4)	(93.8)
Profit on ordinary activities after taxation	160.6	228.5
Minority shareholders' interests	(3.8)	(6.3)
Profit before extraordinary items	156.8	222.2
Extraordinary items	12.9	2.1
Profit for the year	169.7	224.3
Preference dividends	(19.7)	(13.5)
Ordinary dividends	(98.1)	(95.0)
Retained profit transferred to reserves	51.9	115.8
Earnings per ordinary share	18.5p	28.5p

Consolidated balance sheet

As at	X 30 March £ million	Y 31 March £ million
Fixed assets		
Tangible assets	969.4	1031.1
Investments	17.3	66.8
	986.7	1097.9
Current assets		
Stocks and long-term contracts	149.4	180.6
Debtors	553.0	597.2
Investments, short-term deposits and cash	175.9	277.6
	878.3	1055.4
Creditors: due within one year		
Borrowings	(196.6)	(356.0)
Creditors	(592.8)	(687.4)
Net current assets	88.9	12.0
Total assets less current liabilities	1075.6	1109.9
Creditors: due after one year		
Borrowings	(404.3)	(355.8)
Creditors	(19.5)	(38.6)
Provision for liabilities and charges		
Deferred tax	(97.2)	(76.9)
Other provisions	(58.5)	(103.1)
	496.1	535.5
Capital and reserves		
Share capital	189.0	187.8
Share premium account	437.4	447.4
Revaluation reserve	56.0	70.7
Other reserves	(785.3)	(757.5)
Profit and loss account	572.8	532.4
Associated undertakings' reserves	2.9	33.9
	472.8	514.7
Minority shareholders' interests	23.3	20.8
	496.1	535.5

Notes to the consolidated accounts

Creditors

Amounts due	Within one year		After one year	
	X	Y	X	Y
	£ million	£ million	£ million	£ million
Trade creditors	180.9	223.3	–	0.2
Payments received on account	1.5	5.1	–	0.1
Associated undertakings	3.2	0.7	0.2	–
Taxation	43.8	91.2	12.9	11.0
Other taxes and social security costs	82.4	37.5	–	–
Dividends payable	67.8	67.5	–	–
Accruals and deferred income	100.1	126.5	0.2	–
Other creditors	113.1	135.6	6.2	27.3
	592.8	687.4	19.5	38.6

ACTIVITY AM6.4

A COMPANY ASSESSMENT

Activity code
- ✓ Self-development
- ☐ Teamwork
- ✓ Communications
- ✓ Numeracy/IT
- ✓ Decisions

The following trends and ratios have been 'worked through' for you.

Take up the position of an internal accountant to the firm and that of an external advisor to the firm, and write a report on the implications of these trends and sample of ratios for this firm.

Gross profit

	1991 £ million	1990 £ million
$\dfrac{\text{Gross profit}}{\text{Net sales}}$	$\dfrac{89.1}{1208.6}$	$\dfrac{108.9}{1310.3}$
	= 7 per cent	= 8 per cent

Growth

Sales

$$\frac{\text{Sales} - \text{previous year's sales}}{\text{Previous year's sales}}$$

1988	4.5 per cent
1989	4.3 per cent
1990	7.3 per cent
1991	(7.8 per cent)

Gross profit margin

$$\frac{\text{Gross profit} - \text{previous year's gross profit}}{\text{Previous year's gross profit}}$$

1988	(9 per cent)
1989	(43 per cent)
1990	(38 per cent)
1991	(51 per cent)

Rate of return on total assets

	1991	199X
$\dfrac{\text{Net profit}}{\text{Sales}} \times$ total assets turnover	= 0.8 per cent	= 1.4 per cent

Return on assets

Upper quartile	13 per cent
Median	6 per cent
Lower quartile	0 per cent

Total assets turnover

$$\frac{\text{Sales}}{\text{Total assets}} \quad \frac{1208.6}{798.5} \quad \frac{1310.3}{927.9}$$

$$= 1.5:1 \quad = 1.4:1$$

$$= 151 \text{ per cent} \quad = 141 \text{ per cent}$$

Assets utilization	
Upper quartile	279 per cent
Median	202 per cent
Lower quartile	145 per cent

Net sales over net working capital

$$\frac{\text{Sales}}{\text{Current assets} - \text{current liabilities}} \quad \frac{1208.6}{88.9} \quad \frac{1310.3}{127.8}$$

$$= 14:1 \quad = 10:1$$

Liquidity

$$\frac{\text{Current assets}}{\text{Current liabilities}} \quad \frac{340.9}{252.0} \quad \frac{429.6}{301.8}$$

$$= 1.3:1 \quad = 1.4:1$$

Including investments with current assets $\quad = 1.5:1 \quad = 1.5:1$

Gearing

$$\frac{\text{Fixed return capital}}{\text{Equity capital} + \text{fixed return capital}} \quad \frac{77.6}{546.5} \quad \frac{122.3}{626.1}$$

$$= 0.14:1 \quad = 0.20:1$$

$$= 14 \text{ per cent} \quad = 20 \text{ per cent}$$

Debtors to creditors

$$\frac{\text{Trade debtors}}{\text{Trade creditors}} \quad \frac{12.9}{75.3} \quad \frac{26.2}{97.5}$$

$$= 0.2:1 \quad = 0.3:1$$

Current debtors/current creditors $\quad = 0.2:1 \quad = 0.4:1$

MEASURING PERFORMANCE WITH ACCOUNTING INFORMATION

Creditors to debtors

$$\frac{\text{Creditors}}{\text{Debtors}} \quad \frac{252.0}{61.7} \quad \frac{301.8}{119.4}$$

$$= 4.0:1 \qquad = 2.5:1$$

Debtor

$$\frac{\text{Debtors}}{\text{Credit sales}/365 \text{ days}} \quad \frac{61.7}{1208.6/365} \quad \frac{119.4}{1310.3/365}$$

$$= 19 \text{ days} \qquad = 33 \text{ days}$$

Creditor

$$\frac{\text{Creditors}}{\text{Credit purchases}/365 \text{ days}} \quad \frac{252.0}{1119.5/365} \quad \frac{301.8}{1201.4/365}$$

$$= 82 \text{ days} \qquad = 91 \text{ days}$$

Stock turnover ratio

The average stock according to the figures on the balance sheet.

$$\frac{\text{Cost of sales}}{\text{Average stock}} \quad \frac{1119.5}{154.8} \quad \frac{1201.4}{154.8}$$

$$= 7.2:1 \qquad = 7.8:1$$

In days   51 days   47 days

Total assets turnover

$$\frac{\text{Sales}}{\text{Total assets}} \quad \frac{1208.6}{798.5} \quad \frac{1310.3}{927.9}$$

$$= 1.5:1 \qquad = 1.4:1$$

Fixed assets turnover

$$\frac{\text{Sales}}{\text{Fixed assets}} \quad \frac{1208.6}{457.6} \quad \frac{1310.3}{498.3}$$

$$= 2.6:1 \qquad = 2.6:1$$

Fixed assets less investments   = 2.8:1   = 2.8:1

Conclusion

In this unit we have considered a range of financial performance indicators for the organization. These covered responsibility accounting and comparison to budget in earlier units. This unit has had a focus on ratios. They are critical to the financial health of the organization and it is fitting that we end this section by doing an activity on ratio analysis. Please refer to Activity AM6.5.

ACTIVITY AM6.5

RATIO ANALYSIS: DEFINITIONS AND COMMENT

Activity code
- ✓ Self-development
- ✓ Teamwork
- ✓ Communications
- ☐ Numeracy/IT
- ✓ Decisions

Task

Below you will find a type of ratio analysis. You must:
1. Note the formula.
2. Make a comment on each formula.

You should not consult the text.

Many interested parties, from shareholders to consumers, from employees to competitors, take an active interest in the economic performance of an organization. For our purposes the ratio analysis is being used for 'internal consumption' to comment on performance, liquidity and perhaps to help with overall comparisons with budgeted forecasts.

Ratios can be classified into the following groupings depending on purpose:
- profitability
- liquidity
- efficiency
- investment

Although profitability and efficiency may have more 'internal' organizational usage, investment ratios give us a feel for the overall state of the company.

MEASURING PERFORMANCE WITH ACCOUNTING INFORMATION

Profitability/liquidity
    Return on capital employed (ROCE)

    Mark-up

    Return on shareholders' funds

Comment

Comment

    Net profit

    Acid test

    Current ratio

Efficiency ratios
    Stock turnover

    Trade debtor collection period

    Trade creditor collection period

Investment ratios
    P–E ratios

    Dividend per share

    Dividend yield

    EPS

Notes
1. Drury, *Management and Cost Accounting*.
2. Campbell, 'On the nature of organizational effectiveness'.
3. See the series introduction in this book.

Conclusion

One of the writers of this book is an accountant by training, the other is a specialist in management. We have tried to combine our specialisms in writing a book on effective accounting management. The accountant must service his or her clients and the client managers and speak some of the accountant's language to make the interaction and communication meaningful.

We started by giving a context to the subject. Then we moved on to the mechanics of recording financial information. These two units provided the baseline for tackling costs, budgets, accounting information and performance measurement in the next four units.

We attempted to fuse the perspective of the accountant with that of the client, or management of the firm. It is a difficult line to draw between the rigour of accountancy and the more pragmatic stance of management. Planning, control, decision making and performance management were all included as a result.

This book also underpins *Effective Financial Management*,[1] where we apply the concepts from more of a macro perspective. This book dovetails also into another book of the series,[2] where all of the functions of management are considered from a numerical slant.

At the end of the day, the subject matter of this book forms an integral part of the tool kit of an effective manager. Indeed, Massie[3] is correct when he tells us that 'Accounting is, by intent, utilitarian: it is rooted in the pragmatic. As the primary accumulator and communicator of data within the firm, it must respond to the requirements of those using the information.' The response should not be one-sided. Of course, the accountant must make himself or herself intelligible to the user but the client manager has a responsibility to understand the concepts, the techniques and the documentation involved in management accounting. This book has tried to spread this accounting gospel in the context of a wider vision of management, whereby the multi-functional approach of the series is seen as critical to the whole idea of developing effective managers.

Notes
1. Anderson and Ciechan, *Effective Financial Management*.
2. Anderson and Thompson, *Effective Information Management – Decision Analysis*.
3. Massie, *Essentials of Management*.

A Lay Guide to Accountancy Terms

ARR	A method of judging investments using accounting profit, not cash flow, to give the 'accounting rate of return' (see IRR, Payback and NPV).
AVCO	A method of stock valuation based on average costs. The stock is valued by giving each unit held an average value.
Absorption costing	Or full costing. Includes a share of overheads when products are valued (see also variable costing).
Acid test	Also known as the liquid assets test. A ratio which shows the ability to meet obligations in the very short term. As a rough guideline this ratio should be about 1:1.

$$\frac{\text{Current assets} - \text{stock}}{\text{Current liabilities}}$$

Accounting standards	Guidelines of 'best practice', which facilitate a 'true and fair' view.
Accruals (accrued expenses)	Invoices have not yet been processed or received but goods/services have been supplied. An estimate of the cost may therefore be necessary.
Accrued income	This is income not yet accounted for, e.g. the work has not yet been billed.
Activity-based costing	A method of allocating overheads based on identifying the real cost of the activity involved (see also Blanket rates and Predetermined overhead rates).
Administration expenses	Operating costs, such as the personnel department, which are not directly related to the level of output.
Amortization	See Depreciation.
Apportionment	The dividing up of costs to two or more cost centres. This occurs for shared costs.

A LAY GUIDE TO ACCOUNTANCY TERMS

Assets	Resources of value owned by the firm.
Audit	An examination of accounts by an independent party to see whether the accounts have been compiled fairly and properly.
Bad debt	Debt that cannot be recovered, so that the money is lost to the firm.
Balance sheets	A financial 'snapshot' of a business, showing assets, liabilities and capital at any time.
Balancing the account	Calculating the closing balance on the account. This becomes the opening balance for the next period.
Batch costing	Used to value products where they are manufactured in a batch but, when completed, can be separated into individual units, e.g. bricks.
Blanket rates	A single overhead rate given to all products. Also known as a 'factory-wide' rate (see also Activity-based costing and Predetermined overhead rates).
Borrowing ratio	This is the proportion of business financed by loans, calculated by: $$\frac{\text{Fixed interest loans} \times 100 \text{ per cent}}{\text{Net assets}}$$
Book value	The amount at which an asset is placed on the balance sheet and in other accountancy records (see Net book value as an alternative expression).
Break even chart	A graph that illustrates revenues, costs, profit and loss at various levels of activity.
Break even point	The level at which a company makes neither a profit nor a loss, i.e. where total sales revenue equals total costs. This can be drawn on a chart, or it can be calculated: $$\text{Break even output} = \frac{\text{Fixed costs}}{\text{Contribution per unit}}$$
Budget	A quantified, detailed plan, usually covering up to a year in the future.

A LAY GUIDE TO ACCOUNTANCY TERMS

Business expenses	See Overheads.
Called-up share capital	Value of shares in issue (at nominal value, not market value).
Capital allowances	Tax allowable; deductions made from profit for purchases of fixed assets.
Capital budgeting	Appraising/planning fixed asset acquisitions.
Capital employed	Also known as net assets. Capital employed = Working capital + Fixed assets
Capital expenditure	The purchase of fixed assets.
Capital and reserves	How the company has been financed by the investors in the business, i.e. the sources of finance.
Cash at bank and in hand	Any physical cash available to the company. It can be held in cash or in a bank account.
Cash budgeting	Income and outgoings planned in advance to identify any cash shortfalls.
Cash flow	The cash that flows into and out of a business over a certain period of time.
Cash flow forecast	A detailed estimate of cash receipts and outgoings for a given period. The terms cash budget and cash flow forecast are often used interchangeably.
Chart of accounts	Used in computerized bookkeeping to hold the names of the accounts and their numbers.
Consistency	A convention that requires like treatment of similar items from year to year and from one occasion to another.
Cost centre	A physical function/location or piece of equipment in which costs can be determined and related to cost units.
Cost of sales or cost of goods sold	The cost of making items that are sold. This will include the cost of bought-in materials and production costs if applicable. It can be calculated by working out the value of opening stock plus stock purchased less closing stock.

252 A LAY GUIDE TO ACCOUNTANCY TERMS

Costs as a percentage of sales value	A cost ratio: $$\frac{\text{Costs}}{\text{Turnover}} \times 100 \text{ per cent}$$
Contract costing	A larger-scale variation of job costing. Often used in the construction sector over a longer time frame than job costing.
Contribution	The difference between the sale price and the associated variable costs. Therefore, it is the amount each item sold will contribute to fixed costs. Contribution per unit equals price per unit less variable costs per unit.
Creditors	These are part of the 'current liabilities'. Creditors are amounts due to others because goods or services have been bought on credit. Repayment is due in the short term.
Creditors' ratio	The average number of days credit received from suppliers. $$\frac{\text{Trade creditors}}{\text{Purchases}} \times 365 \text{ days}$$
Current assets	Items held by the company in which some benefit is expected, generally within one year. These items are or can quickly be turned into cash, e.g. stock, debtors.
Current liabilities	Amounts owed to outsiders that are repayable within a year, e.g. creditors, bank overdraft.
Current ratio	This is the working capital ratio: current assets ÷ current liabilities. Healthy companies should have a ratio of about 2:1.
Debentures	Fixed long-term loans from an individual to a company, which are paid back in full with regular interest.
Debt	Can be seen as 'borrowings'.
Debtors	Monies which are owed to the company. Debtors are part of the current assets.

A LAY GUIDE TO ACCOUNTANCY TERMS 253

Debtors' ratio	Measures the average credit period given to debtors. $$\frac{\text{Trade debtors}}{\text{Sales}} \times 365 \text{ days}$$
Deferred income	A customer has paid in advance for goods or services but they have not yet been supplied.
Depreciation	A reduction in value of an asset.
Direct costs	Costs which can be *directly* identified with a product or service.
Distribution costs	Cost of delivering items to their point of sale. Includes costs of selling and advertising.
Dividend cover	A ratio which measures the ability to make dividend payments from current earnings, i.e. profit attributable to shareholders ÷ dividend payments.
Dividend yield	$$\frac{\text{Dividend per share}}{\text{Share price}} \times 100$$ This is an investment ratio. It compares the rate of return from a share in dividends with the price paid for it.
Double entry bookkeeping	A method of recording financial transactions based on the duality concept, where every transaction has to have two entries in the books of account.
Drawings	Sole trader or proprietor 'draws' or withdraws money for his or her own use.
Earnings	Company profits.
Earnings per share (EPS)	An investment ratio used to calculate after-tax profits for the shareholder: profit attributable to shareholders ÷ number of shares in issue. This ratio shows how much each share is earning the company.
Earnings yield	$$\frac{\text{EPS}}{\text{Share price}} \times 100$$
Equity	The ordinary shares of risk capital within a firm.

254 A LAY GUIDE TO ACCOUNTANCY TERMS

Entity convention	The business is a separate entity from its owners and wider firms.
FIFO	A method of stock pricing based on 'first in, first out'. That is, the oldest stock is issued to production first, then the next oldest. Also known as historic cost.
Fixed asset usage ratio	An efficiency ratio: turnover ÷ fixed assets.
Fixed assets	Items held by a company to provide an ongoing benefit. The asset should be held for more than one year as a general guide.
Fixed costs	These costs remain the same regardless of the level of activity.
Folio number	The unique reference number of each transaction.
Full cost plus	A method of pricing. All costs are included (estimated) and a profit level is added to find the final price.
Gearing ratio	$$\frac{\text{Loan capital}}{\text{Net assets}} \times 100$$ This is an important internal and external ratio. It shows, for example, to what extent loans have been used to purchase assets. Highly geared companies have high interest repayment commitments.
General ledger	The section of the books where accounts relating to assets and liabilities are found.
General reserve	This is a 'safety net' of funds put aside for a particular purpose.
Going concern	A convention that assumes that the business will continue trading for the foreseeable future.
Goodwill	An intangible asset which may appear on a balance sheet. Often the level of 'value' added to the business over and above the purchase price in case of acquisition.
Gross profit	The trading profit, the excess of the selling price over the direct costs of production: gross profit equals total revenue less cost of goods sold.

A LAY GUIDE TO ACCOUNTANCY TERMS

Gross profit percentage	Ratio used for profitability analysis. $$\frac{\text{Gross profit}}{\text{Turnover}} \times 100$$ This is the percentage of selling price which is profit.
Goods received note	A detailed note of the items received on a delivery.
Historic cost	A convention whereby resources, goods etc. are recorded at original cost price. See FIFO.
IRR	Internal rate of return (discounted cash flow yield or marginal efficiency of capital). This is the interest rate which gives a net present value of zero for investments. Businesses select investments with the greatest internal rate of return. (See ARR, NPV and Payback.)
Income and expenditure account	The equivalent of a profit and loss account for non-profit-making organizations.
Indirect costs	Costs which cannot be directly traced to a product or service. In effect, they are overheads.
Intangible assets	Items which cannot be physically accounted for, e.g. goodwill, research and development.
Interest payable	Monies due on short-term and long-term loans.
Investment appraisal	Businesses use techniques to see if it is worth investing resources into a particular project. Such techniques include ARR, IRR, payback and NPP.
Job costing	A method of costing used when products or different product types are manufactured to customer specification through a job production method.
Journals	Accounting entries not entered from records of prime entry. Used for alterations, corrections etc.

256 A LAY GUIDE TO ACCOUNTANCY TERMS

LIFO	A method of stock pricing based on 'last in, first out'. That is, the newest stock is issued to production first. Also known as the replacement cost.
Ledger	In a manual bookkeeping system, each account is kept in a book – the ledger.
Liabilities	Amounts which the organization owes to outsiders.
Liquidity	Having cash or cash items available to pay short-term obligations.
Liquidity ratios	Ratios which assess liquidity (i.e. they give a 'feel' for the ability to meet payments).
Long-term liabilities	Amounts owed to outsiders that must be repaid in a time period greater than one year. These appear on a separate section of the balance sheet to current liabilities.
Marginal cost	The additional cost incurred by producing another unit. Application of a principle known as marginal costing.
Margin of safety	The excess activity over the break even activity (see break even analysis). That is, the difference between the expected volume and the break even volume.
Mark-up percentage	Ratio used for profitability analysis: $$\frac{\text{Gross profit}}{\text{Cost of sales}} \times 100$$ Percentage by which a product cost is 'marked up' to arrive at a selling price.
Matching convention	Revenues or costs are 'matched' with one another in a calculating profit to determine in which accounting period they should appear.
Master budget	The overall (total set of) budgets of the firm.
Materiality	A convention that accounting information should only concern itself with items of significance.
Material requisition	A note on the detailed items sent out to the factory floor for use in production.

A LAY GUIDE TO ACCOUNTANCY TERMS

Net book value	Gross amount of an asset in the accounts less an allowance for use. This allowance is depreciation.
Net current assets	(Working capital) The difference between current assets and current liabilities: amounts due within one year.
Net present value	A method of appraising investments which expresses future cash flows in today's terms. A year's cash flow is reduced by a discount factor in a manner similar to compound interest in reverse. (See ARR, payback and IRR.)
Net profit	This is what remains after all costs have been taken into account: net profit equals gross profit less overheads (or business expenses).
Opportunity cost	Following one course of action means that the potential value of another course of action not followed is lost.
Other creditors	Anyone owed money (excludes 'trade creditors' and 'creditors'). May include tax authorities, for example.
Overheads	These are all costs incurred by a company which have not been analysed as direct materials, labour or expenses.
PE ratio	This is the price–earnings ratio (inverse of earnings yield): share price ÷ EPS. It estimates the degree of risk. How long does it take to recoup the initial cost of investment?
Payback period	A method of appraising investments showing the amount of time that elapses before initial investment is repaid. Also known as the speed of return. See also IRR, NPV and ARR.
Percentage increases	A cost ratio: $$\frac{\text{Value this year} - \text{value last year}}{\text{Value last year}} \times 100$$
Periodic revaluation	Some assets do not fall in value over time. Assets, such as land and buildings, rise in

258 A LAY GUIDE TO ACCOUNTANCY TERMS

	value, so they should be revalued by a professional valuer. Such a revaluation is treated as an increase in the capital section of the balance sheet.
Posting	This is the term used for the physical act of putting entries into accounts.
Predetermined overhead	This rule is worked out in advance. Estimates of activity and overheads are made. (See also activity-based costing and blanket rates.)
Prepaid expenses	Costs are paid in advance e.g. local government rates for the year.
Prepaid income	This is payment made in advance for which goods or services must be supplied in the future.
Present value	A method of looking at the value of receipts. It examines future values of cash flows and expresses them in today's terms.
Process costing	This is used where there is a continuous flow of goods from start to 'finish'. Often costs are classified here by production departments and process stages.
Profit and loss account	An account that summarizes the flow of income and the flow of expenditure in a given trading period. It is therefore a summary of transactions.
Profitability	How well a business is making profits relative to its size or industry.
Profit margin	The profit element seen as a percentage of the total selling price.
Proposed dividend on ordinary shares	Directors' recommendation for dividends to shareholders.
Provision for bad debt	This is an anticipation of bad debt, so some limited 'writing off' is expected.
Prudence	A careful convention whereby revenue and profits are not anticipated. Accounts are supposed to be compiled with caution – the business should be shown in the least favourable way.

A LAY GUIDE TO ACCOUNTANCY TERMS

Purchase ledger	This is kept to record transactions relating to the buying of goods and services from suppliers. A purchase day book may also be used.
Purchase order	A note which gives authority to the supplier to provide certain amounts of goods or materials.
ROCE	The return on capital employed is a ratio used for profitability analysis: $$\frac{\text{Profit before interest and taxation}}{\text{Net assets employed}} \times 100$$
Rate of stock turnover	The number of times stock is used up and replaced at cost during a period: Cost of goods sold ÷ stock
Realization	A convention that a profit is accounted for when goods are sold, and not when the sale is anticipated.
Records of prime entry	Transactions are entered from an original source document, e.g. an invoice.
Reducing balance depreciation	When depreciation occurs by a fixed percentage every year. The fall in value is not equal in this asset over its life, as the biggest fall in value often occurs at the beginning.
Relevant costing	A technique based on identifying the costs affected by a decision.
Residual value	The amount an asset is expected to sell for at the end of its useful working life (i.e. the value that may be left after depreciation).
Responsibility centres	An area of activity (costs, profits etc.) identified with a particular manager.
Retained profit brought forward from last year	The total profit kept back in previous years. It could legally be distributed to shareholders as dividend but is usually reinvested in the business.
Retained profit carried forward	The amount of profit carried forward to future years.
Revaluation reserve	This shows the increase in value of assets not yet realized. It is not distributed to shareholders.

Revenue	Monies charged to customers for products or services.
Sales day book	This is the record of the left hand side entries in the sales account.
Sales ledger	The section of the company's books that records details of the value of the goods sold. Where sales volume is high, a separate book may be kept.
Share premium account	The 'extra' monies paid by shareholders for the purchase of shares above the face value of the shares.
Standard cost	A predetermined cost used for comparison with actual costs incurred. An estimate of what it should cost to manufacture an item.
Step fixed costs	Fixed costs within a given range. If the range is exceeded, they 'step up' to the next level.
Stock	Items held to be sold at a later stage, e.g. finished goods.
Stock ledger account	A record of the cost of items held in stock.
Stock pricing	The methods of pricing include: FIFO (first in, first out); LIFO (last in, first out); AVCO (Average cost).
Stock records	Details on how many units of each item are held in stock.
Stock-taking	A count and value analysis of the stock.
Straight line depreciation	The writing down of the asset (the fall in value) is spread equally over its life. This can be calculated:

$$\text{Depreciation/year} = \frac{\text{Cost of asset} - \text{residual value}}{\text{Life of asset}}$$

Sunk costs	Costs which have been incurred. They are not considered relevant in making a decision.
T accounts	Individual accounts, so called because of the shape drawn on the page when the account is divided into two.
Tangible assets	Physical items shown in the balance sheet at the net book value.

A LAY GUIDE TO ACCOUNTANCY TERMS

Tax on profit/loss on ordinary activities	Tax is paid on the 'taxable' profit.
Taxable profit	Similar to profit before tax. The main difference is that it is calculated by deducted tax capital allowances and any special allowances.
Total costs	Total costs are variable costs plus fixed costs. (See also break even point.)
Total revenue	Total revenue is the selling price per unit multiplied by the level of output. (See also break even point.)
Trade creditors	Money due to the suppliers of goods and services. Invoices have been received but not paid.
Transaction	An event or activity that requires a record of entry in the bookkeeping system.
Transfer to general reserve	Putting amounts aside into the reserve fund.
Trial balance	An intermediate stage prior to producing final accounts. The total of the debits and credits should be the same, i.e. they should 'balance'.
Turnover	Revenue earned from sales, including sales made on credit but excluding any sales tax.
Turnover ratio	A ratio to show how well a company has utilized its assets: turnover ÷ capital employed.
Variable costs	Costs which increase in direct proportion to an activity, e.g. raw materials.
Variable cost plus	A method of pricing based on a minimum level of costs. Pricing above this level gives some contribution to fixed costs and eventually to profit.
Variable costing	A method of valuing stock that only allocates variable costs to products. (See also absorption costing.)
Variance	Variations from a plan. Differences between a planned budget or standard cost and the actual cost incurred.

Working capital	The difference between current assets and current liabilities.
Working capital turnover ratio	Sales divided by working capital.
Work in progress	Goods or products started but not completed at the time of drawing up the balance sheet.

Select Bibliography and Further Reading

Andrews, P.W.D. and Brunner, E., *Studies in Pricing* (Macmillan, Basingstoke, 1975).
Amigoni, F., 'Planning management control systems', *Journal of Business Finance and Accounting*, 5,3 (Autumn 1978).
Anderson, A.H., *Effective General Management* (Blackwell, Oxford, 1994).
Anderson, A.H., *Effective Labour Relations* (Blackwell, Oxford, 1994).
Anderson, A.H. *Effective Personnel Management* (Blackwell, Oxford, 1994)
Anderson, A.H. and Barker, D., *Effective Business Policy* (Blackwell, Oxford, 1994).
Anderson, A.H. and Barker, D., *Effective Enterprise Management* (Blackwell, Oxford, 1994).
Anderson, A.H. and Ciechan, R., *Effective Financial Management* (Blackwell, Oxford, 1994).
Anderson, A.H. and Dobson, T., *Effective Marketing* (Blackwell, Oxford, 1994).
Anderson, A.H., Dobson, T. and Patterson, J., *Effective International Marketing* (Blackwell, Oxford, 1994).
Anderson, A.H. and Kleiner, D., *Effective Marketing Communications* (Blackwell, Oxford, 1994).
Anderson, A.H. and Kyprianou, A., *Effective Organizational Behaviour* (Blackwell, Oxford, 1994).
Anderson, A.H. and Thompson, M., *Effective Information Management* (Blackwell, Oxford, forthcoming).
Anderson, A.H. and Woodcock, P., *Effective Entrepreneurship* (Blackwell, Oxford, 1994).
Ansoff, H.I., *Implanting Strategic Management* (Prentice Hall, Englewood Cliffs, NJ, 1990).
Banyard. C., 'Value for money: the accountant's contribution', *Management Accounting* (February 1985).
Barnes, K., and Targett, P., 'Standard costing in distribution', *Management Accounting* (May 1984).
Barrett, M.E. and Fraser, L.B., 'Conflicting roles in budgeting operations', *Harvard Business Review* (July–August 1977).
Biggs, C. and Benjamin, D., *Management Accounting Techniques* (Heinemann, London 1989).
Bruegelmann, T. M. et al., 'Variable costing in pricing decisions', *Management Accounting* (April 1985).

Brealey, R. and Myers, S., *Principles of Corporate Finance* (McGraw-Hill, New York, 1984).

Business Technician and Education Council (BTEC), 'Common skills and experience of BTEC programmes' (BTEC, London, n.d.).

Campbell, J.P., 'On the nature of organizational effectiveness', in *New Perspectives in Organizational Effectiveness*, eds P.S. Goodman, J.M. Pennings and Associates (Jossey Bass, San Francisco, 1977).

Chadwick, L., *Management Accounting* (Routledge, London, 1993).

Chartered Institute of Management Accountants, Official Terminology re. Control and Planning.

Cyert, R.M. and March J.G., *A Behavioral Theory of the Firm* (Prentice Hall, Englewood Cliffs, NJ, 1969).

Dearden, J., 'The case against ROI control', *Harvard Business Review* (May–June 1969).

Dew, R. and Gee, K.P., 'Frequency of performance reporting', *Accountancy and Business Research* (Summer 1972).

Dorward, N., 'The mythology of constant marginal costs', *Accountancy* (April 1986).

Drury, C., *Management and Cost Accounting* (Van Nostrand Reinhold, London, 1988).

Gabor, A., *Pricing: principles and practices* (Heinemann, London, 1977).

Ghosh, B.C., 'Fixed costs in break even analysis', *Management Accounting* (May 1980).

Gordon, A.L. and Cook, H.J., 'Absorption costing and fixed factors of production', *Accounting Review* (January 1973).

Grinyer, P.H., 'Financial modelling for planning in the UK', *Long Range Planning* (October 1983).

Hankinson, A., 'Output decisions of small engineering firms', *Management Accounting* (July–August 1985).

Harper, W.M., *Management Accounting* (Pitman, London, 1989).

Harper, W.M., 'The pitfalls in fixing prices', *Accountancy* (January 1972).

Hayes, D., 'The contingency theory of management accountancy', *Accountancy Review*, 53,1 (January 1977).

Hertz, D.B., 'Risk analysis in capital investment', *Harvard Business Review* (January–February 1968).

Hindmarsh, A. and Simpson, M., *Financial Accountancy* (Macmillan, Basingstoke, 1991).

Hofstede, G.H., *The Game of Budgeting Control* (Tavistock, London, 1968).

Hogart, S., 'One man mint', *Business Life* (December 1990/1991).

Horngren, C.T., 'Cost and management accounting: yesterday and today', in *Research and Current Issues in Managerial Accounting*, eds M. Bromwich and A.G. Hapwood (Pitman, London, 1986).

SELECT BIBLIOGRAPHY AND FURTHER READING

Jones, J.A.G., 'Training intervention strategies', ITS Monograph no. 2 (Industrial Training Service Ltd., London, 1983).

Kaplan, R.S., 'Yesterday's accounting undermines production', *Harvard Business Review* (July–August 1984).

Kaplan, R.S., 'The evaluation of management accounting', *The Accounting Review* (July 1984).

King, M., Lee, R.A., Piper, J.A. and Whittaker, J., 'Information technology's impact on management accounting', *Management Accounting* (June 1987).

Koehler, R.W. and Neyhart, C.A., 'Difficulties in flexible budgeting', *Managerial Planning* (May–June 1972).

Largay, J., 'Microeconomic foundations of variable costing', *Accounting Review* (January 1973).

Lee, T.A., *Income and Value Measurement* (Van Nostrand Reinhold, London, 1985).

Lipsey, R.G., *An Introduction to Positive Economics* (Weidenfeld and Nicolson, London, 1975).

Lumby, S., *Investment Appraisal and Financial Decisions* (Van Nostrand Reinhold, London, 1988).

Lynch, R.H. and Williamson, R., *Accountancy for Management Planning and Control* (McGraw-Hill, New York, 1976).

McRae, T.W., 'The behavioural critique of accounting', *Accounting and Business Research* (Spring 1971).

Management Charter Initiative (MCI), *Diploma Level Guidelines* (MCI, London, n.d.).

Manes, R.P., Soong, H.P. and Jensen, R., 'Relevant costs of intermediate goods and services', *The Accounting Review*, 57 (July 1982).

Maskell, B., 'Management accounting and just in time', *Management Accounting* (September 1986).

Massie, J.L., *Essentials of Management*, 3rd edn (Prentice Hall, Englewood Cliffs, NJ, 1979).

Morden, A., 'Zero-base budgeting: a potential revisited', *Management Accounting* (October 1986).

Morse, W.J. and Scheiner, J.H., 'Cost minimisation, return on investment, residual income: alternative criteria', *Accounting and Business Research* (Autumn 1979).

Mott, G., *Management Accounting for Decision Makers*, 2nd edn (Pitman, London, 1994).

Naylor, T.H., Vernon, J.M. and Wertz, K.L., *Managerial Economics and Strategy* (McGraw-Hill, Singapore, 1983).

Otley, D.T., 'Budgets and managerial motivation', *Journal of General Management* (Autumn 1982).

Scapens, R.W., 'Closing the gap between theory and practice', *Management Accounting* (January 1983).

Scapens, R.W., *Management Accounting: a review of recent developments* (Macmillan, Basingstoke, 1985).
Schiff, M. and Lewin, A.Y., 'The impact on people on budgets', *The Accounting Review* (April 1970).
Sikka, P., Puxty, T. and Willmott, H., 'After Maxwell and BCCI, auditors must be audited', *Guardian* (21 June 1993).
Simon, H.A., *Models of Man: social and rational* (Wiley, New York, 1957).
Simon, H.A., 'Theories of decision-making in economics and behavioural science', *American Economic Review*, 49,3 (1959).
Sizer, J., *An Insight into Management Accounting* (Penguin, Harmondsworth, 1980).
Staubus, G.J., 'Direct relevant or absorption costing', *Accounting Review* (January 1963).
Training Commission/Council for Management Education (CMED), 'Classifying the components of management competencies' (Training Commission, London, 1988).
Washburn, S.A., 'Establishing Strategy and Determining Costs in the Price Decision', *Business Marketing* (July 1985).
Wilson, P., *The Barclays Guide to Financial Management for the Small Business* (Blackwell, Oxford, 1990).

Index

absorption costing 105, 106, 172–80
accountability of organizations 6
accountants, types of 6
accounting rate of return (ARR) 203–5, 207, 209
Accounting Standards Board (ASB) 21, 23
Accounting Standards Committee 21
accruals 31
  concept 27
  period end adjustments 63–4
acid test 227
activity-based costing 109
activity ratios 231–5
administrative expenses 34
adverse variance 149
advertising costs 85
allowable expenses 34
assembly department budget 134
assets
  types 30
  valuation 25–8
associate accountants 17
associate companies 28
Associate English Industries 10, 21
audits 16
  history 9
  professional institutions 17
AVCO (average cost) 102

bad debts 64–5
balance sheets 24

accruals 63
companies 73, 76
Companies Acts 28
history 9
layout 29–30
partnerships 72–3
preparation 55–6
sole traders 66, 68–9
stocks 56
balancing the account 40
bank statements 44
batch costing 96
batch production 96
blanket overhead rates 108
bond holders 11
borrowing ratio 235–7
bottom-up budgeting 143
boundary rules 26–8
break even analysis 180–90
budget committee 217
budget manual 127
budgets 119–22
  behavioural aspects 157–9
  cash 138–9
  control 139–43; cycle 122–5
  performance reporting 143–5
  planning 127–8; cycle 122–5; levels 125–7
  preparation 128–38
  variance analysis and reporting 146–7

called-up share capital 32
capital 32
  rationing 205–11
capital account 73

capital allowances 34
capital expenditure budget 128
cash at bank 31
cash budgeting 120, 138–9
cash flow 169
cash in hand 31
chance budgeting 143
chart of accounts 47–8
chartered accountants 17
Chartered Association of Certified Accountants (ACCA) 16
Chartered Institute of Management Accountants (CIMA) 16–17
Chartered Institute of Public Finance and Accounting (CIPFA) 16–17
closing balances
  double entry bookkeeping 40
  trial balance 48
Commonwealth countries 7
communications xix
  budgets for 121
Companies Acts 10, 20–1
  accounting records 39
  financial statements 28–9, 55, 75
competitors 12
computerized bookkeeping 40, 47–8
  checks 49
cost classification 84
concepts, accounting 26–8

267

consistency concept   27
contract costing   93–4
contract production
    93–6
contribution   170–1,
    179–80
  break even analysis
    183
control   121, 122
  budgeting for   139–43
  cycle   123–5
conventions see concepts,
    accounting
coordination, budgets for
    121
corporation tax   73
cost-based pricing
    191–2
cost centres   127
cost of goods sold budget
    135
cost of sales   32
  period end adjustments
    56–8
costing   89–97
  absorption   105, 106,
    172–80
  labour costing   104
  relevant   168–72
  techniques   172–80
  variable   105, 172–80
costs   83
  accumulation   89–97
  behaviour patterns
    86–9
  classification   83–6
  overheads   105–9
  recording   97–105
costs as percentage of
    sales value   224–5
creditors   31
  use of accounts   12
creditors' ratio   233–4
credits
  computerized
    bookkeeping   47
  double entry
    bookkeeping   43–5
  trial balance   49
current account   73
current assets   30
current liabilities see
    creditors

current ratio   226
customers   12

daily rates   103
debenture holders   11
debits
  computerized
    bookkeeping   47
  double entry
    bookkeeping   43–5
  trial balance   49
debtors   31
debtors' ratio   232–3
decision making   xx,
    167–8
  break even analysis
    180–90
  capital rationing
    205–11
  costing technique
    172–80
  investment appraisal
    199–205
  long-term   197–9
  pricing   190–6
  relevant costing
    168–72
deferred income   31
deletion of products
    175–6
depreciation   25–6
  accounting rate of
    return   203–4
  period end adjustments
    59–62
  rate   60–1
differential costs and
    revenues   168
direct costs   84–6
  recording   97–100
  see also variable costs
direct labour
  budget   133
  variances   150–1
direct material variances
    150
directors   5–6
discount factor   198
discounted cash flow yield
    201
disposal of assets   62–3
distribution costs   34
dividend cover   237

dividend yield   238
dividends   73
double entry bookkeeping
    39–47
  history   9
drawings
  financial statements
    66
  separate entity concept
    27
duality concept   28,
    40

earnings per share (EPS)
    238
earnings yield   238–9
economic worth   26
employees   12
European Community
    7, 10, 20
evaluation of tasks   125
expenses   34, 104–5
external environment,
    evaluation   124
extraordinary items   34

factory-wide overhead
    rates   108
favourable variance   149
'featherbedding'   157–8
feed-back control   140,
    141
feed-forward control
    140, 141
fellows   17
FIFO (first in first out)
    101, 102
final accounts   54–6
financial accounting
    13–14
  computerized systems
    48
Financial Reporting
    Council (FRC)   22
Financial Reporting
    Review Panel   23
Financial Reporting
    Standards (FRSs)
    21–2
  extraordinary items
    34, 220
  Reporting Financial
    Performance   23

INDEX

financing ratios 235–7
finished goods 31
   valuations 57–8
finishing department
   budget 134
fixed asset usage ratio
   231–2
fixed assets 30
fixed budget control 142
fixed costs 87–8
   semi- 89
folio numbers 42
fixed overhead variances
   152–3
flexible budget control
   142
frauds 6
full cost plus pricing
   192–3
future costs and revenues
   169

gain on disposal 62–3
gearing ratio 235–7
General Electric
   Company 10, 21
general ledgers 47
general reserve 32
going concern concept
   27
gold 8
goods received notes
   (GRNs) 98
government 13
gross profit 32
gross profit percentage
   222
groups of companies
   28–9

historic cost 25
   concept 28
   less depreciation
   25–6, 59
history of accounting
   7–11
hourly rates 103

imperfect markets 190
implementation of tasks
   125

income tax 11, 69, 73
incremental costs and
   revenues 168
indirect costs *see*
   overheads
industrial revolution 9
inflation 199
Inland Revenue 11, 34
   and partnerships 66
   and sole traders 65,
   69
   stock pricing 101, 102
'inside out' budgeting
   143
Institute of Chartered
   Accountants in
   England and Wales
   (ICAEW) 16–17,
   21
Institute of Chartered
   Accountants in
   Ireland (ICAI)
   16–17
Institute of Chartered
   Accountants in
   Scotland (ICAS)
   16–17
intangible assets 30
interest cover 237
interest payable and
   similar charges 34
interest rates 199
interim dividends 73
internal rate of return
   (IRR) 201, 206–9
interpolation 201
investment appraisal
   methods 199–205
investment centres 127
investment ratios 237–9
investors 11
invoices 104–5

job cards 104
job costing 92
   labour costs 104
job production 91–3
   overheads 107, 108
job sheets 92–3, 104
joint stock companies 9
journals 53

Ken College 50–2

labour costs 102–4
land and buildings 30
ledgers 40
legal costs, provisions
   65
legislation
   framework 20–1
   history 9–10
lenders 11–12
LIFO (last in first out)
   101–2
limited liability companies
   9
liquidity 225–31
liquid ratio 227
local authorities 6
long-term decision
   making 197–9
long-term lenders 11–12
loss on disposal 62–3

machine utilization
   budget 133
management 13
management accounting
   14
   computerized systems
   48
   job and person profiles
   18–19
manufacturing costs 84
manufacturing industries
   89–91
margin of safety, break
   even analysis
   182–3, 189
mark-up percentage
   222–3
mark-ups 191–2
master budget 127–8
matching concept 27
material costs 97–100
materiality concept
   27–8
materials purchases
   budget 132
materials usage budget
   132

INDEX

money measurement concept 27
monitoring of tasks 125
motivation, budgets for 121, 159
multiple overhead rates 108–9

National Health Service 6
National Insurance contributions 103
negative variance 149
negligence 16
net book value (NBV)
 and depreciation 59, 60–1
 and disposal of assets 62
net current assets 31
net present value (NPV) 200, 202, 206–8
net profit percentage 223
net realizable value 26
nominal ledgers 47
non-manufacturing costs 84
not-for-profit organizations 6
notes to accounts 30
numeracy/IT xix–xx

objectives, setting 124
objectivity concept 28
opening balances
 double entry bookkeeping 40
 trial balance 48
opportunity costs 168
organization of tasks 125
overdrawn bank accounts 31
overheads 58, 105–9
 budgets 133–4
 classification 85
 contributions 170–1
 and pricing 192
 standard cost of product 148

variances 151–3
overtime 103
owners 11
owner's equity 69

parent companies 28–9
partnerships 10, 55
 financial statements 66, 69–73
payback period 201–3, 206–7, 209
pension funds 11
pension plans, company 12
percentage increases 224
performance, company
 budgetary evaluation 122
 reporting 142, 143–5
 and share value 5–6
period end adjustments 53–4, 56–65
predetermined overhead rates 108
piecework 103
planning 120, 122
 budgeting for 127–8
 cycle 123–5
 levels 125–7
policy, budget 129
positive variance 149
posting entries 41
postulates *see* concepts, accounting
predetermined overhead rates 108
prepayments 64
present value approach 197–8
pressure groups 13
price – earnings (PE) ratio 239
price elasticity of demand 190
pricing 190–6
probability budgeting 143
process costing 96–7
process production 96–7

product costing 89–97
 labour costs 104
production budget 132
production overhead budget 134
professional institutes 16–17
profit and loss account 24, 32
 accruals 63
 bad debts 65
 budgeted 135
 companies 73, 75
 Companies Acts 28
 depreciation 59, 61
 disposal of assets 63
 history 10
 layout 33
 partnerships 71–2, 73
 preparation 54–5
 principles 77
 stocks 56, 57, 58
profit before interest and taxation (PBIT) 220
profit centres 127
proposed dividend on ordinary shares 34, 73
profit margin 191–2
profit measurement 24–8, 220–7
 costing techniques 172–5
profits and pricing 190–1
provision for bad debts 64–5
prudence concept 27
purchase day books 43
purchase ledgers 43
purchase orders 97–8, 104

ratio analysis 217–19, 237–47
 activity 231–5
 financing 235–7
 investment 237–9
 liquidity 225–31
 profitability 220–5

INDEX

raw materials 31
  valuation 57
realization concept 27
recording costs 97–105
records of prime entry 53
reducing balance depreciation 60–2
reference numbers, double entry bookkeeping 42
regulation of accounting framework 17–23
  history 9–10
regulators 141
relevant costing 168–72
relevant range 186–8
replacement cost 26
requisitions, material 98–9
reserves 32
residual profit 73
residual value of asset 59
responsibility centres 126–7
restrictive factors and budgeting 129
retained profit 34
return on capital employed (ROCE) 220–1
revaluation reserve 30
revenue 32
roll over budgetary control 142

safety margin, break even analysis 182–3, 189
salaries 103
sales 32
sales budget 129–30
sales day books 43
sales ledgers 43
sales margin variances 153–4
scarce resources 178–80
secured loans 11
self-development xviii
self-regulation 10, 20–3
semi-fixed costs 89
semi-variable costs 88

sensitivity analysis, break even point 188–90
separate entity concept 27
service industries 89–91
share premium account 32
shares 5
short-term lenders 12
sole traders 10, 55
  financial statements 65, 66–9
special orders 177–8
stable monetary unit concept 28
standard cost of product 48
standards 21–2
Statements of Recommended Practice (SORPs) 21
Statements of Standard Accounting Practice (SSAPs) 21–2
  contract costing 93
  stock valuation 58
step costs 89
stewardship function 8, 10
stock exchange 23
stock holders 11
stock ledger account 99, 100
stock pricing 101–2
stock records 99, 100
stock taking 101
stock turnover, rate of 234–5
stocks 31
  period end adjustments 56–8
stolen goods 57
straight line depreciation 59–60, 62
strategies, selection 124–5
subsidiary companies 28
sunk costs 169
suppliers 12

T accounts 40

takeovers
  history 10
  use of accounts for 12
tangible assets 30
tax on profit or loss on ordinary activities 34
taxation 11, 69, 73
teamwork xix
time clocks 104
time sheets 104
time value of money 197–9
top-down budgeting 143
trade creditors 31
transfer to general reserve 34
trial balance 48–52
turnover 32
turnover ratio 223–4

unfavourable variance 149
unit trusts 11
Urgent Issues Task Force (UITF) 23

variable cost plus pricing 193
variable costing 105, 172–80
variable costs 86–7
  semi- 88
  see also direct costs
variable overhead variances 151–2
variances 121, 146–57

wealth measurement 24–8
work-in-progress 31
  valuation 57, 58
working capital 225–6
working capital ratio 226
working capital turnover ratio 232

zero-based budgeting 143